EAST ANGLIA 1939

by

R. DOUGLAS BROWN

TERENCE DALTON LIMITED
LAVENHAM . SUFFOLK

1980

Published by
TERENCE DALTON LIMITED

ISBN 0 86138 000 2

Text photoset in 11/12 pt. Baskerville

Printed in Great Britain at
The Lavenham Press Limited, Lavenham, Suffolk
© R. Douglas Brown 1980

Contents

Publishers' Note

The publishers regret that the reproduction of certain illustrations is below the quality that they would normally demand.
The *East Anglian Daily Times* and the *Norwich Mercury*
series, who kindly permitted us the use of their files, were
unfortunately unable to provide original photographs and,
consequently, the pictures shown are reproductions from the
printed newspapers. The same applies to those photographs
acknowledged to the *Cambridge Evening News* that were so
kindly provided by the Cambridge Collection of the Cambridgeshire Libraries. Where applicable, it was considered
preferable to show illustrations, even if below our usual
standard, rather than no pictures at all. This volume is the
first of a series which will fully document the events in East
Anglia, year by year, and we would welcome any photographs
that apply to 1940 or subsequent years. These would be
forwarded to the author for his use and, of course, returned in
due course.

*   *   *   *   *

To William Bensley,
East Anglian, Neighbour and Friend

Index of Illustrations

INDEX OF ILLUSTRATIONS

Introduction and Acknowledgement

MANY books have sought to recapture the flavour of the period imme-diately preceding the outbreak of war in September 1939, and even more have related the events and circumstances of the early months of hostilities. Generally, the authors have concerned themselves with the drama played out on the national or international stage, with a cast of men and women of national or international status; or else the stories have been personal and autobiographical.

This book is concerned with ordinary people, living ordinary lives, in one particular region of England. It is more concerned with what went on in the parish councils than in the Parliament at Westminster. It is more concerned with the problems of the local market place than with those of national economic strategy.

Those old enough to remember life in 1939 tend to view it through the eyes of the present, drawing contrast between then and now. I have abjured this approach, and have simply described things as they were, leaving readers to make their own comparisons. Younger readers, however, may need to be briefed to this extent: in 1939 there were no jeans, denims or ladies' tights, no high-amplification music or magnetic tapes, no detergents or laundrettes, no deep-frozen foods, no ball-point pens or aerosols, no electronic gadgetry such as pocket calculators, virtually no plastic materials of any kind, very few combine harvesters, no motorways or parking meters. These examples indicate how far our world has changed in a few decades; the list could be extended indefinitely.

This is not a comprehensive and definitive account of life in East Anglia in 1939. Research on this subject might well continue throughout a lifetime, and yet remain incomplete. I have had to work within a time-scale, and I have had to be selective with the material I have examined. On the other hand, many of the things I have described were characteristic not only of 1939 but of the whole pre-war society as it developed during the late 'thirties. The result, I hope, is a summary which deals with the most significant features of regional life during a period of special interest.

My principal sources have been the daily and weekly newspapers published during 1939 in Norwich, Cambridge and Ipswich, and I am indebted to the Eastern Counties Newspaper Group Ltd and to Cambridge Newspapers Ltd., and to the editors of the various newspapers for their valuable co-operation and for permission to quote from their reports and to reprint some of their photographs. Directories and yearbooks for these and other towns have been consulted, and the volumes listed in the selected bibliography have provided valuable material. I acknowledge with thanks the co-operation of publishers who have permitted me to quote short extracts from some of them, as indicated in footnotes. I have interviewed at length about a dozen men and women from among a large number who responded to my published appeal for recollections of 1939; their names will be found in footnotes whenever they are quoted. I thank everyone who wrote to me, and particularly those who agreed to be interviewed. Within the limits imposed by a publishing schedule, I have gathered additional material from original documents deposited in library archives, and information about these is also given in footnotes. I wish to record my appreciation of the co-operation of staff at the Suffolk Record Office both at Ipswich and Bury St Edmunds, at the Cambridgeshire Local History Collection at Cambridge Central Library, and at the Local Studies Department of the Norfolk County Library at Norwich.

The task of securing suitable photographs to illustrate the text has been a difficult one. The regional newspapers provided the obvious source, but, unfortunately, in every case, the negatives and original prints have not survived. It has been necessary, therefore, to re-photograph from the pages of newspaper files, a process which inevitably involves some loss of quality. In most other commercial photographic libraries I have found that material has rarely been documented adequately in terms of place and date. I am grateful to all those who have assisted, and acknowledgement is made beneath each illustration. My experience leads me to urge all those who have photographs of potential historical interest to record on the back of each print the fullest possible information about subject, locale and date.

If this book stimulates others to delve more deeply into the archives and the memories of those who survive, that will be my main achievement. I shall be glad to hear from readers who are able to elaborate my account in any important or significant way.

R. DOUGLAS BROWN

Stoke-by-Clare, Suffolk
July 1980.

CHAPTER ONE

Bleak Prospect

EAST ANGLIA has been called "the oaken heart" of England.[1] It was the nursery in which the English people learned to construct the earliest forms of social organisation. It was the crucible in which many new elements were fired to create the English character: Celtic, Roman, Scandinavian, Norman, Flemish influences absorbed in turn. It was the fortress from which warriors emerged to fight for their special concepts of freedom: Boadicea against the Roman Legions, Hereward the Wake against Norman invaders, Cromwell against absolutist monarchy. East Anglia has the oldest recorded town in England, Colchester, which the Romans made their headquarters when they occupied the country; at Cambridge it has one of the oldest universities in the world; its manufacturers and merchants in Norwich set the pace through many centuries as England established its place in the world.

The year 1939 was a hinge-year in British history, and there is no better place to find the proof of this than East Anglia. This giant tongue of land, stretching north-eastward from London and the Thames to the North Sea, had all but forgotten the alarms and excitements of its ancient past. To the 1,700,000 people living there, nothing seemed to have changed significantly within the time covered by their memories and the tales they had been told. Now, quite suddenly, the stage on which they played was swung aside. Nothing was ever again to be quite the same. We are going to try to join in spirit this East Anglian community on the first day of January in 1939.

As dawn broke over the North Sea, a grey light spread across a frozen East Anglian landscape, its saltings and sandbanks blighted, the farmlands barren, the flat Fens at their bleakest. "Infection and the hand of war" could be sensed on the wind.

The wind blew hard. A sullen sky poured down snow and rain, until the ground was sodden, the ditches over-flowed and the rivers flooded. In the bitter cold, men and women tried hard to maintain their customary routines, but their spirits sagged low.

Later, this could be seen as an augury of what lay ahead; but it was also a symbolic culmination of what had already occurred. The year 1938 had been a sombre period in Britain's history, the events of which had left many people troubled or perplexed. Everyone knew that, in Europe, the dogs of war had

1. The novelist Margery Allingham wrote an account of life in a North Essex village on the eve of the war, which was published under the title *The Oaken Heart* by Hutchinson, in 1941.

slipped their traces. The German army had marched into, and occupied, Austria and was now threatening Czechoslovakia. Synagogues were being burned down and Jewish business premises plundered in Germany itself. Britain's response to these events had been equivocal, to say the least. The Prime Minister, Mr Neville Chamberlain, had flown three times to visit the German leader, Adolf Hitler, and seemed resolved to keep Britain out of war, at any price. His Foreign Secretary, Mr Anthony Eden, had differed so profoundly with this policy that he had resigned from office; others, notably Mr Winston Churchill, forecast catastrophe unless the British government changed course.

Amid the continued professions of hope for peace, there were increasing portents of war: the Navy had been mobilized in September 1938 and convoys of troops moved ostentatiously about the countryside, while everyone was urged to volunteer for some form of National Service. It was not surprising that many people felt confused, anxious, or numb. Particularly, on this damp and chilly New Year's Day, numb.

There were other reasons for gloom. The number of unemployed in Britain hovered around two millions — higher than it had been for three years. The resultant hardships were felt most cruelly in the industrial areas of the country, but East Anglia did not escape. Agriculture, horticulture and fishing, the great food-producing activities of the region, were in dire trouble: prices at rock bottom, farmhouses falling into dereliction, fields over-run by scrub, fishing boats tied up in harbours.

Unusual traffic in Princes Street, Ipswich.
East Anglian Daily Times

Those who switched on B.B.C. wireless to follow the hard news of that New Year's Day would have found it equally dis-spiriting: General Franco's forces in Spain made a push on the Catalonian front, launched an air raid on the centre of Barcelona, and lobbed shells into Madrid. The fact that *that* war might be something of a rehearsal for another, bigger conflict was not yet universally accepted, however. Spain was a long way from East Anglia, and there were pressing problems at hand.

The weather had set in badly over Christmas and robbed that festival of some of its relaxed pleasures. So, as the New Year began, the air was full of complaint. The tradesmen of the little Suffolk town of Sudbury, for example, were castigating their town councillors because "the town was allowed to be snowed in and practically icebound for ten days", so that Christmas trade was ruined. The unemployed in the seaside resort of Clacton, who had been found temporary work clearing snow from the streets, were protesting loudly because they had been paid only one shilling an hour and had not had their insurance cards stamped.

During the first week of January the weather became worse. Heavy snow fell on most of East Anglia: five inches in a single day on the port of Great Yarmouth, twelve inches during the month in many areas of Cambridgeshire. On 6th January, Norwich, with 18.8 degrees of frost, was the coldest place in England. In the ports around the coast, vessels were glazed with ice. Inland, a damp grey mist drifted over the snow. Local authorities had insufficient horses and carts with which their labour gangs could clear the roads. And everywhere, as the snow began to melt, the rivers began to rise menacingly.

The geography of East Anglia makes it peculiarly liable to flooding; it shares many of the features, and the problems, of the Netherlands, which face it from across the North Sea. Along most of the coast erosion has been a serious problem throughout history; whole towns and villages have been lost beneath the sea. A considerable inland area in the so-called Fens lies below the level of the waterways as they run down to the sea. Vast sums of money have been spent over centuries to seek protection. Back in the seventeenth century the Dutchman Cornelius Vermuyden spent most of his life, and a large part of the local landowners' fortunes, building dykes and cutting drains.

North of Cambridge, for a distance of 70 miles to the sea at the Wash, and across a breadth of 35 miles, most of the countryside was marshland until Vermuyden came. The cathedral town of Ely and a few other small settlements — March, Chatteris, Littleport, Thorney, Whittlesey — stood up as islands in this great fenland. Vermuyden drained the area, supplemented the outflow of its languorous curving rivers with a network of embanked canals, and opened the way for farming. The countryside is, of course, dead flat. The canals are dead straight. There are few trees or hedges. The dykes limit lines of sight. Away from the main roads, access is by "droves": tracks beside the waterways, green and spongy in summer, but muddy and rutted in winter. The Fenmen of 1939 covered most of their territories in punts.

In a winter like that of 1938-9 they were full of apprehension. They had suffered serious flooding in 1936 and 1937, after which efforts continued unceasingly to raise the river banks. Now, as 1939 came in, the water in the principal river, the Great Ouse, was rising by a foot each day. Day after day, week after week, the threat continued; sometimes the water fell a few inches, but never sufficiently to relieve anxiety, and usually some roads in the region were deep under water. On Saturday, 28th January the Chief Engineer of the Great Ouse Catchment Board concluded that the drainage system of the area nearest to Cambridge, the "South Level", could take only another eight inches of water before disaster would occur. On the Sunday the town crier went out into the streets of Waterbeach, a small town on the Cam just north of Cambridge, to call for volunteers to work on the banks. The next day the water was over the main road and railway links between Cambridge and King's Lynn and was flooding homes in Littleport.

Trains travelling through the Fens had to contend with flood water on the permanent way — a typical scene near Littleport station.

Cambridge Evening News

Now men were out all day and all night, patrolling, measuring, shovelling. Whole villages turned out to help; the Salvation Army organised food and hot cocoa to fuel their efforts. "Three hundred men with lanterns patrolled nearly 400 miles of Fenland waterways on Wednesday and Thursday nights, as the first two of three high 'Spring tides' blocked the outlets into the Wash," the *Lynn Advertiser* reported on 3rd February. "As they patrolled, scrutinising every yard of the banking, hundreds of other men were stopping with clay any small holes as they appeared, or piling sandbags on parapets where the water was already lapping . . ."

The tension, and indeed the terror, of those nights is implicit in the recollection of a man who more than once joined in fighting the floods:

> "The river was level, full of water. We carried a spade and a torch and we went up towards Brandon Creek. My brother was with me, and the bank was leaking, and he left me all on my own in the dark to go and report it. The wind was a-howling; we had to tie our hats on with string. That was the worst night I've ever had in my life."[2]

In the last hours of January two dams gave way. Thousands of acres of cultivated land were inundated. Spring wheat, celery, mangold and clamps of potatoes lay under two feet of water. Farmhouses and farm buildings stood isolated, deserted and forlorn amid the floods. In many cases they had been abandoned two or three weeks earlier, as the threat developed.

Suddenly, the whole situation changed. On 1st February the water fell by as much as a foot in a day and some families returned to their homes by boat. On the following day there was a fall of several inches everywhere in Fenland. It went on falling and before the week-end an official of the Great Ouse Catchment Board felt confident enough to say "We are getting on top now".

Meanwhile, on the eastern side of the region in the counties of Norfolk, Suffolk and Essex, the weather inflicted comparable hardships. Whenever high tides and easterly gales coincided, land here was liable to inundation. A stretch of many miles of coast immediately east of Norwich was being barricaded with bags of concrete and great metal stakes after tragic floods early in 1938. Many trees were dead, the land was stained and salted. Further south, the port and seaside resort of Lowestoft had spent something like half a million pounds on its sea defences; though there was a bonus in the form of fine marine parades for the holiday-makers, the local ratepayers were appalled and restless about the expense. Southward again, at the smaller resorts of Southwold and Aldeburgh, possible defence works were being discussed in a general atmosphere of apprehension that the sea might make major breaches that might change the whole landscape. The repair and extension of sea walls was a problem of every East Coast public authority.

The flood of January 1939, however, did not come from the sea, but from exceptionally heavy rainfall inland. Ipswich fared the worst. On 25th and 26th January the town had about two and a half inches of rain, the river Gipping burst its banks and hundreds of homes were quickly flooded. In some parts of the town the water was five feet deep. Furniture floated in the streets. Police, aided by firemen and Boy Scouts, rescued bungalow dwellers in rowing boats; those in houses moved upstairs. It was four days before the flood began to recede, by which time widespread distress had been caused. The Mayor of Ipswich opened a fund for the victims and over £11,000 was subscribed in a few weeks.

---

2. Recalled by Mr C. R. Everitt, of Southery, in an interview with the author in 1980. This recollection did not refer specifically to the 1939 floods.

The task of building the sea defences at Horsey was completed in January.

Norwich Mercury series

Elsewhere, traffic was halted on many roads, trains ran seriously behind schedule, electricity and telephone services were interrupted and much farmland was inundated as storms continued and rivers burst their banks. It was, the greybeards said, the worst weather for forty years.

And then Nature made its amends. There were very few days in February when the sun did not shine. Some days in March were the warmest for a decade. By 12th April the temperature in Ipswich reached 77 degrees Fahrenheit in the shade — the hottest day at that time ever recorded there.

*   *   *   *   *

East Anglia in 1939 seemed remote from the remainder of the country, and very much self-contained. Its major centres, Norwich, Ipswich, Cambridge and Colchester, had a continuous and varied contact with the outside world, and its holiday resorts — Clacton, Great Yarmouth, Cromer and half a dozen others — drew in large numbers of visitors from the industrial cities during the summer months. But few people went to East Anglia without a specific destination and purpose. It was not *on the way to anywhere else,* and most of its rural acres remained undiscovered by outsiders.

Nor did East Anglians, the majority of whom lived in the villages and small agricultural towns, travel far themselves: usually only to the nearest market town, perhaps once or twice during the summer for a day's outing at the coast. Summing up their characteristics in 1939, an honest but sympathetic observer, Doreen Wallace, wrote:

"Nothing in their lives causes them to examine their established habits and beliefs."[3]

Ways of life, and social attitudes, had changed much more slowly in East Anglia than in most other parts of Britain. Agriculture still employed the majority of the people, and farmers showed considerable resistance to change in equipment and techniques. Cambridge University might have absorbed the thinking and practice of the Renaissance, but in many villages the social climate seemed to have changed very little since medieval times. It remained a hierarchical and inward-looking society.

There was a significant royal presence in East Anglia, for the Sandringham Estate in Norfolk was a home well-liked by King George VI and his Queen. They spent the whole of January 1939 there, with the old Queen Mary and the young Princesses Elizabeth and Margaret. The King enjoyed the shooting. Queen Mary liked to be driven through the countryside, to see the sea at Hunstanton or to visit a favourite antiques shop in Cambridge. The whole family attended the village church at Sandringham each Sunday. There was a full programme of house parties. The Duke and Duchess of Kent were among the guests for the New Year; later in the month there was a big party with Crown Prince Olaf of Norway, the Princess Royal, the Earl of Harewood and the Lascelles children. The Royal family were received by leading county families into the stately homes of Norfolk; on one such occasion during that bitter month of January the local British Legion band played selections on the terrace outside the dining room.

A temporary footbridge in use to replace the road bridge that was washed away during the flooding near Ditchingham Station. *Norwich Mercury* series

3. See Doreen Wallace: *East Anglia*, Batsford, 1939.

The region had a second focal point of royal interest at Newmarket, the headquarters of the Jockey Club since its foundation in the eighteenth century. Among the thousand or more horses kept in training there were some owned by the King, and when he returned to London from Sandringham on 1st February 1939 he made a wide detour to Newmarket to watch fifteen of them at exercise. The Queen went with him and for ninety minutes they admired the horses and chatted with their trainer, Mr W. R. Jarvis. It had only just become "Royal Newmarket" again; King George V did not race there after 1928 and his son made his first visit in April 1938. But 1939 was to be an important year in the history of the turf: two classic events, the Cambridgeshire and the Cesarewitch, were to be run for the one hundredth time, and the Jockey Club would be celebrating its 190th anniversary. The King's visit at the outset of the year was, therefore, of special significance.

Much of East Anglia in 1939 was in the hands of titled landowners. Some of them devoted themselves energetically to agricultural experiment and improvement, maintaining a tradition which went back to Coke of Norfolk, the first Earl of Leicester, who, rather more than a century before, had revolutionised the farming scene. Some of them, in the generally depressed state of agriculture at the time, were in financial difficulties. One of the biggest of the noble landowners, the Duke of Grafton, who had only recently inherited the Euston Estate in Suffolk, observed sadly at the annual banquet of the London Society of East Anglians in April 1939: "Some of the big estates have gone, which I look upon as nothing less than a tragedy — and this caused almost entirely by the short-sighted policy of our government, who drain all the capital from the unfortunate landlords by way of taxation and death duties."

As a general rule, however, the landed gentry were maintaining their position well enough. They preserved their closely-knit class distinction. They inter-married. They were members of, and often dominated, every kind of elected public authority and they provided patrons, presidents and chairmen (and chair-women) for every kind of voluntary organisation. They let their farms to tenants, who usually identified their interest with those of their landlords. They provided employment, directly or indirectly, for a majority of the East Anglian population, who felt dependent upon them. This applied as much to the women as the men, for most girls in 1939 left school to go into domestic service.

An unusual insight into this world is provided by the Journals of Sir Robert White, who was the Chairman of the East Suffolk County Council in 1939.[4] In the first week of January he presided at a County Council meeting, at a meeting of the Woodbridge Public Health Committee, and at the Quarter Sessions at Ipswich. He entertained guests at the weekend in his Queen Anne mansion, Boulge Hall, and four of them went out on the

---

4. Sir Robert White; Journals. Suffolk Record Office, Ipswich.

Saturday morning and bagged 42 pheasants. Later in the month he lunched with the High Sheriff, took under his roof a neighbour who had handed *his* house over to the judge who was presiding at Ipswich Assize Court, and was then invited by another neighbour to travel as a guest on a trip to Egypt. Sir Robert was seventy-four, but he seems to have been indefatigable. Day after day throughout the year he attends rural, district and county councils, committees of every kind, conferences about drainage schemes, meetings of school governors, sessions with the bishop to discuss religious instruction. He presides at the meeting of the Suffolk Horse Society and he opens a succession of local fetes and similar events. The young members of his family bring their guests to his home, there are week-end parties, hunt balls to attend and tennis to play. The domestic staff make demands on his time, too. One Sunday in July, he records, he went specially to the parish church: "Monks, the head gardener, Mrs Hodges, the chauffeur's wife, and Jean, the under-housemaid, attended, having just been confirmed."

These activities he combined with the management of his estate, noting in his diary each significant event. In March he made plans to plant extra potatoes "in the small meadow against the Cypress Court, in case of war". In June he records that "some corn has been knocked about by the rain . . . There is a plague of little frogs from the pool." When the war comes he supervises the ploughing up of his parkland. His public and private activities and responsibilities dovetail snugly together at every point. The most remarkable demonstration of this was provided when his son married and joined the Army for war service.

"Everyone voted it a perfect county wedding," reported Sir Robert when his son, Richard, married the only daughter of the Dowager Marchioness Townshend, whose family had owned one of the greatest Norfolk estates for something like five hundred years. Richard's regiment, the Loyal Suffolk Hussars, provided a Guard of Honour.

Almost immediately afterwards, on 2nd September, Richard was called to join his regiment full-time. For a period he remained, with his unit, in the neighbourhood. One morning in early November Sir Robert White set off across his park to see what progress was being made with the clearance of a great hedge between the Rose Meadow and an osier bed. Before he reached his objective, an Army lorry approached, carrying his son and another officer. "They want their battery to come for a night," Sir Robert recorded in his journal that evening. "The guns will be in the South Park, with a guard, and the rest of the men probably in the Court Room . . . " Within the week, the battery arrived, took up positions, and Richard flew over the park to judge if the camouflage was effective. The Officer Commanding the regiment turned up, too, with other top brass, made an inspection, and stayed to dine at the Hall with Sir Robert. On the Saturday before these manoeuvres began Boulge

Hall staged its own celebration of the recent marriage. "We had a party for them — or really two parties, one for the neighbours at which there were about 50, and another in the servants' hall and billiard room for the tenants and employees . . . Afterwards the tenants and wives came into the other party and had sherry before leaving."

The sense of duty and responsibility of men like Sir Robert White was immensely impressive and when later we dip again into his journal of 1939 we shall find further reason to accord him profound respect; but what emerges clearly is that, for Sir Robert and his kind, the literal defence of hearth and home which began in 1939 was also an instinctive expression of a patriotism which embraced an absolute belief in the social structure of the time. Most people could not be expected to share such a belief; certainly not the woman who recalled:

"My father died when I was nine. He was an engine driver. I can remember my mother saying she had ten shillings then for herself, and five shillings pension for me. The day I was fourteen — I remember it now — this money stopped. So she said: 'I'm afraid you've got to go out to service now.' I had to have my first little job. I believe I cried the whole night. Then I earned five shillings a week. I used to have to pay back for what she'd spent on me. That's how hard things were then . . . "[5]

That woman's husband, recalling the same period, said: "My brother was called up. He went about a month after. *They took him to the war* and he was in France, after six weeks' training . . . "[6]

Between these two extremes, there was a so-called middle class: the more prosperous farmers, shop-keepers, professional men. Something of the special quality of their lives is captured in this recollection:

"I was earning the average salary for qualified men in a responsible position — £250 per annum, plus about £15 bonus and a Christmas box. My wife had a small private income of about £50 a year and we had no mortgage on our house, as my father-in-law gave it to us as a wedding present.

We were paying to educate two boys at the best private school in Norwich — the Grammar School. We had a hut on the beach at Gorleston and my two weeks annual holiday was spent on my brother-in-law's farm near Halesworth, where I was expected to be, and enjoyed being, a labourer during the harvest. We had a car, but we never, at any time, tried to keep up with the Joneses. We did not go out for an evening meal except on the most special occasions, and then there was no question of drinking wine — we couldn't afford it on our salaries."[7]

5. Mrs C. R. Everitt, of Southery, in an interview with the author in 1980.
6. Mr C. R. Everitt, interviewed.
7. Mr Edward J. Cunningham, of Barnham, in an interview with the author in 1979.

"Pride in their craft" — Mr H. Richardson, a thatcher of Monks Eleigh, shown covering a stack at Hill Farm, Chelsworth. *East Anglian Daily Times*

11

Undoubtedly, snobbery was a feature of life in the larger towns, where all classes of society were in close contact. Most people seem to have known how to "keep their place" and the hierarchical pattern among the better-off seems to have had a mirror-image among those who were dependent upon them. Mistresses and their staffs were doubtless equally keen to be listed in the report of the seventh annual Domestic Staffs' Ball, held at the Dorothy Cafe in Cambridge in February 1939. The *Cambridge Independent News* reported: "A buffet provided delicacies which ranged from veal and ham patties to reception fancies . . . Among those present were staffs of the following households: Lady Wentworth Stanley, Lady Hiley, Lady Briscoe, Captain Sykes, Captain Thornhill, Lord Fairhaven . . . " There followed a long list of professors, doctors, clergymen and others with titles. A more explicit suggestion that the worth of the humble was to be measured by the distinction of the master is to be found in a report of a ploughing match at the village of Eyke, near Woodbridge, in May. The horsemen expended all the effort and displayed all the skill, but the results were announced thus: 1. Sir Charles Bunbury (horseman, A. Airey); 2. J. P. Flemming (E. A. Fuller); 3. Lord Alastair Graham (S. Smith).

It would be quite wrong to suggest that social stratification meant either happiness for the privileged or misery for the oppressed. It would have been difficult to find many people in East Anglia who saw the situation in such terms. The evidence of how they voted shows that only a minority positively wanted to see any big changes in their society. Though their hours were long and their home conditions primitive, country dwellers displayed a deep spirit of contentment and found pleasure in the calm and beauty of their surroundings, the rhythmic pattern of the seasons, and the close relationships of families and friends in self-contained communities. Their pride in craft traditions enabled most of them to get real satisfaction from their work.

In the towns, people enjoyed most of these things, and more. In these urbanised communities there was organised dissent, there was a high rate of unemployment, and there were still some slums. Nevertheless, they were lively, colourful, bustling places, where a visit to the big open-air markets, the relatively new chain stores, and the great variety of specialist shops created a weekly excitement in which all shared. Because the streets were narrow, and therefore congested, they seemed to pulsate. Ancient hostelries fulfilled their ancient role as centres of activity: bargains were struck, village carriers came and went at intervals, news was systematically exchanged.

People enjoyed more home comforts and conveniences than ever before. New housing estates had been built by local authorities on the outskirts of the towns, and bathrooms and modern kitchens had become commonplace. New schools were being built. Most people had the entertainment provided by the radio, and cinemas offered a quick escape route to a form of luxury and excitement. Sport, particularly football and greyhound racing, engaged the enthusiasm of the men. For the better-off minority, the motor-car and the telephone added a new dimension to living. For the intellectual élite, there were theatres and libraries and a remarkable number of voluntary organisations dedicated to music, art and drama, and most types of specialist interest.

An advertisement during January for the Ford 8 at the new price of £115.
Cambridge Evening News

But the economic life of East Anglia in 1939 was dependant upon agriculture. In Norfolk and Suffolk, for example, nearly 30 per cent of the male working population was directly employed on farms.[8]. Many of the manufacturing and service industries in the towns depended entirely upon the local or regional market, and their fortunes were thus linked to agriculture.

From 1925 British agriculture had been in a seriously depressed condition. Despite the provision of some subsidies in the 'thirties, imports of farm products into Britain rose steadily and by 1939 we were importing over seventy per cent of the food we required. In East Anglia farmers were in despair. Their 1937 and 1938 harvests had been particularly disappointing, and even wheat, sugar beet and potatoes had failed to cover their costs.

8. See T. Eastwood: *Industry in the Country Towns of Norfolk and Suffolk,* Oxford University Press, 1951. This report was the result of a survey commissioned by the Development Commisioners and financed out of the Development Fund.

Some of the Fenland farmers were more fortunate. Their reclaimed land, with its rich black soil, was some of the best in Britain; it was said that their wheat grew a foot taller than anyone else's. They did not carry much stock, for this land did not require manure, and they concentrated on sugar-beet and potatoes. A Ministry of Agriculture census of 1937 showed Cambridgeshire, including the Isle of Ely, with one of the highest totals of tractors in use of any county in England. This happy picture was not seen everywhere, however. There was much Fen skirt land, where sand overlay the peat, with low productivity. It was cropped for about three years and then abandoned for two or three years, except that the grass was cut for hay; it would then be ploughed and sown to mustard and in this way the soil was expected to recover to carry wheat again, without the use of fertilisers. There was also a good deal of other Fen land which was permanently derelict and waterlogged.

In Norfolk and Suffolk, however, things were even worse. The traditional pattern had been mixed farming: most of the land used as arable, some pasture, sheep moving over the arable in folds, and cattle and pigs kept in yards. A four-course rotation of clover, wheat, fodder roots and barley was usual. This was labour-intensive (even in 1939, when the pattern had changed a great deal, Suffolk farms employed three men per hundred acres, compared with two, taking England and Wales as a whole) but it kept the land in good heart and it was believed to be the way to produce the maximum food per acre.[9]

From 1928-29 depression began to undermine the four-course rotation as the areas under wheat and barley declined. The sheep population was dramatically reduced and so the need for turnips and swedes was reduced. Farmers sought to cut production costs and to collect their returns more quickly. Some of the land was bought by farmers who moved in from Scotland and built up dairy herds, and their example was widely followed. In Suffolk dairy herds increased by twenty-five per cent during the depression years. The area of permanent grassland was extended. Pig populations increased. Some areas turned to fruit-growing. But the most significant change came with the introduction of sugar-beet. A sugar-beet factory opened at Bury St Edmunds in 1925 was, at the time, the largest in Britain. Others were opened all over the region: at King's Lynn, Ely, Cantley (near Norwich), Sproughton (near Ipswich) and Wissington (between Sudbury and Colchester). By 1939 the Bury St Edmunds factory was contracted to take the production from 42,590 acres, and contracts such as these kept afloat many farmers who would otherwise have gone under.

Less significant for the region as a whole, but important to the areas in which they were sited were the canneries opened at Woodbridge, North Walsham and Swaffham during the 'thirties to handle the increased production of fruit and vegetables.

9. See T. Eastwood, as before; and also P. J. O. Trist: "A Survey of the Agriculture of Suffolk", Royal Agricultural Society of England, 1971; and also "Norwich and its Region", British Association for the Advancement of Science, 1961.

There was one other change in land use which had greatly affected the appearance of part of East Anglia by 1939: afforestation. The so-called Breckland around Thetford had never yielded good crops before the Forestry Commission took it over in the early 'twenties and began to plant enormous areas of spruce. Thetford Forest, one of the largest in the country, was planted during the 'twenties and The King's Forest had been fully planted by 1939.

None of these changes brought real prosperity to the farming community as a whole. The Farm Economics branch of the Department of Agriculture at Cambridge University surveyed two hundred representative farms in twelve separate districts in the Eastern Counties over a number of years during the 'thirties and it produced a general picture of losses which in no way could have been avoided.

Harvesting with a self-binder during the summer of 1939. Horse-drawn machinery was still commonplace on the farms. *B.B.C. Hulton Picture Library*

By 1939, in fact, there were thousands of acres of heavy land in Suffolk which had reverted to thorn bush and there were thousands of acres of light virgin heathland which there was no prospect of cultivating at a profit. No further capital was being invested in the land. Something like a quarter of the total acreage had passed into the possession of owner-occupiers as the big estates had been broken up after the First World War; these small men had used all their resources for the original purchase. In Suffolk during the 'thirties most farms of more than 150 acres acquired a tractor—but there were fewer than 1,500 such farms, compared with nearly 6,300 of less than 150 acres. In 1939 there were fewer than a dozen combine harvesters in the whole of Suffolk

15

and single-furrow horse-drawn ploughs were a much more familiar sight than two-, three- or four-furrow ploughs behind a tractor. There were 18,238 horses used for agricultural purposes in the county.[10] Significant changes were taking place in the numbers employed on the land, as the following table shows:

Numbers of Agricultural Workers in Norfolk and Suffolk. [11]

	TOTAL	REGULAR			CASUAL
		Males under 21	Males over 21	Females	
June 1931	64,840	9,232	44,613	1,842	9,153
June 1939	63,216	8,796	40,503	1,579	12,338

*   *   *   *   *

The preservation of a traditional social structure, combined with the decline of the basic economic activity of the region, inhibited most developments which might have affected the visual beauty and the pace of life. The low standard, indeed very often the total absence of, water, sewerage and electricity services, discouraged new industries from moving in. Transport, on the other hand, was relatively good. There was main road access to East Anglia from London by the A10 to Cambridge and King's Lynn, the A11 to Newmarket and Norwich, and the A12 to Ipswich and Lowestoft. Within the region, a number of towns were by-passed during the 'thirties including Colchester and Woodbridge and construction was proceeding on the first sections of a Norwich ring road. Cambridge was lively with controversy about its proposed ring road; at a public enquiry in March 1939 critics objected to the proposed line of road near Grantchester and much anxiety was expressed about the future of the Gogs and Madingley Woods. Bus services and carriers operated from all the principal towns to serve their satellite villages; there were nearly 200 carrier services operating in and out of Norwich and Ipswich, for example, and about 60 motorbus services and carriers served Bury St Edmunds and its neighbourhood.[12] Many firms had gone over to using their own road transport—in 1939 there were believed to be about 50,000 goods vehicles operated by 17,000 owners in East Anglia. This was a development at the expense of the railways, which in 1939 had a heavy network of lines serving every part of the region. They operated under restrictions imposed by governments in the days when the railways enjoyed monopoly conditions; now they were campaigning strenuously for a "square deal". Most of the lines in East Anglia belonged to the London and North Eastern Railway Company—one of the "big four" railways in 1939.

10. See P. J. O. Trist, as before.
11. Table reproduced from T. Eastwood, as above.
12. See *Suffolk County Handbook and Official Directory, 1939*, published by the *East Anglian Daily Times*, Ipswich, and *Kelly's Directory of Norfolk, 1938*.

The L.N.E.R. tried very hard to improve its fortunes. After 1936 the government offered loans to the railways at the low rate of interest of two and a half per cent, and one of the biggest improvement schemes which resulted was for colour-light signalling to Chelmsford, as a preliminary to later electrification of the line. Virtually all motive power was provided by coal-fired steam locomotives, but they were capable of high performance on tight schedules. A luxury six-coach train, with specially streamlined locomotives, was introduced in September 1937, named "The East Anglian". It linked Norwich with Ipswich in 48 minutes and with London in 130 minutes. At the same time five-coach buffet-car trains were introduced between London and Cambridge, running three times a day on a 65 minutes schedule. Until 1939 Cromer enjoyed five trains each day running through to London, and they were speeded up for Saturday holiday traffic to give running times of 173 minutes for the up journey and 187 for the down. Continental visitors arriving at Harwich could ride in new coaching stock introduced in 1938 or in the older but more elegant Pullman cars. There were Sunday Pullman excursions from London to Clacton in the summer of 1939, running in 90 minutes.

Luxury train: the six coach "East Anglian", with specially streamlined locomotive, linked Norwich with London in 130 minutes. *Crown Copyright: National Railway Museum*

East Anglia also had a number of railway links across the region, the most important of which was the Midland and Great Northern Joint Railway, the 182 route miles of which linked Peterborough, King's Lynn, Cromer, Norwich and Yarmouth. Other east-west lines linked Norwich-Thetford-Ely, Ipswich-Bury St Edmunds-Cambridge, Colchester-Sudbury-Cambridge, and Maldon-Witham-Braintree-Bishop's Stortford. Communities such as Framlingham, Eye, Thaxted, Dunmow, Long Melford, Halstead, Lavenham and Swaffham all had their regular passenger trains. A single-track railway ran to the village of Laxfield, in deepest mid-Suffolk, and there stopped dead.

The L.N.E.R. bravely struggled to improve its services. It called a press conference in May 1939 to draw attention to the improvements it had made in the course of the previous year. It had straightened out the main line and provided extra platform accommodation at Colchester; it had improved facilities in the terminus at Clacton and it had in hand the duplication of the line between Clacton and Thorpe-le-Soken; King's Lynn station was in course of reconstruction, with a new booking office and refreshment rooms; refreshment rooms had been improved in the stations at Cambridge, Ipswich, Ely and Felixstowe. The railway company owned the top-ranking Felix Hotel at Felixstowe and, anxious to keep abreast of the times, it had installed a cocktail lounge there.

The cruel truth, however, was that these railways were in decline. Some of the branch lines never had paid their way, but were justified as "feeders" to the trunk routes. By 1939 the internal combustion engine offered commerce and individual travellers a form of door-to-door transport which steam-propelled trains could not match. According to an historian of the region's railways, "from the 1920s even holiday traffic tended to decline and by the late 1930s agricultural patronage was falling steadily away. Rural passenger levels and overall seasonal fluctuations remained as disheartening as ever — in 1939 the estimated number of tickets collected in the whole of Suffolk reached only 21,000 in January and 97,000 in August . . . "[13]

Those who used the roads and railways to explore the region in 1939 saw a good deal of change in progress. Most of it was cosmetic, but some was surgical. In Ipswich, Colchester and Cambridge it was a matter of heart surgery. Julian Tennyson noted in 1939 that in Ipswich many fine old timbered houses had been pulled down or engulfed and that the timbered and crooked old taverns which had once set the tone of the town were rapidly disappearing; "I believe that more than 30 have been pulled down in the last two years alone," he wrote.[14] In April 1939 another notable hostelry disappeared with the closure of the Cross Keys, a Victorian rebuild of an important coaching inn which dated back to the seventeenth century. In Colchester the local Civic Society tried vainly to save a number of old houses

13. D. I. Gordon: *A Regional History of the Railways of Great Britain, Vol. V: The Eastern Counties*, David and Charles, 1968, reprinting 1981.

14. Julian Tennyson: *Suffolk Scene*, Blackie and Sons, 1939; reprinted and republished by E. P. Publishing Ltd, with an introduction by Ronald Blythe, 1973. No more sensitive and

which were demolished in 1939 to permit town centre re-development at Culver Street; the best they could achieve was the preservation in the Castle Museum of one bay of a timber-framed hall.

The major development in Cambridge during 1939 was the completion and formal opening of a new Guildhall dominating the south side of Market Hill, but this was the culmination of a big scheme of demolition and reconstruction which affected a large proportion of the centre of the town. The north side of Market Hill had been transformed a few years earlier when all the old buildings had been replaced by a modern block owned by Caius College. Then, to clear the site for the new Guildhall, a row of old timber-framed houses and shops in Peas Hill was demolished, one of them dating from about 1450 and containing massive oak timbers from an old ship and fine linen-fold panelling hidden beneath twenty-seven coats of paint. Two other streets in the centre of the town, Bridge Street and Sussex Street, were rebuilt and widened, to provide the university with improved accommodation and the town with a better traffic flow. There were some critics of these schemes. The Cambridgeshire County Council passed a resolution in January 1939 regretting the continuation of the policy of street widening in the town centre (for which the Town Council carried responsibility, though the County Council met forty per cent of the costs). It was argued, in response, that assessment values had increased so much as result of the re-development that the whole of the cost would be quickly recouped in increased rates. The architecture of most of the new buildings, however, aroused general admiration. The Cambridge Preservation Society considered the new Guildhall made "an important contribution to the dignity of the town".[15]

Norwich also completed a dominating new public building at this time: a redbrick City Hall of austere design, with a tall tower with gilded clockface. It echoed the lines of the much-admired hall in Stockholm, but the citizens of Norwich at first made it the source of lively controversy. Soon, however, it was featured on the picture postcards sold to tourists as worthy to take its place beside the cathedral and the castle, and it was accepted as an impressive backscreen to the kaleidoscopic market scene before it.

In most other towns in East Anglia it was a sense of permanence, rather than of change, that impressed the visitor. Those who went to King's Lynn, for example, usually entered through a castellated gate built in 1437 and then found themselves in one of the most splendid examples of a medieval borough surviving in Britain. The great market place was surrounded by fine houses, few of which were less than two hundred years old. Large churches rose above narrow streets. Granaries and warehouses served a port where the little ships had come and gone with grain and timber for many centuries. Great Yarmouth was the most important herring fishing port in the United Kingdom, but when the catches had been cleared and tranquillity settled on

15. See F. A. Reeve: *Cambridge*, Batsford, 1964; and John Steegman: *Cambridge as it was and as it is today*, Batsford, 1940.

the quays, and the thirteenth-century Toll-House and the fourteenth-century Cloister and the Elizabethan merchants' houses were illumined by a sun shining from those immense East Anglian skies, then it had the timeless quality of a Vermeer or a van Ruisdael painting. The fishermen's quarter of Old Lowestoft was intact, more or less as Charles Dickens had described it, with tightly-packed cottages below the cliffs and tarred sheds dotted along the shore and nets stretched on the drying grounds.

Inland, Bury St Edmunds was a perfect example of a county town serving a purely agricultural community, and entirely unconcerned with outside opinions or modes of behaviour. All of its activities seemed to move with a relaxed grace. There was little evidence of unrestrained commercialism. Houses of every period blended harmoniously in a composition which embraced two enormous abbey gateways, an outstanding example of late eighteenth-century Assembly Rooms (though in 1939 one visitor reported that "its cracking and stained plaster and large black windows look miserable")[16] and a massive colonnaded Corn Exchange. Newmarket was another town of grace and charm, though the style was different. It was set in wide, green heathland and ringed by superbly-maintained stud farms. Generations of well-to-do devotees of the turf had built fine houses and the headquarters of the Jockey Club gave tone to the town while suggesting a certain aloofness from those who thronged the wide main street and who were less concerned with purity of pedigree. Peterborough, at the eastern rim of the region, had less distinction, but a remarkable twelfth-century cathedral, Norman-Romanesque in style, with a horizontal emphasis to its design which matched it to the plain in which it stood. Ely Cathedral, also largely twelfth-century, exemplified Late Romanesque but was also richly Gothic and stood high above the Fens to attract travellers to the slumbering streets around it.

A corner of the Cornhill, Bury St Edmunds, before alterations for the bus park. *East Anglian Daily Times*

16. Doreen Wallace, as before.

In general, however, the western side of the region, as we have already remarked, was not of outstanding natural beauty. The Fens were flat and treeless. Moving eastward, Breckland was barren or, where the Forestry Commission was at work, changing into a dark landscape of tall, dense timber. Eastward again, the huge flat farms of Norfolk glowed yellow at harvest time, but could look flint-grey when winter winds whipped across from the North Sea. Between Norwich and the sea the meres and marshes of the Broads brooded mistily through most of the year, to spring to life when the first holiday makers arrived in the spring and the pleasure boats were launched for a new season of cruising. Change *was* noticeable here, as each year more boats were available for hire, more advertising signs appeared, more shops and shacks served the needs of the young men and women in rollneck sweaters, slacks and canvas shoes. Along the Norfolk coast, too, southward from Cromer, there was something new: small colonies of summer bungalows and a number of "holiday camps" offering a new kind of all-in escape formula.

Rural Suffolk was resistant to all change. It was a country of far vistas and secret places. There was nothing neat and tidy about the images it offered, yet they were richly harmonious. Julian Tennyson wrote of its "pattern of disorderliness". In 1939 one thought one saw exactly the countryside which Constable had painted, in essence if not in precise detail. It is impossible to improve on Tennyson's description of hedgerows . . .

". . . fascinating, extravagant and dramatic. Hazel, may, bramble, blackthorn, anything than can find a place in them, runs amok in a dizzy tangle until the hedges tower twelve feet about their banks and the over-burdened lanes seem to contract to half their real width.

Like the country itself, the buildings are quite irregular and illogical in their placing and character. Cottages and farmhouses, even churches, often seem to exist without any human contact at all, connected with the nearest road by an almost unrecognisable and wholly impassable cart-track. On a walk of a dozen miles you will find scores of them, desolate, untended, making their last, long stand against decay; today they seem even farther from civilisation than they were three hundred years ago, and rather than their beauty it is their stubborness and their courage that will attract you . . . "[17]

Throughout this East Anglian countryside — not only in Suffolk — there were buildings in series of a kind which were characteristic of this part of England. First to catch the eye were the windmills, probably a couple of hundred of them in total. When the Suffolk Preservation Society staged an exhibition of photographs in Ipswich in June 1939 it included photographs of 150 windmills in that county alone, most of which were said still to be standing though some were derelict. A county council sub-committee reported at about

17. Julian Tennyson, as before.

the same time that Suffolk had more post mills in working order than there were in the whole of the rest of England together. There were also smock mills and tower mills, and efforts were being made to preserve a representative collection of all kinds.

Along the coasts of Norfolk, Suffolk and Essex, often at the most desolate parts, there were the remains of fortifications which, by 1939, had no practical significance but were a symbolic reminder that these were the shores upon which, through many centuries, invaders had landed. Most of them were circular fortresses, about forty feet high, which had been built by the Royal Engineers in 1810-12 against the threat of Napoleonic invasion. They were called Martello Towers because they were inspired by a fortress of similar design in Corsica, the Torre della Martella, which had withstood a bombardment by an English fleet under Lord Hood in 1794.

Another characteristic building in many towns were the maltings for, although the acreage of barley was decreasing, it was still a principal crop and East Anglian brewers such as Adnam, Greene King, Cobbold, Lacon, Tolly, Dales, Morgans and Steward and Patteson were producing some of the best beer in Britain. Some of the maltings stood disused in 1939, but there were still many towns where the first greeting to the visitor came in the distinctive whiff of barley being steeped and germinated.

The windmill at Eye: one of those included in the Suffolk Preservation Society's exhibition of photographs in Ipswich during June 1939.

H. Norman Collinson

The richest architectural treasures of the countryside, however, were those which had been created with the wealth of East Anglian landowners and merchants who had controlled the production and sale of wool and woollen cloth: the glorious clerestoried churches and the magnificent manor houses, which were often moated. These were the artistic triumphs of a society which had preserved its essential features since time immemorial; but, in 1939, some of these buildings and some of the features of the old society showed signs of crumbling.

*　　*　　*　　*　　*

In the homes, the schools, the churches, the council chambers and the factories, what happened during the course of 1939 cannot be adequately described in terms of actual dates and specific events. It was the trends and the developments which were significant.

Neville Chamberlain with Lord Halifax and Mussolini during his visit to Rome.

B.B.C. Hulton Picture Library

On the world stage dramatic events occurred all too frequently, and not even the dullest cottager in the most isolated hamlet of East Anglia could ignore them. The battery radio set, the local newspaper and the visiting politician poured out news and views as Britain and France, on one side, and the European dictators, on the other, took up positions for the coming conflict. In January Prime Minister Chamberlain went to Rome to talk with Mussolini. "The result of the visit has been entirely negative," the diplomatic correspondent of the *East Anglian Daily Times* told his readers afterwards. In February the British and French governments formally recognised the insurgent Franco regime in Spain. In March German forces occupied the whole of Czechoslovakia, Mr Chamberlain put the Territorial Army on a war basis and guaranteed the independence of Poland. In April the Italians invaded Albania, Hitler abrogated German treaties with Britain and Poland, and Mr Chamberlain announced conscription for all twenty-year-olds.

The political organisations in the East Anglian constituencies received regular guidance from their M.Ps and candidates. In March Mr John Hare, the prospective National Government candidate for Woodbridge, sobered a series of meetings with his declaration that "by bringing seven million Czechs, proud of their land, under the rule of Germany, Hitler has shown for the first time that he is out for world domination". This was a time for the stiff upper lip. On 4th July Captain Frank Heilgers, the Member of Parliament for Bury St Edmunds, told a Newmarket audience that "he did not believe that war was imminent and he thought it was a great mistake for people to pass on rumours that war was likely to break out". At Stowmarket a few days later Mr Edgar Granville, M.P. for Eye, explained how Mr Chamberlain was handling matters: "He is in complete control of the situation. He is playing a great game of poker with Hitler and he cannot tell everyone what cards he is going to play. But I believe he is going to get through, and it is our duty to support him . . . " Mr Somerset de Chair, M.P. for South-West Norfolk, was still confidently predicting on 8th August at Dereham: "There will be no war for Britain this year".

The House of Commons adjourned on 4th August for its two-months summer recess. It was hastily summoned on 24th August to hear the Prime Minister declare: "The country finds itself today in imminent peril of war." Thereupon, on that same day, it debated and passed an Act which gave the government almost absolute powers. There were some last-minute exchanges with Hitler, but the die had been cast, and war was declared on 3rd September.

Obviously, these were the matters which made the principal headlines in the newspapers of East Anglia, as elsewhere. There was also a diligent coverage of the predictable routines of community life: the local authority debates, the petty crime, the marriages and deaths, the amateur dramatics, the sporting events. We shall explore these fields in later chapters.

Damage estimated at £100,000 was caused by the fire which destroyed business premises in Pier Avenue, Clacton.
East Anglian Daily Times

The out-of-the-ordinary events which make news are, unfortunately, often disasters, and East Anglia had its quota. A striking feature of the year was the number of serious fires. Early one morning in April a policeman patrolling the centre of Cambridge found the Central Cinema well ablaze. This was the first in-town cinema and one of the largest in the town. Before firemen, working with a 70 foot water tower, could bring the flames under control the whole site between Hobson Street and Sidney Street had been gutted. In June there were three spectacular conflagrations. One of Clacton's main shopping centres, in Pier Avenue, and its largest department store were destroyed on 4th June in the biggest blaze the town had ever suffered. The Clacton Club, the Bohemian Restaurant, the International Stores, a tobacconists and a provision merchants were completely lost as the flames leapt up fifty feet and masses of masonry crashed into the street. Many other buildings were seriously damaged and sparks drifted all over the town, starting small fires elsewhere, in one case a quarter of a mile away. On 8th June the Empire Cinema in Chelmsford caught fire; its stage was gutted and its roof seriously damaged. On 11th June the end portion of Hunstanton's 800 foot pier was

25

gutted, its massive timbers falling into the sea and its metalwork left a crumpled mass. A crowd of fifteen thousand people watched this Saturday night spectacle and the glow was seen thirty miles away. There were a number of smaller fires at farms in the region, and there was another major blaze on 27th July at Dedham, when the East Anglian School of Painting and Drawing was gutted and paintings and a valuable art library were destroyed. On 10th September one of the principal Nonconformist churches in Norwich, St Mary's Baptist Church, was almost completely destroyed when fire broke out immediately after a morning service.

There were two serious rail accidents during the year, and they occurred within a couple of days of one another. On Whit-Monday as a Cromer to London train was passing through Witham five coaches left the track, but were kept upright by the platform. A hundred yards of track was torn up, but none of the 700 passengers was seriously hurt. Things did not turn out so well on 31st May when a Hunstanton to London train crashed into a lorry laden with straw at Hilgay, near Downham Market. The locomotive and five coaches were wrecked and four women passengers died.

One evening in March a large rat running over the equipment in the power station at Great Yarmouth landed with his forepaws on one terminal and his hind feet on another, ten inches away. He caused a 6,000-volt short-circuit which led to a transformer break-down, two explosions, the death of one employee and injury to five others, and a complete blackout of Great Yarmouth, part of Lowestoft and hundreds of square miles of surrounding countryside. In July there was a short-circuit, followed by a fire, on the main switchboard of the Norwich Corporation power station and that cut off supplies to the city and a large rural area for several hours. Another unusual occurrence in Great Yarmouth made headlines later in the year: what the *Norwich Mercury* called "an event unparalleled in medical history". It explained: "Two girls in one local family have become boys. The sisters were Marjorie and Daisy. Friends who knew them by those names will now have to call them Mark and David." It seems that the elder, who was seventeen had received treatment at a London hospital, a prominent local lady having raised a fund to meet the cost, and needed one final operation. The younger child was fifteen and had not, at the time, received medical treatment.

The year provided one outstanding example of good news making big headlines. The *East Anglian Daily Times*, indeed, used a heavy three-columns "banner headline" of a kind which appeared on no other regional story during the year. It read: "Great archaeological find in Suffolk". It was one of the most important and richest discoveries ever made in Europe.

The story began in 1938 when Mrs E. M. Pretty, of Sutton Hoo, near Woodbridge, agreed to permit the excavation of several burial mounds on her estate. The Curator of Ipswich Museum supervised the dig, three barrows were investigated, and one of them produced remains of an 18 foot long boat and evidence of a cremation. Thus encouraged, the Curator sought permission to open another barrow in 1939. Mrs Pretty made available several of the regular workers on her estate and employed a foreman, and digging began on 8th May. Soon they exposed what was evidently the stern of a ship, it seemed likely that a discovery of significance was at hand, and the Ministry of Works in London was advised. They promised to send an expert, but there was some delay and meanwhile the dig proceeded under the careful supervision of the Ipswich curator. When midship was reached, metal objects were found on the floor of the vessel. The curator knew that they had found an unrifled burial deposit and, despite the intense excitement, he ordered the men to cover everything again until experts from London could be present. They arrived on 8th July to take charge and work proceeded. Within three weeks there was unearthed what Nikolaus Pevsner called "the richest and most brilliant treasure ever found on British soil".

Reconstruction of the Sutton Hoo helmet in the British Museum. Visor, cheek-pieces and neck-guard hang from an iron cap which has a crest of iron cased in silver. The eyebrows, nose and mouthpiece are of bronze, with silver decoration.

British Museum

No superlative could do justice to the find. There were 41 objects of solid gold, heavily encrusted with garnets. These included a belt buckle, hinged shoulder clasps and mounts for suspending a sword which all formed part of the elaborate armour, including helmet, shield and chain-mail, of a high-ranking warrior. There was a purse, decorated with seven gold plaques, which contained gold coins of the Merovingian period of European history, which enabled the date of burial of the treasure to be fixed at about 625 AD. There was a hoard of silver objects, including dishes and bowls made in Byzantium. One large silver salver carried the control stamp of Anastasius I (491 to 518 AD), there was a pair of late classical silver spoons, and silver shoe buckles. There was a heavy bronze bowl, made in Alexandria, decorated with a lion, a tiger and a camel, and bronze hanging bowls from Ireland and western England. There were the remains of a six-stringed harp, in a beaver-skin bag; drinking horns with silver-gilt mounts; iron-bound wooden buckets; sheet-bronze cauldrons; a pottery bottle; wooden cups or bowls; remains of combs, leather slippers, a leather bag, and clothing. A wrought-iron standard of authority, 6 foot 4 inches high and carrying on the top a stag, and a giant sceptre or ceremonial whetstone provided the conclusive evidence that it was the burial treasure of a warrior king.

It had been deposited in what had been a gabled cabin amidships of an 89 foot vessel designed for thirty-eight oarsmen; little remained of it, but the pattern of iron clench-nails in the ground provided the archaeologists with the evidence they needed. This ship must have been dragged up from the river Deben, deposited in a deep trench and covered with an oval mound over one hundred feet long and twelve feet high, to form a cenotaph commemorating the dead chieftain. This practice of boat burial was known from the Swedish province of Uppland. The initial conclusion was that this was a memorial to an early Anglo-Saxon king who had come from Scandinavia.

Police protected the site while the treasure was retrieved, the whole area was scheduled by Whitehall as an Ancient Monument, and by 4th August everything had been removed to the British Museum for laboratory examination. On 14th August most of it was brought back again in a motor van to the Village Hall in Sutton and the great pile of gold and silver was set out in display cases borrowed from Ipswich Museum. Fourteen local residents were summoned to form a jury and, sitting with a Coroner, they were called upon to decide if this was a case of treasure trove. The law, as the Coroner explained, was that treasure trove could be retained by the Crown, which would pay to the finder the full market value. If it was *not* treasure trove the first finder would be deemed to be the owner. The jury found that it was not treasure trove and that Mrs Pretty was the finder.

The site of the excavation of the burial ship at Sutton Hoo, near Ipswich.
British Museum

Mrs Pretty donated everything to the British Museum, provided only that it was loaned for a period to Ipswich Museum, and arrangements were made to display it there on 2nd and 3rd September. By that weekend, however, the people of East Anglia were more concerned with a new threat of invasion from the Continent.

CHAPTER TWO

Homes and Hearths

A LMOST half the population of East Anglia in 1939 lived in villages. It has been estimated that in Norfolk and Suffolk forty per cent lived in large towns, ten per cent lived in small country towns, three and a half per cent lived in small coastal towns, and the remaining forty-six and a half per cent lived in the rural districts.[1] In the whole sweep of countryside from Chelmsford northward to the Wash and from Peterborough eastward to the North Sea, rather less than one hundred miles in each direction, there were only three large towns: Norwich with 118,000 inhabitants, Ipswich with 100,000, and Cambridge with about 80,000 within its borough boundaries. There were about forty other towns with populations ranging from a few thousand up to about 50,000 in each of Colchester, Great Yarmouth and Peterborough.

We will do best to meet these people first in their homes, around which their lives revolved. We shall consider later the economic realities of life: how they earned their money, and how they spent it; but, if we are to avoid serious misunderstanding, we must here emphasize that money values are meaningless unless they are related to the labour required to earn a pound as well as to the goods which it will purchase. We must note, too, that the British currency of 1939 comprised, pounds, shillings and pence, with twelve pence to a shilling and twenty shillings to a pound.[2]

We may now run our eyes over the advertising columns of the local daily newspapers early in 1939, where the following representative properties are listed:

> Bungalow-type detached house (well-built), Oulton Broad, main road. Two good living rooms, scullery, bathroom, 4 bedrooms, electricity. Good garden, shed, garage. Freehold, £550.
> £650 — For sale: semi-detached residence, freehold. 4 Bedrooms, 2 sitting, kitchen, bathroom, separate WC. Gas, electricity, City water. Well planted garden. No road charges. 3 miles City. Thorpe End, Norwich.
> Typical Queen Anne period residence. Secluded in own timbered grounds. Lounge, 3 spacious sitting rooms, cloakroom, 6 bedrooms, bathroom. Main services. Garage, greenhouses, etc. Charming gardens, one acre, £1,650 freehold.

---

1. T. Eastwood, as before.
2. The present metric penny is equivalent in face value (but not, of course, in purchasing power) to 2½ of the pennies of 1939.

Farm, in the picturesque Constable country on the Essex and Suffolk borders. 6 bedrooms, bathroom, 3 reception rooms, etc. Main electricity, prolific water supply, telephone, hot water system. Together with registered cowhouse for 17 and other buildings and 45 acres including 37 acres of rich pasture with running brook. 2000 guineas, with possession.

A Cambridge newspaper, at about the same time, published a feature: "Be your own landlord" which included an advert for the Fendon Estate offering "architect-designed houses, built with best materials and labour . . . every house is different, from £985". Smaller properties all over the region were bought and sold for a few hundred pounds each and many cottages were virtually unsaleable. At an auction at Ilketshall St Lawrence, near Bungay, in May a modern freehold bungalow with two living rooms, an entrance hall, three bedrooms, a large garden and immediate possession was withdrawn because no-one offered more than £240 for it.

Only a minority could consider buying and hope to own (after paying off mortgages) the homes in which they lived, but there were a number of locally-based building societies in the Eastern Counties offering finance at an interest rate of four or five per cent.

Most people either rented, from private landlords or local authorities, or lived in "tied cottages" which were owned by their employers and made available as part of the reward for the work they did. There were plenty of private landlords with property to let, and there were firms which found it profitable to build specifically for the purpose, as at Fen Causeway in Cambridge, advertised in January 1939 as "the best of all flat schemes in Cambridge . . . overlooking open fields on all sides . . . kitchen equipment on a lavish scale . . . refinements that are not offered in the ordinary flat . . . " These included central heating, constant hot water and a fitted refrigerator, a lock-up garage and a resident porter. The rents began at £80 a year for a single-bedroom flat and ran up to £125 a year for three bedrooms. This was luxury, and relatively expensive. More typical of the accommodation on offer were these:

Felixstowe. House to let, minute sea. 4 bedrooms, bathroom, 2 reception rooms, scullery, electric. 25s. inclusive.

Ipswich, New 3-bed house to rent, £75 p.a.

When the Colchester Area Assessment Committee met in May it was told that there were 82 houses for sale and 49 to let in Frinton-on-Sea, which was more than fifteen per cent of all the houses in the town. On the other hand, Bury St Edmunds Town Council was told at its meeting in March that there were 175 applicants on its waiting list for Council houses, and the majority of local authorities had comparable lists. Many of the available houses were not in the areas where they were needed, or else the rents were beyond the means of those who needed them. Those on the council waiting list were living in tied or rented houses which were, at best, sub-standard and, at worst, quite dreadful slums.

Housing was recognised to be a national problem. Since 1919 central government had made grants to assist housing schemes. An Act of 1924 offered grants specifically to assist the building of houses to rent and in 1930 what became known as the "Slum Clearance Act" extended the system of Exchequer grants. Both these measures were devised by Labour governments and until the mid-'thirties, at least, the concept of public aid for housing, with administration by local authorities, was a matter of acute political controversy. Some local authorities embarked on very ambitious slum clearance schemes and programmes of house building for tenants, but others believed the whole problem was best left to private enterprise. A correspondent of the *East Anglian Daily Times* in May complained of "the latest mad rush of slum clearance" in Ipswich, but by this time most East Anglian local authorities were deeply involved in their own housing programmes. Rings of red-brick estates encircled most of the bigger towns, and there were very few villages without a group of council houses. The Duke of Grafton, who had the resources to build a "model village" on his Euston Estate, remarked in April: "On my own estate I think we are almost unique in that we have not even got a rural district council house."

Once known as the Norwich Football Social Club, this building in Golden Ball Street was demolished to permit road widening.   *Norwich Mercury* series

Norwich had cleared over 4,000 slum properties by the beginning of 1939, as a result of a decade of activity, and many two- and three-storey blocks of flats had been built to replace them. Away from the City centre, the great housing estate at Earlham had been created. In Ipswich, the President of the local Chamber of Commerce and Shipping told his members at their annual dinner, slums had been a serious problem in their town, but "during the last five years the aim of wiping them out has been vigorously urged, with the result that there are now many happy and good homes where formerly these people lived in terrible conditions." Swaffham U.D.C. in the course of five or six years, had made demolition or clearance orders in respect of a quarter of the 600 cottages in its area. Bury St Edmunds Council had built and let a total of 520 houses by 1939, and moved 2,200 people into them; it planned to build 75 more over the following five years. Most of the rural district councils were building steadily. Blyth, for example, had built 265 council houses in its villages by February 1939. Newmarket seemed to be less dedicated to the task, for its Medical Officer of Health in his annual report presented in August pointed out that no land had been acquired for housing by the Council during 1938 and so far in 1939. Negotiations to purchase some land had failed and the council had shown reluctance to use its compulsory acquisition powers. Meanwhile, the doctor observed, some houses in the town "are not merely unfit to live in — they are, in many instances, unfit even to die in". This sad situation was not unusual. The Norfolk County Medical Officer of Health reported 300 houses unfit for human habitation in the Downham R.D.C. area, while a member of the Wells U.D.C. drew attention to a slum in that town where "people are taking food upstairs to keep it away from the cockroaches, rats and mice".

Local authorities in the Eastern Region which were affiliated to the National Housing and Town Planning Council held a conference in June at which the region's requirement at the beginning of 1939 was estimated to have been 200,000 new houses to replace slums, 180,000 to relieve over-crowding and 50,000 for agricultural workers. This was estimated to represent work for the following five years.

In order to qualify for Exchequer grants toward the cost of their houses, local authorities were required to build to certain minimum standards. This was sometimes a cause of friction. The Duke of Grafton, in the address from which I have already quoted, said: "I am somewhat nervous about the government's housing policy in the country districts. It seems to me that we are much too much in the hands of our county surveyor. They come with all sorts of rules and regulations as to cubic space per foot of ventilation, etcetera, which are all very well as far as the towns are concerned, but the same rules do not seem to me to apply in the country." The Halstead Rural District Council was involved in a contretemps with Whitehall early in the year: the rooms in

the houses it planned to build for farm workers in its villages were considered
to be too small. The Ministry thought that sitting rooms should be at least one
hundred square feet in area and the third bedrooms at least seventy square
feet. Eventually, a compromise was agreed at ninety square feet for the sitting
rooms.

Agreement having been reached, a subsidy of £10 per house was to be
paid by the government and Halstead Council then proposed to charge rents
of five shillings a week, plus 1s. 3d. or 1s. 6d. rates. At Diss, Norfolk, the
Urban District Council decided in April to fix its council house rents (exclusive
of rates) at 1s. 6d. a week for single-bedroom houses, 2s. 6d. a week for those
with two bedrooms, three shillings for three bedrooms, four shillings for four
bedrooms, and 7s. 6d. a week for six-bedroomed houses. The figures tell us
something about the absence of birth control facilities in the countryside at the
time.

But what about those for whom there were, as yet, no council houses, a
high proportion of them living in cottages tied to the farms on which they
worked? The farmers were in dire trouble; even the farmhouses were
crumbling to ruin. The cottages, almost invariably, lacked every kind of
amenity. They had no indoor water supplies and used wells, streams and
sometimes even ponds. They had no indoor sanitation and used "privies" in
sentry-box-sized sheds in the gardens. They had no lighting other than
paraffin oil lamps. They had no heating but the cast-iron kitchen range, the
great open hearth or, sometimes, a paraffin burner.

"I lived in Sedge Fen Drove in 1939. There were fourteen houses down
that fen. They had big families. We used to have to carry four gallons of
paraffin on our shoulders from the top of the drove. When you went out
on Thursday or Saturday to catch a bus to Ely or Downham Market,
you'd go in your water boots — your Wellingtons — and you'd change into
your best shoes when you reached the main road.

Mother used to wash from a local fen drain, wash the linen. The
water you caught from the roof of your house was your drinking supply.
In the summer when it was a dry time you'd go up to the top of the drove
and take a horse and cart and fill the soft water tank up from the hard
water tap — it cost you sixpence.

Lighting was by paraffin lamp. Goats was your main milk supply.
Bread was carried down by two men, baked in the village, every other
day. If it got rough and they couldn't get down, mother would sometimes make some."[3]

In such circumstances, many local authorities were concerned about the
right order of priorities; should general provision of water and sewerage
services come before new housing? Some councils were anxious about inad-

3. Mr C. R. Everitt, as before.

equate protection against fire, particularly if they had a lot of property with thatched roofs. Councillors spent many hours in 1939 grappling with such problems. The government made a million pounds available in 1934 to help to provide rural water supplies but even with this aid, many local authorities believed they could not afford to undertake schemes on the scale which was called for. All sorts of inadequate ameliorative action resulted. The following examples are from the *East Anglian Daily Times:*

"The Sanitary Inspector reported that the Stour Brook at Withersfield water supply was out of use after a dead cat and a dead rat had been found in it. Villagers were being allowed to use the wells belonging to the Rector and the doctor. A special committee reported it had looked into the possibility of sinking boreholes at Hundon and Lidgate and for the extension of piped water mains from Withersfield to the Thurlows and Bradley and from Clare waterworks to Poslingford and Cavendish. The estimated cost was £48,000. The matter was referred back." (*Report of Clare R.D.C. meeting, 7th January*).

"At a Ministry of Health public enquiry at the Shirehall, Bury St Edmunds into Thingoe R.D.C's proposal to borrow £3,050 for a water scheme for Bradfield St George, the Clerk to the R.D.C., Mr A. F. Chamberlayne, said there was no water supply in the area other than private sources. At times the ponds on which certain inhabitants depended dried up. It had been said that they often had to drain tadpoles out of the water before they could use it. The Medical Officer of Health said the scheme would take pure water within easy distance of 79 houses with 262 residents and would allow a satisfactory supply to the school, which had 62 pupils and three teachers. Of the 33 wells, 15 had either dried up in drought periods or become so low that water could only be used very sparingly, and these 15 supplied 171 of the 322 inhabitants, as well as the school. The Chief Sanitary Inspector said in 1938 all wells gave out and for a month the Council had to provide a water cartage service." (*Report of a Ministry of Health Public enquiry at Bury St Edmunds, 3rd May*).

It will be noted from the last report that the ambitions of those councils which felt able to proceed with water supply schemes did not extend to provision of supplies to individual homes; most of them were concerned only to lay on a piped supply to standpipes and taps in the open, which could then be shared by cottagers. The examples we have quoted are from Suffolk, but the same conditions existed throughout most of East Anglia. In Huntingdonshire, for example, St Ives R.D.C. sought to borrow £14,000 to provide a water supply for the 1,800 inhabitants of the villages of Houghton, Wyton, Hemingford Abbots and Hemingford Grey and at a public enquiry in July the

BIG REDUCTIONS IN ALL DEPARTMENTS.

ROBERT SAYLE & Co. Ltd., St. Andrew's Street, Cambridge - - - - 'Phone 4286

Wilton Carpets 9' × 12' for less than £6. This advertisement indicates the general level of prices. *Cambridge Evening News*

36

chairman of the Houghton and Wyton parish council described the local wells: "They are putrid and strangers would risk typhoid or some other disease if they drank it. Natives are immune." The school well has been condemned, and others were shallow and sometimes dry. The Sanitary Inspector told the enquiry that cottages had pail closets and the contents were buried in the gardens where the wells were situated.

Without proper water supplies, sewerage was everywhere a serious problem. Lavenham villagers protested to the Cosford R.D.C. in January at the system of collecting night soil during daylight hours which had been recently introduced as an "improvement". Pails often had to be carried through rooms to bring them to the front of the houses, they pointed out. Cosford councillors, rejecting the complaint at their April meeting, said the new centralised scheme which covered all their villages was similar to that operated by other local authorities, who had been canvassed and who reported that *they* had received no complaints. At Thedwastre R.D.C.'s July meeting the Medical Officer of Health reported problems over drainage and sewage, with many houses discharging into ditches or cesspools, the latter often not functioning in clay soil. "Until Exchequer aid becomes available important extension of sewerage is beyond the district's financial resources," he said. "Indeed, it would be cheaper in some instances to rebuild the whole village to a new plan at a more suitable site rather than attempt to introduce water supplies, drainage and sewage works into existing parishes." The Medical Officer's annual report to Swaffham R.D.C. in June reported that in their area there was absolutely no system of drainage and sewerage.

Samford R.D.C., at a special meeting in August to consider protection against fire in its district, received a report on available water supplies. The district had been divided into two, with fifteen parishes in the western part and thirteen in the eastern. In the western part there were 1,097 houses with running water within 500 yards, 152 houses with running water within 1,000 yards, 426 houses with still water within 500 yards, 51 houses with still water within 1,000 yards, and 181 houses (or nine per cent of the total) with no water near. In the eastern area, sixty per cent of the houses were within 100 yards of running water and 75 per cent within 1,000 yards, while five per cent had no water available. The council chairman appealed to the people of the whole district to secure as much dry sand as possible to keep by them in case of fire.

Even in the towns adequate water supplies and associated works had not been completed. Not until June 1939, for example, was Bury St Edmunds assured that the northern area of the town was reasonably well served. A new main had just been brought into use, but the deputy mayor observed that "every effort is being made to ensure a satisfactory supply to all parts of the town and in the transitional stage it is somewhat difficult to supply the higher levels if indiscriminate use is made of hoses in the lower levels". Harwich, at this time, had only just resolved to proceed with a £43,000 scheme to provide low-level sewerage disposal works. Colchester reported that it had a great deal of work still to be completed on water supplies and sewers. Stowmarket estimated that sewerage would take half of its £106,000 capital works programme over the following five years. Ipswich set aside £42,000 for sewerage in the same period.

Frequently, however, the daunting cost of schemes led to prevarication. Halstead R.D.C., informed in May that no government grant was immediately available, postponed consideration of the matter for six months. Bungay U.D.C. decided to call in an independent expert to advise on the best way to ensure complete and permanent protection against pollution of its water supplies—but it also resolved to pay this consultant not more than fifteen guineas for his advice. No-one was prepared to come for so little. The first quotation received was for forty-four guineas; they shopped around until they found someone who would come for twenty guineas plus certain expenses. The council then resolved to take no further action.

Perhaps it was remarkable that anything was achieved, but there were not many communities able to match the achievement of Melford R.D.C. which, on one triumphant day in June 1939 charged twenty-six miles of new mains with running water. In the House of Commons on 31st July the Minister of Health disclosed that the government had given grants totalling £47,725 under the provisions of the 1934 Act to assist 114 Suffolk parishes with their piped water projects.

Even the phlegmatic East Anglians were becoming restive over the water problem. What fanned the discontent in some areas was the fact that defence establishments newly arrived in the region were demanding, and getting, supplies of water, though the local inhabitants had been demanding in vain. When Gipping R.D.C. learned in June that two new borings had been made to provide a supply for an aerodrome at Great Bricett, the Vicar of Needham Market, who was a member of the council, showed considerable indignation. For six years, he said, he had been pressing the claims of the people of his parish. He received a dusty answer: the Air Ministry were ratepayers, they would require practically all the supply available, and no date could be given for a scheme for Needham Market.

Protest meetings were not always in the same mould. In Suffolk, one hundred villagers of Earl Stonham packed a protest meeting because they had only two wells and some people had to walk a mile for their water; they sent a petition to the Ministry of Health demanding water. But in Cambridgeshire a public meeting in the village of Shepreth passed a resolution "that this meeting of local government electors wholeheartedly disapproves of the proposal put forward by the South Cambridgeshire R.D.C. to supply the village with a main water supply, as being utterly and entirely unnecessary and unwanted by the majority of residents of the village and as being a wanton waste of public money". Of one hundred who attended, only six dissociated themselves from this point of view.

The South Cambridgeshire R.D.C. had prepared a scheme to supply ten villages with water. It was to cost £23,500 and was expected to mean an additional rate of one shilling in the pound. That was the cause of the indignation. Other big schemes were also in hand in the county and in July the County Council came to the conclusion that it had best assume full responsibility for carrying out these future schemes, placing the charge on the general county rate.

A feature of the countryside in the conditions we have just described, though it was so commonplace as rarely to be considered worth mentioning at the protest meetings and the public enquiries, was the large population of rats. In a campaign against them during November and December 1939, 66,561 were killed in East Suffolk and over 22,000 in West Suffolk. At Stowmarket U.D.C. in November the vice-chairman said that one section of that town was infested. "They are attacking private houses now and getting into people's bedrooms," he declared.

Wymondham's new Post Office, nearing completion.

Norwich Mercury series

Practically all local government operations came to a standstill when war began in September 1939. The general rule was that the government would approve completion of council house schemes only when construction had already reached roof level. Other types of work had to have some important war-time justification if it was to go forward. So October and November were months of agonising for many local authorities and they were forced to makeshift solutions. As an example, Woodbridge U.D.C. put work on its new sewerage scheme into abeyance indefinitely and decided to instal two large tanks, each big enough to hold one week's night soil collected from earth closets.

The supply of electricity in 1939 was in the hands of a number of concerns, some publicly owned, some private enterprise organisations. Electrical power was, generally speaking, a town luxury. In rural areas, even street lighting was unusual. When Blyth R.D.C. tried, early in the year, to secure electricity for a group of villages south-west of Southwold, the East Anglian Electricity Supply Company refused to supply. The Council appealed to the Electricity Commissioners; they decided that the Company could not be expected to supply unless the Council was prepared to contribute towards the £4,700 estimated capital cost. In the towns, however, electricity was established as the most satisfactory means of lighting homes, offices and shops and of providing power for the factories and workshops. Ipswich in 1939 had a project for a new 90,000 kilowatt power station to meet the growing demand; it was to cost two million pounds. At the fourth annual Ipswich Ideal Homes and Trades Exhibition in February the Ipswich Corporation Electricity Supply Department displayed a wide range of "labour-saving electrical appliances" which included, for the first time and amid a certain degree of scepticism on the part of the visiting public, an electric dish-washing machine.

Many of the older cottages and certainly most of the farmhouses had open hearths with ancient bread-ovens built alongside them.

"I remember my grandmother at Ashen had one. When she baked bread, everything had to go out into the garden — the mats came off the floor and the furniture was shoved to one side. Then in came the bush faggots and they were shoved in the oven. You could go in the door and crawl round that oven, there was plenty of room. In the back wall there was a black stone and when you got the fire going, when that stone turned white the oven was hot.

Then you used to shove all the ashes right round the sides and then have a long stick with a damp cloth on the end and wipe it all over the floor of the oven. The bread would be all ready to go in and you shoved the loaves in on a peel — a flat bit of board on a long handle — and put them on the floor, then shut the door. You left them there, I suppose about half an hour. When you took them out, you had to thump them on the bottom to see if they rattled right; if not, they had to go in again.

Then out came the bread and in went the big old rice puddings, rabbit pie with a bit of pork in it. You wanted a ham cooked in one of those ovens. They used to cover the ham with dough, that kept all the goodness in. Any cake, or anything else they wanted, used to go in.

After things were done cooking, in would go the clothes to be aired."[4]

4. Mr William Bensley, of Stoke-by-Clare, in an interview with the author, 1979.

Electric House, Ipswich.   *Eastern Electricity*

Farmhouses and cottages usually had brick or stone floors, with no damp courses and no insulation over the earth immediately below the brick. The traditional way of cleaning these floors was to sift sand over them through a cullender; the normal traffic of feet did the rest, and the sand was then swept up. Cleanliness and comfort was secured in most of these East Anglian cottages as a result of great effort.

"My mother had a little black stove, with the oven at the side. She used to clean the bright parts with emery paper and the black parts with blacklead—Zebra and Zebo. It used to look lovely. There was always the guard round, on hooks, if you had children.

The shelf above the fireplace had a nice piece of velveteen put round it: wine colour or rust. On the mantelpiece people put china dogs, photographs of mother when she was twenty and of her husband, probably in his Great War Uniform, and lots of people had a Scottish scene of Highland cattle—they used to send away for those prints.

People used to make peg rugs with old sugar sacks and pieces of . . . anything, old clothes, an old coat, cut into little pieces. You got a pegger and you just pulled them through. People made lovely patterns.

They used to sit there in the evenings with this old sacking on their laps. These peg rugs were put down over lino. When they cleaned, they swept up with a long brush, wiped the lino round with a bucket of water, and shook the mat outside—but they were very heavy. Houses looked fresh and lovely when they'd been done like that and the stove black-leaded."[5]

Though these were the exceptions, there is no question but that it was a society of vivid contrasts, as another picture of urban life-style makes clear:

"The best houses in Norwich were in Newmarket Road and in Thorpe. My grand-father had a nice, roomy house in two-thirds of an acre of garden in Newmarket Road, which he had bought in 1918. In 1939 he was 94 and he was looked after by his housekeeper, a maid and a chauffeur odd job man. There was little company at the house, so the work was not too hard. The maid had to get up about 6.30 a.m. to light the kitchen range, clean out and light the dining room fire, cook breakfast and take tea up to my grandfather. The odd-job man was in every day, often on Sunday included, dealing with the garden and driving my grandfather down into the city when necessary in a big old Wolseley car"[6]

These were the homes that people struggled hard to create, to improve— and, before 1939 was out, to defend. We shall examine now the way they shouldered and discharged these responsibilities.

---

5. Mrs K. R. Taylor, of Littleport, in an interview with the author, 1980.
6. Mr Edward J. Cunningham, as before.

Coach fares during May 1939.
Norwich Mercury series

Norwich Amusements during August.
Norwich Mercury series

CHAPTER THREE

Earning and Spending

FEW people have made fortunes in East Anglia. Many have worked hard throughout their lives and achieved little better than a bare subsistence level. It was always a low-wage region, as the official statistics plainly show. In 1939 average earnings in England and Wales by men over twenty-one were sixty-nine shillings a week, and the average for women was thirty-two shillings and sixpence. When, in July 1939, the Farm Economics Branch of the School of Agriculture at Cambridge University surveyed earnings of those employed in thirty small country towns in Norfolk and Suffolk they established the following weekly levels, in shillings:[1]

Industry	Men	Women
Agriculture (minimum rates)	35	—
Brush and mat making	46½	29
Food and drink	47½	29
Woodwork and furniture	53	45
Chemicals	53½	30
Textiles	55½	35
Engineering	56½	35
Clothing	60	34
Printing	60	31

Agriculture, of course, employed far more men than any other industry. It also employed several thousand women; no weekly average wage is shown for them in the table above because they were traditionally hourly-paid workers. In December 1939 Cambridgeshire farmers agreed, for the first time, to fix a weekly rate of 27s. 6d. for women, but the other eastern counties refused to follow this example.

Farm workers' wages varied from county to county. After the First World War, they rose generally by 1920 to forty-five to forty-six shillings a week, but then fell back dramatically to only twenty-five to thirty shillings. By January 1939 the weekly rate in Cambridgeshire was thirty-five shillings, in Norfolk it was thirty-four shillings and sixpence, and in Suffolk it was only thirty-four shillings. These rates applied to a standard working week of forty-eight hours in winter and fifty hours in summer. Special classes of worker, such as horsemen, cowmen and shepherds, received a few shillings more — a Cambridgeshire horseman, for example, was paid forty-one shillings a week. Women were employed on the farms at sevenpence an hour in Cambridgeshire and sixpence an hour elsewhere.

1. T. Eastwood, as before.

Not surprisingly, the National Union of Agricultural Workers maintained a constant pressure to improve wages and conditions. As 1939 opened, they were concentrating on the issue of holidays. Parliament had passed a Holidays with Pay Act in 1938; it provided for seven days holiday each year for agricultural workers, exclusive of such public holidays as were already granted in different counties. In East Anglia, however, the Agricultural Wages Committees (which included farmers' and union representatives, plus some independent members) decided that the Bank Holidays must form part of the seven day's entitlement. On 27th January the Suffolk Committee decided that horsemen, cowmen and shepherds should get four days holiday with pay after twelve months service with the same employer, and all other workers three days holiday. Those with four months service would be entitled to one day, those with eight months to two days. The Essex Committee fell into line, but when the Norfolk Committee met on 30th January the farmers insisted that they could not afford more than three days holiday for anyone. A few weeks later, however, they changed their minds and followed the example of neighbouring counties.

For the weeks of harvest special hours and a special bonus were negotiated each year. When the Suffolk Agricultural Wages Committee met at Ipswich on 31st May, the union representative proposed that the harvest bonus for 1939 should be £7 and the working hours eleven each day—compared with £5 and eleven-and-a-half hours in the previous harvest. The farmers' spokesman opposed this suggestion vigorously. The conditions of the countryside, as he saw them, did not point to any degree of poverty at all, but rather to a very reasonable and happy standard of living. The position of the worker, he argued, had improved relatively, and that of the farmer had deteriorated. The economic wage, if related to the condition of agriculture at the time, would be 24s. 6d. a week, he suggested. Farmers were clearly paying already more than they could afford. And further, the spokesman added, eleven-and-a-half hours work was not a hardship. Eventually, after much discussion, it was agreed that the bonus should be £5. 7s. 6d. and that the hours worked would remain unchanged.

Not until after the outbreak of war, when the government had begun to improve the income of farmers, did the union achieve any significant improvement. Emphasizing the need for a better deal for those upon whom the nation's food supplies increasingly depended, the union demanded a minimum wage of forty shillings for a forty-hour week year-round. The farmers opposed any increase. The Cambridgeshire Agricultural Wages Committee, however, resolved on 14th October to grant an increase of two shillings a week—to thirty-seven shillings, though hours were to remain unchanged at forty-eight in winter and fifty in summer. The rate for horsemen, cowmen and shepherds was increased by two-and-sixpence to 43s. 6d. a week. Women workers achieved for the first time their flat rate of 27s. 6d. for a forty-four hour week and their hourly rate went up from sevenpence to sevenpence-halfpenny. The Norfolk Committee, nine days later, also gave a two shillings increase, to produce a new minimum of 36s. 6d., and it increased the hourly rate for women from sixpence to sevenpence. A week later the Suffolk Committee advanced the minimum by two shillings to thirty-six shillings a week, but shied at the prospect of giving more to the women. It met again on 1st December, however, and voted them an extra penny an hour, in line with Norfolk; but it firmly refused to contemplate a weekly minimum.

All wool camel cloth coats for £1.   *East Anglian Daily Times*

Other workers familiar in the rural scene and earning low wages were the roadmen and the railwaymen. Essex roadmen were relatively well-off with fifty shillings a week, but those in East Suffolk received less than two pounds. Early in 1939 the County Council decided to pay an extra eighteenpence to those whose wage was below thirty-nine shillings. Railway porters were paid forty-five shillings a week, but there were fifteen thousand railwaymen in other grades who received less. In July 1939 the minimum for adult males was raised to forty-five shillings and in October, in the new war-time circumstances, the Railway Staff National Tribunal accepted the union claim for a fifty shilling minimum for all adult male employees.

Not many who worked in towns were as poorly paid as the countrymen. Workers in the Norwich boot and shoe industry had minimum rates of 58 shillings a week for men and 38 shillings for women, but they were on piecework and could hope to earn up to a quarter more than the minima. In December 1939 the rates were increased by three shillings for men and two shillings for women and were linked to the cost-of-living index. The hairdressers of Ipswich, however, fared no better than the farm worker. A letter published in the *East Anglian Daily Times*, signed "Snip", said:

> "In Ipswich the assistants work between 55 and 60 hours per week. The average wage paid is thirty-five shillings to two pounds per week . . . The average labourer earns tenpence to 1s. 2d. per hour. Surely the hairdresser should be entitled to more money, taking into consideration that one has to serve three years' apprenticeship and a further two years improving?"

The master hairdressers of Ipswich, however, were still charging only fourpence to sixpence for a haircut and *they* were keeping their shops open until eight o'clock in the evening in order to get *their* living. In March 1939 the local branch of the National Association of Hairdressers resolved to improve matters, by agreeing that all members would increase their charges by two pence and by seeking from the local authority an order to regulate closing hours. The occupiers of eighty-four shops supported this move. From June 1939, the order having been secured, barbers' premises had to be closed by 7 p.m. on Mondays and Tuesdays, by 1 p.m. on Wednesdays, and by 8 p.m. on Thursdays, Fridays and Saturdays. The local branch of the National Shop Assistants' Union, which was actively recruiting members in Ipswich at the time, seems to have had a good deal to do with these developments.

To provide perspective, we may compare the lot of the hairdressing assistant with that of the junior employee in local government, an area of employment in which "good, steady jobs" were considered highly desirable. A Salaries Sub-Committe of the West Suffolk branch of the National Association of Local Government Officers proposed in February 1939 a new scale of salaries which the union should seek to negotiate for its members. The proposed scale was designed "to give more rapid progression through the scales in order ultimately to secure for officers a salary of £200 per annum, at which it is considered that they could reasonably afford to marry".[2] To achieve this result, the sub-committee proposed a starting salary for clerks of sixteen of £50 a year, increasing by £10 a year until they were twenty, and then by £15 a year.

The rewards for those who settled to a career in local government are indicated by the January 1939 advertisements for a Clerk of Works to supervise a new sewerage scheme at Eye, Suffolk, at £6. 10s. a week, and for a Highways and Public Health Clerk of Works for the same council at £7 a week, and by the decisions of the Newmarket Urban District Council in May fixing its Rent Collector's salary at £6. 10s. a week, its Rating Officer's salary at £300 a year, its Deputy Clerk at the same figure, and its Clerk — the top post — at a maximum of £500 a year. At Cambridge, a couple of months later, the Town Council increased its Deputy Town Clerk's salary from £600 to £650 a year.

In March 1939 a spokesman of the Ecclesiastical Commissioners revealed that "it is more or less accepted standard that in a country parish of about 700, a clergyman's stipend shall be £500 per annum". But the Vicar of Haughley, near Stowmarket, declared at the same time that the rule of the St Edmundsbury diocese was to bring the salary of an incumbent up to £300 a year, if it did not reach that figure, plus an additional allowance for each child. Soon afterwards, he dramatically staged an auction of the contents of his home on the vicarage lawn because, he said, he had not received the grant he had expected, his net income was only £252, plus the use of the vicarage, and he had four children to support.

We have noted elsewhere that well-qualified artisans and professional men earned between £250 and £500 a year. The Norfolk and Suffolk National Fitness Committee advertised for a Secretary for that organisation at £500 a year, rising by annual increments of £20 to £600 (for a man — if a woman was appointed, the salary was to be £400 rising to £500). The Essex Education Authority offered £600, rising to £700, for a Principal Assistant Education Officer with responsibility for elementary education in that county, while the new Chief Education Officer who was appointed early in 1939, from among thirty-nine exceptionally highly-qualified candidates, was paid the princely salary of £1,600 a year; it was one of the highest-paid professional posts in Britain.

The principal employment for women was domestic service. A sample survey of women in employment in the smaller towns of Norfolk and Suffolk showed fifty-eight per cent in domestic service, compared with thirty-five per cent in England and Wales as a whole. The situations vacant columns of the local newspapers in East Anglia carried many announcements such as this:

2. N.A.L.G.O. West Suffolk Branch, Minutes, 1939. Suffolk Record Office, Bury St Edmunds.

"Capable woman wanted, all duties. Elderly couple. State age. 10 shillings weekly." One in the *Norfolk Mercury* read: "Cook-general and house parlour-maid wanted. One in family. Generous outings. Wireless. Wages, £50 and £45. Highest references essential." An employment agency in Cambridge advertised in February 1939 for a House Parlourmaid at £50 a year, a Cook at £52 a year, a Head Housemaid at £60, an Under Parlourmaid at £36, a Working Housekeeper at £40, a Nurse for two children (one month and one year) at £60, and a married couple as Chauffeur-gardener and Cook at £2 a week for the two. Nursing was a career enjoying great public esteem, but despite this, and the hard work it involved, the rewards were modest. Cambridgeshire Mental Hospital at Fulbourne, for example, offered probationer nurses aged eighteen to thirty a weekly salary of £1. 13s. 11d., rising, subject to passing the mental nursing examinations, by annual increments to £2. 13s. 2d. a week. From these salaries, however, 14s. 3d. was deducted each week for board, lodging and washing, if the nurses lived in the hospital. Uniforms were provided. Nurses had two days off duty each week, and three weeks annual holiday. Wardmaids, of course, did not do so well; Norwich Isolation Hospital advertised for some in January 1939, offering £29 a year, with uniform provided.

The influence of recruitment upon advertising in March 1939. *Norwich Mercury* series

There was a minority of revolutionary thinkers in 1939 who advanced the idea that women should be paid the same wages and salaries as men; indeed, even, that they should be treated as equals. The local government officers in Bury St Edmunds, for example, drafting the proposed new salary scales already referred to, insisted "that the principle of equal pay for equal work as between male and female officers shall continue to be recognised". Cambridge University had progressed to the point at which it elected, in May, its first woman professor, Miss Dorothy Annie Elizabeth Garrod, of Newnham College, who became Disney Professor of Archaeology.

But repeated attempts during the 'thirties to allow women into the debates at the Cambridge Union were defeated. Another attempt in January 1939 was still-born; the house was "counted out" when a member tried to move a resolution that they should invite "not more than two lady speakers" to one meeting in each term. Marriage was a bar to employment of women in many jobs; one education committee in Cambridgeshire agonised during 1939 over the problem of a headmistress whom it did not want to lose, but who was insisting that she intended to get married.

Wages and working conditions were influenced by the limited range and variety of employment available in the region, by the level of unemployment, and by the general ineffectiveness of the trades unions.

> "I had no trouble with the trades unions. If a man was slacking, I told him to wake up and if he still insisted in being a slacker he was discharged, generally at the Saturday lunch-time, unless he was very bad—then the two-hour notice applied.
>
> All classes of workers showed respect for supervisors. The unwritten law was that overtime was payable only when asked for by the employer, for urgent work." [3]

Taking the region as a whole, the total number of men employed in manufacturing industry matched fairly closely the number working on the land, but service industries employed more than either of these productive sectors. Within the service sector, clerical, commercial and financial operations provided most jobs, with building and decorating and transport close behind. The most important sectors of manufacturing industry were engineering, woodworking and furniture making, and textile goods.

Norwich was the biggest employment centre, with a number of large firms founded a century or more earlier by prominent local families and still controlled by them. Messrs Colman employed about 2,500 in their factory at Carrow, making mustard, starch and foodstuffs. Messrs Boulton and Paul, who until 1934 had included aeroplane construction in their activities, had reverted to the more prosaic business of constructional steelwork and buildings. Messrs Laurence, Scott and Electromotors was a substantial concern in the

3. Mr Edward J. Cunningham, as before.

electrical machinery industry. Messrs A. J. Caley and Son were well-known manufacturers of chocolate, cocoa and Christmas crackers, but in 1932 they had been bought out by John Mackintosh and Sons and in 1939 they lost their identity in a complete amalgamation of the two firms. There were also significant tailoring, wood-working, printing, brewing and wine bottling activities in the city. The Norwich Union Life Insurance Company was an important employer and there was a highly-developed range of commercial activities to serve the population. One of the leading stores, R. H. Bond and Sons, employed over 200 and was just celebrating its diamond jubilee.

Thousands of barrels of herring ready for transport at Great Yarmouth.
B.B.C. Hulton Picture Library

The Norwich shoe industry deserves special attention. There were about a dozen different companies, including the Norvic Shoe Company, Southall and Co. and W. Hurrell. The industry employed between 11,000 and 12,000 men and women. Elsewhere in Britain a process of concentration had led to larger units employing fewer operatives; Leicester, Kettering and Northampton, between them, lost 3,800 jobs in the industry during the decade to 1939. But Norwich, while introducing the new machinery and methods to step up productivity, had also successfully expanded its market for women's and children's shoes, with the result that its labour force had increased by 600. Again, in 1939, it proved its resilience and efficiency. It had completed its preparations for a spring 1940 range of fashion shoes — "models in louis heels from 1½ to 2¾ inches in height, in a wide range of colours — blues, browns, greens, each with many varying shades — both in glacé kids, baby calf and suedes" — when war intervened. New machines were immediately brought in, operatives re-trained and production concentrated on stout footwear for the women's auxiliary Services and for a sobered home market which was suddenly denied American and Continental products.

Ipswich, too, had its old-established family firms. Messrs Ransomes, Sims and Jefferies employed 3,000 at its Orwell works, spread over forty acres at the dockside, and remained pre-eminent in the manufacture of agricultural machinery of every kind, as well as producing omnibus bodies and electrical machinery. Messrs Ransomes and Rapier manufacturered cranes, sluices and railway equipment. Messrs E. R. and F. Turner were well-known for their steel roller milling machinery. There were many others.

Ipswich, Felixstowe and King's Lynn all had busy docks. Lynn, for example, was served by a Dutch line with a weekly sailing in each direction to link with Rotterdam, and it also imported timber direct from Archangel and Leningrad. There were five big timber companies operating there, employing several hundred men.

> "The main shipping season was between April and September; they couldn't get away from Archangel until the ice melted. The timber was all loose and a lot of it on deck, which made it very difficult for the crew, especially in bad weather.
>
> Every piece of timber had to be manhandled. It was mass-dumped on the quay. The porters used to erect trestles and running planks and carry every piece on their shoulders — they had shoulder pads of leather. They had to sort it out and carry it about 250 yards to the pile in the timber yard." [4]

Some small towns had traditional industries centred upon them: textiles and clothing at Haverhill, Hadleigh and Sudbury, silk-weaving, mat-making and corset-making at Sudbury, printing at Bungay, brush-making at

4. Mr Reg Dexter, of King's Lynn, in an interview with the author, 1980.

Wymondham, engineering at Leiston, flint knapping and rabbit fur at Brandon. Some of these industries were in decline and employing fewer people each year.

There were large numbers of people who could not find employment. At the outset of 1939 there were in Britain as a whole twelve and a half million men with jobs, and well over two millions without. As the months passed, and war came closer, the unemployed total began to drop — until it was down to 1,230,000 by August. Most of the towns of East Anglia suffered. The *King's Lynn Advertiser* reported on 6th January:

> "Clerks at the Lynn Employment Exchange had a busy day on Friday . . . There was a long queue of applicants outside the Exchange when paying out started at 9.45 a.m. and business continued on equally busy lines until 9 p.m., two hours after normal closing time. Usually employees have a two hours break at noon and a further hour for tea, but both these breaks had to be given up owing to pressure of work."

There was a National Unemployed Workers' Movement with a militant leadership and an ability to organise demonstrations which secured large headlines. In January it co-operated with the Cambridge University Socialist Club in a campaign against the government because it was not more active in combating unemployment. Over two thousand signatures of members of the university were collected on a petition. When a delegation from the N.U.W.M. visited the town to speak at a crowded meeting in St Andrew's Hall, it was met by a large group of undergraduates who formed a torchlight procession from the railway station to the hall. A fortnight later fifty unemployed marched through Clacton behind a drummer carrying posters: "Appease the unemployed, not the dictators". There were about one thousand men on the unemployment register at Cambridge at the time, and about eight hundred in Clacton, which had, however, fewer than than a third as many employable males. Lowestoft was even worse hit, with one in six of its employable residents out of work and six hundred of them claiming relief. Ipswich had the most serious problem. In February its Town Council set up a special committee to investigate the circumstances in which the number of local unemployed had doubled within a year, to a total of two thousand, and to consider what might be done. Ten months later, despite the probing and the planning, there were still 1,900 unemployed in the town.

The Mayor of Ipswich had presided over a Committee for the Welfare of the Unemployed for some time. During January he organised a draw to select fifty of the workless for free rail tickets to travel to Birmingham to watch Ipswich Town play Aston Villa in the third round of the F.A. Cup. In February the Committee distributed six hundred loaves which had been produced for a competition sponsored by Hovis Ltd. A little later it established a Cheap Milk Depot in a shed behind a clinic on one of its new housing estates and opened it for a couple of hours each morning to sell milk at twopence a pint to pensioners and families on relief. The peak of all this effort was reached each year with the "Poor Children's Outing", organised by the Ipswich Motor Cycle and Car Club and described as the biggest event of its kind in the country. On 24th June, 1939, a Saturday afternoon, thousands of people lined the pavements to watch a cavalcade of 2,600 cheering and singing children leave for the country. They travelled in 350 cars and lorries loaned by local residents and decorated with bunting, and they made a fifty-miles round trip to Yoxford, where they were given tea, played games, and received the benediction of the Mayor and Mayoress, the Chief Constable and various other local dignitaries. The Norfolk Motor Club organised a similar event for crippled and poor children in Norwich. In June 1939 over a thousand of them were taken out to Necton Hall for the day.

The importance attributed to the gas mask in the early days of the War.

Norwich Mercury series

The pattern of misfortune which blighted so many lives at this time had no more touching feature than the gesture made by Czechoslovak refugees who found their way to the East Coast and were temporarily settled in camps there. They heard of the condition of local unemployed and they produced and performed two concerts and donated £22 of the proceeds to the Clacton Unemployment Assistance Committee. But sympathy was not always showered on the down-at-heel. When two men appeared before the Bury St Edmunds bench in May, summoned for begging in the street, the Chairman of the Bench, sentencing each of them to fourteen days' hard labour, commented: "Begging in Bury is becoming an intolerable nuisance. There is too much of it, and it must be stopped."

If there were problems in getting one's hands on money, there were certainly none about spending it. The shops were heavily stocked with a wide range of well-made goods, and luxuries of every kind were temptingly on offer. Woolworths ("nothing over sixpence"), Marks and Spencers and a number of other chain stores were in business in several of the larger towns, but most shops were still in the hands of small businessmen, offered personal service— and chairs for customers to sit on, and had "atmosphere".

"Shops in the main street were personally owned and the owners and their families lived above them, although, as they got more prosperous, some of them moved out into the suburbs. There was a very nice grocers' shop where they had lovely biscuit racks: seven-pound tins of biscuits side by side, under a glass cover which lifted on brass hinges, and you could have a handful of biscuits out of each tin to make up a pound, or you could just have a pound of ginger nuts. Then there was a corner shop with pickled cabbage, loose piccallilly, Strongbow vinegar, milk in the jug, and beer from the off-licence."[5]

"One of the most important grocers' shops in Norwich was Eddington, where the ladies of quality would walk down the few steps, and be greeted by name by the assistants behind the counter, which ran from front to back of the shop. They would hand in their lists and perhaps be given a little piece of something to taste and sample. Everything was collected from the shelves and brought to the counter by an assistant. Cabbages, leeks, carrots, potatoes and similar items would not have been washed or packed. When everything had been checked against the shopping lists and priced, the order was set on one side to be delivered later. Then the ladies in their gloves—ladies were not properly dressed unless wearing gloves—went into the Corner House opposite Jarrolds for tea or coffee . . . and to discuss their friends."[6]

5. Mr Reg Dexter, as before.
6. Mr Edward J. Cunningham, as before.

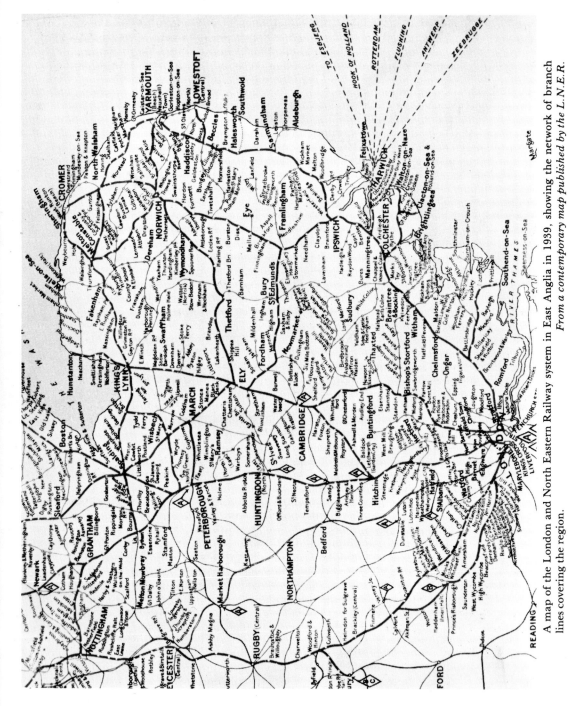

A map of the London and North Eastern Railway system in East Anglia in 1939, showing the network of branch lines covering the region. *From a contemporary map published by the L.N.E.R.*

The Day Books for 1939 kept by Thos Ridley, old-established grocers in Bury St Edmunds, provide examples of typical weekly orders delivered to well-to-do customers and provide evidence of 1939 prices. A major at the local barracks gave this order:

Butter, 4 lbs @ 1s. 6d.		6s.	0d.
Mustard, ¼-lb tin			8½d.
White pepper, ¼-lb			4d.
Echo margarine, 2 ½-lb packets @ 4½d.			9d.
Compound, 2 @ 5½d.			11d.
Currants, 1 lb			6d.
2 lbs strawberry jam		1s.	7d.
2 lbs apricot jam		1s.	6d.
Suet, 1 lb.			11d.
Fowlers syrup, 1 lb			11d.
Cheddar cheese, 2 lbs 6 ozs @ 1s. 1d.		2s.	7d.
Potatoes, 2 qtrs. @ 6s. cwt.		3s.	0d.
Tins of fruit, ½ doz @ 12s.		6s.	0d.
Rice, 1 lb.			4d.
¼-lb Ven. curry			10½d.
Birds Custard Powder, 1 tin		1s.	2d.
Rashers, ½ and ½, 2 lbs @ 1s. 6d.		3s.	0d.
Marmalade, 4 lbs @ 7d.		2s.	4d.
Lee & Perrin sauce, 1 bottle			11d.
Tomato sauce, 1 bottle		1s.	0d.
2½s. Peas, ¼-doz @ 10s. 6d.		2s.	7½d.
Prunes, 1 lb			7½d.
½-tin Cheese Assorted, 2 lb @ 1s. 4d.		2s.	8d.
Tin ?			8d.
Grnd. coffee, 1 lb		1s.	8d.
Sausages, 3 lbs @ 1s. 4d.		4s.	0d.
Granulated sugar, 3lbs @ 4½d		1s.	1½d.

£2. 8s. 8½d. [7]

Another order, delivered just before Christmas, suggests a big party and a lady with a sweet tooth. In part, it was as follows:

Clear consommé,	1 tin,	1s.	4d.
Lobster,	1 tin,	1s.	6d.
Prawns,	1 tin,	1s.	5d.
P & N tongue,	1 tin,	6s.	0d.
Muscadets,	1 packet,	2s.	0d.
Jordan almonds	¼ lb,		8½d.
Glacé pineapple,	½ lb packet,	1s.	2d.
Nigger dates,	1 packet,	1s.	7½d.
Turkish Delight,	1 packet,	1s.	7½d.
Barley sugar,	1 packet,	1s.	7½d.
Apples,	1 lb,	1s.	1d.

7. Thomas Ridley, of Bury St Edmunds, Grocers: Day Books, 1939. Suffolk Record Office, Bury St Edmunds.

At Christmas, too, an Ipswich shop advertised Duoro port at 5s. 9d. a bottle, twenty-five different kinds of sherry at 5s. 9d., whisky at 14 shillings, gin at thirteen shillings, and three-star cognac at 16s. 6d. a bottle. A leading King's Lynn retailer advertised throughout the year: "Cru de Carillon—a delightful dinner wine of exceptional value and highly recommended. Per dozen bottles, 48 shillings."

There was perhaps rather less contrast in clothing between the classes. Montague Burton, which had opened a shop in Cambridge, advertised: "Four guinea value suits for 45 shillings, to measure". High-quality, made-to-measure three-piece suits in the up-market shops were priced at £5 to £7. The sales offered special bargains, particularly to the ladies. A big Ipswich store advertised in January: "Coats—exceptional quality, now 63 shillings. Gowns—this season's day and evening, now 20 shillings. Furs—moleskin, pony calk coats, now £9. Skirts—good-quality plains and checks, Now five shillings."

Standards of dress were well defined:

"Nearly everyone, male and female, wore hats, the male being bowler or trilby. The local plumber considered a bowler hat was part of his trade. Men wore shirts with detachable collars. Most gentlemen carried umbrellas."[8]

"Men wore leather lace-up boots, and drain-pipe trousers. They kept their Sunday clothes in a box at the foot of the bed—a tin box or a wooden box—and they got the suit out just for Sundays. Women didn't put the men's clothes away; the men folded them up carefully and did that, they were so precious, you see. My dad used to put his bowler hat in there as well."[9]

There was a remarkable choice of furnishings and equipment for the home. In most of the larger shops there was a selection of oak dining room suites from about £14 upwards, and of real-hide three-piece suites for the drawing room from about seventeen guineas. Or one could shop in the local auction rooms. In July 1939 a Colchester auctioneer disposed of the residue of the effects from Woodham Mortimer Place, near Maldon, and the "good prices" which were announced afterwards included a Chippendale mahogany writing table at £9, four Hepplewhite mahogany dining chairs at £14. 10s., a pair of Dresden groups for £7, a Queen Anne mahogany bureau bookcase at £21, a seven-ounce silver sugar basin of 1790 at four guineas, and a pair of pastel portraits of ladies, attributed to Sir Joshua Reynolds, for £6. 10s.

In Cambridge in the early months of 1939 one could buy a twenty-six piece dinner service with "hand-painted coloured bands, etc" at prices from 13s. 11d. and a twenty-one piece tea service "in semi-porcelain with modern handcraft decoration" from 4s. 11d. A Cambridge music shop announced in

8. Mr Edward J. Cunningham, as before.
9. Mrs K. R. Taylor, as before.

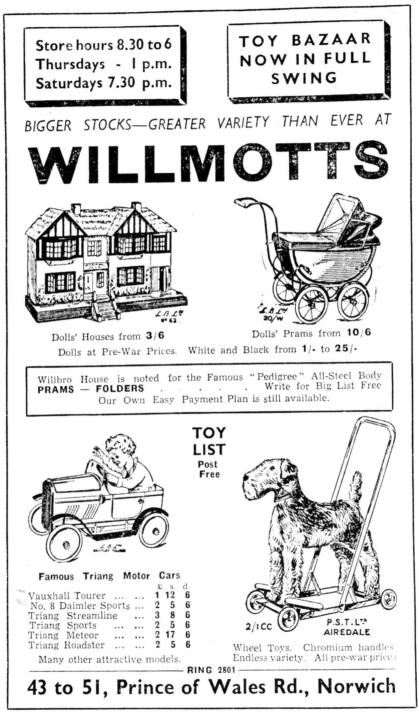

Toys were still available as Christmas presents during December.
Norwich Mercury series

March a new upright piano at twenty-four guineas, and had a selection of grands from ninety-nine guineas. The point had already been reached, however, when more people wanted radio sets in their homes than pianos, and these were priced from ten to eleven pounds upwards, with an H.M.V. automatic radiogram priced at fifteen guineas. By 1939, over 373,000 "wireless licences" had been issued by the Post Office in its Eastern District, an increase of 18,400 in one year. In the countryside, most of these wirelesses had to be powered by dry cell or accumulator batteries, in the absence of mains electricity. The idea that a wireless was essential in every home was not established fully, as is shown by the comments of a County Court judge at Colchester, when he admonished a debtor in these terms:

> "If people in your walk of life pay £12. 10s. for a wireless set, you deserve all the trouble you get into. People in my position think twice before they buy a wireless set for £12. 10s. You people do this sort of thing, and then you come here and want to get off from your bargain. What right has a man in your position to pay £12. 10s. for a wireless set?"

There was no television service generally available in East Anglia to provide further temptation but a few enthusiasts found they could receive programmes transmitted from London. One Cambridge retailer had erected a special mast in order to receive programmes for demonstration purposes and there was one enthusiast in rural Suffolk who caused quite a stir. He was a 35-year-old bachelor farm worker living in a small cottage in Long Melford and his imagination had been so fired by the wonders of television that he had somehow got together £126 to purchase a television set and a 60 foot aerial. With this he successfully received programmes transmitted from London and over a period of two years over a thousand people beat a path to his cottage to see what the *East Anglian Daily Times* described as "the world's latest wonder". Early in 1939 the *Radio Times* published a feature about this enthusiast and one result was the arrival of eight hundred letters from would-be brides. This seems to have quickly broadened his interests, for within a matter of weeks he was married at Sudbury Register Office (on 1st April) to a London domestic servant, with press photographers and a considerable crowd on hand.

Another relatively new device in the home, quickly becoming popular with the middle class, was the telephone. Some local newspapers regularly published full lists of new subscribers, which was undoubtedly of great practical value, but had the incidental attraction of establishing a new kind of social register. In January it was reported that there had been 34 new connections in the county of Suffolk in a month, six of them in Bury St Edmunds, five in Lowestoft and one each in Beccles, Bungay and Haverhill. Norwich reported 31 new subscribers and Great Yarmouth nine. Ipswich,

Television was a technological wonder of the time and was not generally available in East Anglia. With special aerials, however, reception could sometimes be achieved. Millers, at Cambridge, set up their own studio to show programmes.

TELEVISION...

DEMONSTRATIONS DAILY

AT *Miller's* STUDIO

OR FREE HOME DEMONSTRATIONS ARRANGED

RING CAMBRIDGE 2253

"HIS MASTER'S VOICE" 1939 EXHIBITION RELEASE MODELS

From **31** GNS.

Arrange your H.P. Terms with us.

You are Cordially Invited to inspect our Complete Television Range.

Miller's SIDNEY STREET, CAMBRIDGE.

Cambridge Evening News

Colchester and Chelmsford between them produced 13, but Clacton only one. Felixstowe telephone exchange in 1939 was able to handle 900 subscribers. At Thetford, a new post office and telephone exchange made provision for 400 subscribers, but only 200 were connected at that time. Attleborough provided for 240 subscribers at its new exchange. Histon's new exchange was designed to serve 200 subscribers. Other new exchanges were built at about the same time at Wymondham and in St Andrews Street, Norwich. The important thing about these new exchanges was that they were automatic, and no longer called for operators sitting at the plugs. This meant that many villages secured

61

24-hour telephone service for the first time and it meant that subscribers everywhere could dial many more numbers direct. Another improvement during 1939 was the provision of telephone boxes in most villages with a post office.

The motor-car was a symbol of personal prosperity. Doctors, some shop-keepers, some professional men had them; ordinary wage-earners rarely harboured a hope of ever owning one. The public transport system was supplemented by bicycles, which cost from £5 to £6. 10s. each, and motor-cycles, which often had "sidecars" for a passenger. Cars, however, were heavily advertised, and there was keen competition in the lowest price range. Ford whose manufacturing base was at Dagenham, in Essex, sold their eight-horse power car at £115, a new Standard Eight was priced at £139, the Hillman Minx at £175 and a Morris Ten "saloon de luxe" at £185. Probably the most popular of all the small cars was the famous Austin Seven range. Representative of bigger cars, there was the new Wolseley Fourteen at £285. In Ipswich market second-hand cars went for a song: a 1929 Riley Nine saloon for £10, a 1930 Austin Sixteen for £15, a 1934 Vauxhall Twelve for £40. Botwoods, a leading dealer operating in several of the region's largest towns, offered a dazzling selection: a 1927 Rolls Royce 40/50 h.p. Open Limousine at £110, a 1933 Delage 30 h.p. Binder Sports Coupé at £145, and a four-years-old Bentley 3½-litre ME Sports Saloon at £575. To tempt the customers into the showrooms, this firm advertised: "Cars over £100 guaranteed for three months. Free driving tuition. Free oiling and greasing once monthly for three months."

It was, however, a narrow market. When, in July, the Aldeburgh Trade Association ran the first of a series of old people's outings, taking thirty-four of them for a ride in seventeen of the members' cars, it was noted that "many of the old people had not been in a motor-car before".

The East Anglian society of 1939 was one of dramatic contrasts. A handful of silver would buy a dinner service or a suit, but many men and women had to toil for forty-eight hours in a week to fill their hands with so much silver. A handful of notes would buy a motor-car, or even a small house, but few people believed that in a whole lifetime they could save that many notes, after meeting the costs of food and clothing and shelter. Most people's expectations were as modest as their incomes.

CHAPTER FOUR

Bodies and Minds

MEDICAL and educational services in 1939 were very firmly in the hands of the local communities in which they functioned; the role of the state, though it had been increasing, was still minimal. There were many critics of this situation and a national survey of public opinion early in the year showed a large majority favouring state intervention in the hospital service. A leading article in the *East Anglian Daily Times* argued against this view:

> "There would be none of that local pride and enthusiasm in an institution founded in the first place by private beneficence and maintained by the local community for more than a century such as were manifest at this week's annual meeting of the Ipswich representatives of the Contributory Scheme of the East Suffolk and Ipswich Hospital."

The scheme referred to was run by dedicated volunteers. They acted as honorary collectors in factories, shops and offices and they made regular household calls; there were eighty-seven in the town area of Ipswich alone knocking on doors. The annual general meeting of the Contributory Scheme, in March 1939, heard that it had been a record year, with £37,679 collected, and the chairman observed with pride: "The threepence-a-week contribution is the best money that anybody can spend, especially when you realise that a man, his wife and family under sixteen can be conveyed to the hospital, treated, sent to Felixstowe for a fortnight and brought back to Ipswich." Two-thirds of the patients admitted to the hospital were members of the Contributory Scheme, or their dependents.

This was but part of the story. The total collection covered little more than half the cost of running the hospital. There was at that time "a waiting list of tragic proportions". There was urgent need of a new ward block for women and for an extension of the gynaecological ward. At virtually every hospital in the region — indeed, in the whole country — the same story could be heard: a desperate battle to balance the books. The Norfolk and Norwich Hospital reported in April that its income for the year had been £63,000 and its expenses £68,000. Its Contributors' Association, collecting subscriptions of twopence a week, had raised £37,300. The hospital had a waiting list of eight hundred. In the following month the Essex County Hospital at Colchester reported a deficit for the year of £5,671 and an overdraft of £18,000. At

Cambridge, Addenbrooke's Hospital collected £53,004, and spent £53,507, including one thousand pounds on cleaning, painting and overhaul which had had to be much delayed. The chairman of the maintenance fund committee there commented: "To meet the still-increasing demands on the hospital, we should really be starting on further extensions to give more beds, accommodation for more nurses, and all the consequent items that go with it . . . Dare we start to think about it? It is necessary for the benefit of the people, but can the money be raised to do it?"

In their early days the local hospitals had depended principally upon charitable gifts and bequests, and in 1939 these remained an important source of income. At Braintree, in Essex, the local hospital had been donated to the community in 1921 by one man, Mr William Julian Courtauld, and had been named after him. He had met all subsequent capital expenditure, including £8,000 for a maternity block added in 1938. At the hospital's annual meeting in March 1939 Mr Courtauld warned: "If the people of Braintree really want a hospital of this kind, they will have to pay for it in the near future. I have paid for it very largely in the past, but that cannot go on for ever. I am not immortal . . ."

The Carnival Queen in a landau leads the Norwich Hospital Week procession past Victoria Station in June. *Norwich Mercury* series

More typically, the Norfolk and Norwich Hospital aimed to meet its running costs from the proceeds of its Contributors' Association plus a variety of special fund-raising events, and to earmark legacies for extensions to the hospital and other capital commitments.

No conceivable method of raising money was overlooked. One saw regularly in the press advertisements such as this:

ESSEX COUNTY HOSPITAL
COLCHESTER (174 beds)
Our work for the sick: 2,500 in-patients,
64,700 out-patient attendances.
OUR NEED: £33,000 annually.
Please help by sending an annual subscription or donation,
and remember the Hospital when making your will.

In May 1939 the Mayor of Colchester sent out twenty thousand personal appeal letters and then sat at the entrance of the Town Hall for two days to receive donations. Each of the hospitals organised a supporters' association of some kind and these, working with other local organisations, did their best to keep money rolling in. Some of the events for which they were responsible were not simply fund-raising; they became important and enjoyable social occasions in the various communities. Through the summer months, there was rarely a weekend when a big hospital's event was not being staged somewhere in the region and they vied with one another not only to break money-raising records but also to provide maximum entertainment value. On August Bank Holiday 1939 nine thousand people attended a hospital fete in the grounds of Culford School, near Bury St Edmunds. At the top of the bill were "Les Cosaques Djiguites, led by Captain Korolkoff", offering "thrilling displays". They were already well-known and popular in the region, usually presented less pretentiously as "The Cossacks". There were also at Culford the band of the Royal Army Service Corps and the more home-spun amusements of open-air boxing, a village tug-of-war contest for a silver challenge cup, clay pigeon shooting, Punch and Judy, roundabouts and sideshows. The programme continued late into the evening, by which time "Lennie Sewell and his band" were playing for dancers on the lawn. Finally, before everyone staggered home exhausted, there was a firework display. Another formula was the hospital carnival, with a Carnival Queen, a procession through the town, and a programme of events which, in the case of Clacton, stretched over three days or, in the case of Chelmsford, for a whole week.

Similar activities were maintained throughout the year. In the winter there were hospital balls—one at Bury St Edmunds in February raised over £200. Whist drives were organised on an astonishing scale. Also in February, the press reported, "three halls were needed to accommodate nearly 1,200 whist players at Colchester, on the occasion of the culmination of the annual whist tournament in aid of the Essex County Hospital. Throughout the winter many drives have been held in the villages in the large area served by the hospital, and it is calculated that in these local drives and on Wednesday no fewer than 8,000 people have supported the cause." The amount raised totalled £500. This example was followed elsewhere. The East Suffolk and Ipswich Hospital organised a similar competition for the first time during the winter of 1938-39. Over ten thousand whist players attended drives in one hundred and one Suffolk parishes and a total of £872 was collected. In Norfolk one of the big efforts of the year was the Hospital Egg Week. In 1939 it produced a total of 220,456 eggs, collected in 400 parishes throughout the county and distributed among 28 hospitals and charitable institutions. Ipswich hospital had its own well-established "Egg Day" and in March 1939 three hundred and fifty-six Girl Guides made a house-to-house collection of 23,381 eggs; these were stored in large tanks of waterglass at the hospital until they could be used.

Addenbrooke's Hospital at Cambridge had its Linen League, the members of which each paid at least 1s. 6d. a year subscription and promised to send at least two garments or articles of household linen for hospital use.

Every hospital published a weekly list of gifts received, acknowledging eggs and rabbits, fruit and groceries, toys and books, papers and magazines, stamps and tinfoil (for re-sale in bulk), and sometimes clothing. On one occasion in 1939 the West Suffolk General Hospital announced its gratitude for "a gift of jellies and food from Culford Hall".

The basis upon which hospitals admitted patients was succinctly stated in a prospectus of the Ipswich Hospital, in these terms: "Free treatment is provided for necessitous cases only. Each In-Patient is expected to contribute as his or her circumstance will permit, and to reimburse the Hospital the whole cost of maintenance if in a position to do so." Members of the Contributory Scheme, however, were covered by their regular threepence-a-week payments. At the West Suffolk General Hospital at Bury St Edmunds a more complicated system operated. Anyone who subscribed two guineas a year was entitled to receive one "In-Patient Letter" and one "Out-Patient Letter", and an "In-Patient Letter" was an entitlement to six weeks' treatment in the hospital. That was one means of securing admission. Another was to join the Contributory Scheme, paying one penny a week; this offered free treatment and maintenance for the member, his wife and any children up to the age of sixteen. The third way was to pay cash — not the complete cost, but £1 a week contribution towards the cost of maintenance for patients over six years of age, or ten shillings a week for young children. "The amount may be remitted in whole or in part in necessitous cases," the hospital stated.

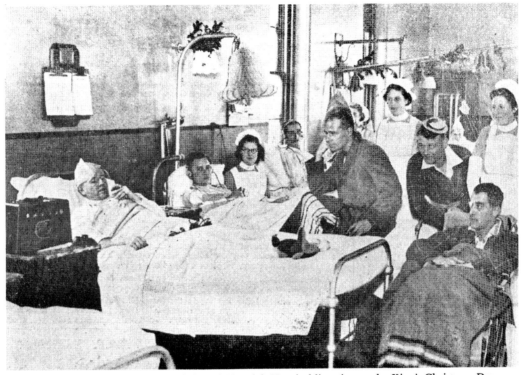

Patients and nurses at the Norfolk and Norwich Hospital listening to the King's Christmas Day broadcast to the Empire.   *Norwich Mercury* series

There was, of course, a private sector too. At Addenbrooke's in Cambridge a bed in a private single ward was charged at twelve shillings a day, and one in an open ward of the private wing cost ten shillings and sixpence a day. The West Suffolk Hospital at Bury St Edmunds was planning to extend its private accommodation when the war stopped all such work; it explained: "there is a very large class of people nowadays who, while desiring greater privacy than can be given in the public wards, are perfectly willing to pay something towards the amenities of a private ward, but cannot always meet the extreme expense of a private nursing home".

There was no payment for treatment, but only for maintenance in hospital. The principle embodied in the foundation charters of all the big voluntary hospitals remained in force: they were charitable institutions for the sick poor and the specialists who served them gave their services free, depending for their living on building up lucrative private practices in the area. Patients, interviewed by a hospital almoner to see how much they could contribute, did not always appreciate the finer points of this system.

Considerable attention was given to keeping costs down in every possible way, and the West Suffolk Hospital was particularly proud of its achievement in handling patients at an average cost of £2. 12s. 2½d. per head per week, compared with a figure of about £3 in most other hospitals. We have already noted the modest rewards of nurses who, after paying for their keep, had between £1 and £2 a week left for everything else, most of them at the lower end of the scale. Support staff were considerably less well paid—the commencing wage for a cook required for a nurses' home in Ipswich was £40 a year, and for a kitchen-maid £28 to £38.

There was no militancy, however, nor even active discontent. There was a sense of service and dedication, with overtones of religiosity about it. When the Assistant Matron of the Essex County Hospital told the members of the Colchester Rotary Club in August something of the nurses' life and work, she explained:

> "Each nurse had three hours off duty daily, not including meals, and one whole day weekly, when they might sleep away from the hospital. A nurse's hours were fifty-two a week . . .
>
> A probationer's salary, perhaps, to those who did not weigh everything, did not seem much, but when one considered that she was learning a profession, fed, housed, given uniform after the first three months and numerous other advantages, she really was in a fortunate position as compared with many other branches of work where one had to pay to be taught."

By the summer of 1939 one distinct improvement in nurses' conditions had been achieved: their hours were reduced to ninety-six in each fortnight.

By that time, too, plans had been made for an expansion of hospital facilities, for the improvement of their equipment, and for a measure of government financial assistance. These were part of the preparation for war; they were to prove, in time, to be the beginning of the end of the whole system described above. The immediate objective was to increase the number of hospital beds available in the region. Before the measures took effect, in that last peace-time summer, there were 440 beds in the Norfolk and Norwich Hospital, 315 in Addenbrooke's at Cambridge, 285 in the East Suffolk and Ipswich Hospital, 174 in the Essex County Hospital at Colchester, 112 in the West Suffolk General Hospital at Bury St Edmunds, and several hundreds more in smaller hospitals at Lowestoft, King's Lynn, Peterborough, Huntingdon, Saffron Walden, Felixstowe, Beccles, Sudbury and other towns of similar size.

Hospitals were only one element in the care and treatment of health. The experience of the majority of people was limited to home treatment by nurses and doctors. Nursing associations and Friendly Societies were the means of providing such services. The soberly-uniformed district nurse on her bicycle, with her medical equipment in a bag on the carrier, was a familiar sight in every town and village. She delivered babies; she cared for the elderly infirm; and she looked after those who, while not requiring hospital treatment, needed professional attention. The eight district nurses working in the borough of Cambridge, four of whom were midwives, made a total of 22,000 visits in a year. Four nurses in Bury St Edmunds made 15,584 visits in a year; even on the basis of a six-day week and fifty working weeks in the year, that means that each nurse averaged more than a dozen cases each day. One nurse working alone at Cromer made 5,064 visits to 170 cases in a year. In Ipswich the nursing services made well over 40,000 visits in the year. An enormous number of these were to poor homes, and no charges were made. The result was that all public subscriptions, donations and church offertories, as well as a £500 grant by Ipswich Corporation, were completely expended and there was a deficit at the year-end of £240. The system of financing the nursing associations was very similar to that for the hospitals: a contributory scheme for members, fund-raising and supplication of donations on the widest possible scale.

The arrangements for general practioner treatment of the sick were the subject of considerable debate and some experimentation in 1939. A system of national insurance first introduced in 1911 and subsequently amended in various ways provided insurance against both ill-health and unemployment, but this cover did not apply to the whole working population. The State scheme involved working arrangments with the Friendly Societies, the activities of which had for more than two centuries been woven into the texture of the lives of the poor. Quaintly named as, for examples, the Rechabites, the Oddfellows, the Sons of Temperance, the Foresters, and the Loyal Order of Ancient Shepherds, they sometimes had a quasi-religious character or a special concern with social and economic emancipation. Some had begun life in the seventeeth century essentially as burial clubs, but in general their activities had been extended to offer sickness and disablement benefits, maternity grants, burial grants and medical insurance in varying degrees. When a State system of insurance against illness was introduced these "approved societies", as they became known, were permitted to handle much of the administration.

In each county, an Insurance Committee was set up including members *appointed* by the County Council, the Minister of Health, the local medical practitioners, and the approved societies, and others *elected* by approved society members.

The Lord Mayor of Norwich, Mr Fred Henderson, reading to the children at the Llandaff House Children's Home on Christmas Day. *Norwich Mercury* series

The Friendly Societies had substantial memberships in East Anglia. The Bury St Edmunds District of the Independent Order of Oddfellows Manchester Unity, at its annual meeting at the Atheneum, reported 26,000 members organised in forty-two lodges in its area. Before the State intervened, each Friendly Society made its own contracts with general practitioners to provide services to its members. But by 1939 there was a growing apprehension that new developments were steadily eroding the role of the Societies. The British Medical Association had devised a new Public Medical Service structure and general practitioners in many towns had by 1939 created such an organization. These schemes gave a free choice of doctor (and freedom to the doctor to refuse a patient) and also covered the services of the district nurses. In Ipswich, at the beginning of 1939, there were twelve thousand members of the local Public Medical Service, paying fourpence to elevenpence a week, according to the size of families. In Cambridge and in other areas in the region, the doctors had created similar schemes, but had not yet reached agreement with the Friendly Societies as to how they would work together.

East Anglia was a relatively healthy region of Britain. In the borough of Cambridge thirty babies died before their first birthday for every one thousand live births; in Norfolk the mortality rate was 35.04 and in West Suffolk 40 per thousand; in Cambridgeshire it was 53. These figures compared with fifty-eight deaths per thousand births for England and Wales. People also lived to a ripe old age. The 1931 Census (the last one before the war) showed over eleven per cent of the population of the small country towns of Norfolk and Suffolk to be over the age of sixty-five, compared with only 7.4 per cent in England and Wales. Tuberculosis was still a menace, though it was slowly being brought under control. Cambridgeshire had one of the lowest rates for tuberculosis in the country, but in March 1939 it opened a new county tuberculosis clinic in Cambridge. The number of deaths in the county had dropped from 172 in 1918 to 71 in 1937. Suffolk had a County Tuberculosis After-Care Committee, with a growing network of sixteen district committees under its wing. At the annual meeting of this organisation in June 1939 it was reported that 160 patients had been given help during the year, in the form of milk, eggs, patent foods, coal, clothing, travelling expenses or convalescent home treatment.

If the demand on medical resources was being reduced in this field, it was rapidly increasing in another. Traffic accidents were now a regular occurrence. The East Suffolk and Ipswich Hospital reported during 1939 that it had admitted 214 accident victims in a year and that they had spent a total of 6,456 days in hospital; in the previous year the figures had been 153 patients and 5,409 days of treatment.

There were plenty of under-nourished people in the region. When the East Suffolk County Association of the National Union of Teachers held its annual meeting at Southwold, a local alderman declared there were many local children who had to go without a midday meal. The physique of Southwold youth was poor, he said; their average height was much below the average for the whole country. When he travelled to the north of England, the children there seemed giants by comparison. But the School Medical Officer for Health for Norfolk in his annual report, in June 1939, said that only 14 children had been found whose nutrition was "bad" and 1,781 (15.1 per cent) whose nutrition was slightly sub-normal. His main concern seemed to be that 69 per cent of the children examined needed dental treatment. The West Suffolk Education Committee was told in February that only fifty of the 9,463 children attending its schools had been found to be suffering from malnutrition and later in the year the Chief School Medical Officer reported that the nutritional standard was improving. In Cambridge schools 180 children who were considered to be in need were being given a wholemeal bread sandwich with their mid-morning milk and, the School Medical Officer reported, "the great majority enjoy them and are very often the envy of those who are not on the sandwiches list".

71

It was sometimes easier to cope with problems of health than with those of hygiene. With the housing conditions in which many lived, cleanliness was virtually impossible.

"Most people in the Fens had fleas. Washing facilities were not good. Nobody had a bath, nobody had a flush toilet. When you went to school, they looked in your hair every day. I had fleas, me and my brother. My mother used to have what we call a bug comb, a very fine toothed comb, and she combed our hair on paper. Clean as you was, you couldn't avoid being lousy. I think nearly every family was lousy."[1]

"Then the weekly bath . . . in the zinc bath. It was carried in by the husband and wife on the Friday or Saturday night. The water had to be heated by kettles, saucepans, anything handy. The little children had to bath first, then the mother, then the father, all in the same water. There was only one towel for the lot. Only well-to-do people had proper bath-rooms . . ."[2]

In the urban areas, however, things were definitely getting better. The Norfolk Medical Officer of Health commented in his annual report that, while social conditions did not change much from year to year, over a period of years a great change had taken, and was taking, place. The homes of many people, he said, had been improved out of all recognition through the city's housing activities, and the mentality of certain classes was improving. "It used to be said that if people were given baths, the baths would be used for storing coal," he wrote. "This, as far as Norwich is concerned, is now a myth. It does not happen."

A classroom in the new area school at Beccles, which was built to accommodate over 400 senior pupils.
East Anglian Daily Times

So much for the care of bodies; now what of the minds, particularly of the young? The Education Act passed in 1936 provided that the school-leaving age should be raised to fifteen from September 1939; because of the war this policy was not implemented at that time and, except for the minority which went to grammar schools, children went out to work at fourteen.

The majority learnt little more than the basic skills of reading, writing and simple arithmetical calculation during the nine years they spent in school. As most schools had begun their existence as church foundations, the religious influence remained strong, even though local education authorities had taken over some of the costs of running them. In the village schools, in particular, the vicar remained almost as great an influence on the children as was the teacher.

School buildings were, in most cases, without adequate amenities. Central heating, with large cast-iron pipes along the walls to carry the hot water, had come to some town schools, but those in the country usually had very old stoves into which coal or wood had regularly to be shovelled. There was the same sort of contrast with lighting: electricity was normal in the town schools, but many in the villages still used paraffin lamps. Earth closets were also commonplace, as few village schools had running water.

But new schools were being built and Norwich was setting a fast pace. In April 1939 a new elementary school for 500 senior boys was opened at Catton and a similar girls' school in the same area was reconstructed. A fortnight later a nursery school for 120 children between two and five years old was opened at Earlham — the first nursery school in the city. A week after that primary and infants' schools nearby were officially opened, so that "amid the houses of the great building estate of Earlham there has arisen a group of fine bright buildings covering, with their grounds, an area of eleven acres, which will provide continuous observation, care and training for children from ante-natal period to the time they leave for the post-primary part of their education". A maternity and child welfare clinic was constructed as part of the same complex. Norwich also came forward with a bold project — not to be realised at that time — for a new technical college with university status, which would offer not only engineering degrees, but a full range of commercial and professional courses.

Lowestoft opened a new junior school for 420 at Oulton Broad in June and, as an imaginative gesture, had the opening ceremony performed by a six-year-old pupil. At eleven, children moved on to senior schools, usually travelling in from villages to a town centre; the pattern was demonstrated by a new area school opened at Beccles which took 456 children from thirteen schools in the area, and Wymondham was another centre which provided a new senior school in 1939. It was at the age of eleven that every child confronted a fateful parting of the ways ahead. The ambitious (and those with

1. Mr C. R. Everitt, as before.
2. Mrs K. R. Taylor, as before.

When this new Junior School was built at Dell Road, Oulton Broad, the earlier school on the site was modernised and incorporated. *East Anglian Daily Times*

ambitious parents) were keen to secure a place in a grammar school; it was universally accepted that only those who did so could look forward to a worth-while career, and that the others were destined to be "hewers of wood and drawers of water". Grammar schools accepted paying pupils and scholarship pupils and during the years immediately before the war the ratio between the two groups had changed radically. At the annual dinner of the old boys of Thetford School in March 1939 the headmaster reported that between 65 and 70 per cent of pupils at that date paid no fees. It had had a sweeping effect on the school, he said: from being fifty per cent a boarding school, it had become ninety per cent a day school.

Scholarships to grammar schools usually covered the costs of tuition, leaving parents to meet the costs of books and stationery and uniforms. "Special places" were made available at some schools and the parents of those to whom they were awarded were expected to pay partial fees, according to their income. In Ipswich those with earnings of less than £3. 10s. a week were entirely exempted from payment. The system aroused strong emotions, and the controversy drew in politicians as well as educationalists and parents. The idea that cash could buy educational privilege and the career prospects associated with it came under fierce attack. In January 1939, for example, a

A firework night guy at H.M.S. *Ganges.*

The H.M.S. *Ganges* mast dressed overall.
A. Frost for B. A. Davies, official photographer to H.M.S. Ganges

A parade at H.M.S. *Ganges* during 1939.

Joint Committee of Ipswich Teachers criticised the scholarship system, because many children had been denied secondary education because of the financial circumstances of their parents. The teachers demanded changes. When the letter came before the Education Committee for consideration, it was told that the governors of the local grammar school had already decided to increase the number of special places there from fifty per cent to eighty per cent of the total, in stages of ten per cent each year from September 1938. When the eighty per cent level was reached, the matter would be reviewed again. Meanwhile, the Education Committee was assured, of 123 children offered special places during 1938 only five failed to accept them.

Another indication of the fundamental changes under way came when one of the oldest grammar schools in Britain, the King Edward VI School at Bury St Edmunds, decided to surrender the independence it had enjoyed since its foundation in 1550 in exchange for the economic security offered by absorption into the state system. The West Suffolk Education Committee resolved in July that it would take over the school from the following year.

Similar problems arose all over the country during the 'thirties and the government accepted that the secondary education system required a searching examination. It appointed a committee under the chairmanship of the Master of Corpus Christi College, Cambridge, Mr Will Spens (he was knighted in the 1939 New Year's Honours, immediately after publication of the Spens Report, as it became known). The Committee recommended that as soon as possible admission to grammar schools should be solely on merit, and that fees for secondary education should be abolished. It suggested multi-lateral schools, sharing teachers and facilities, and many other far-reaching changes, and it proposed the creation of technical high schools. Unfortunately, the preoccupation with preparations for war meant that the recommendations received inadequate consideration and led to no early action.

An important innovatory idea originating in Cambridge had brought into existence by 1939 four Village Colleges — at Sawston, Bottisham, Linton and Impington — which were intended to spread the gospel that education was a continuing process throughout life. Each College was intended to be both school and community centre and the first four sought to engage the interest and enthusiasm of a population of about thirty thousand scattered in forty-one villages.

The educational privilege which by 1939 was under assault was most starkly epitomised by Cambridge University. Grant-aided students had first appeared in the colleges during the 'twenties, but they had had no significant effect upon attitudes and practices, and class distinction was maintained as strongly as ever. An author who knew the university well stated matters bluntly when he wrote in 1939:

The May Week Balls formed one important feature of an elaborate social calendar at Cambridge University: this dawn picture of undergraduates and their partners was taken after the Trinity College ball.   *Cambridge Evening News*

"The poor man from the elementary school really does not get very much out of Cambridge. He is not likely to make many friends and will almost certainly remain a fish out of water. He would be much wiser to go to one of the newer universities where he would feel less discontented with his lot. Discouraging though it may be for social reformers, the man from the elementary school is unquestionably excluded from everything that makes Cambridge worth while."[3]

Cambridge, thought this critic, was for "the father who wishes his son to have a few years of intellectual pubescence". Doubtless, this was a somewhat idiosyncratic view, for the 'thirties had witnessed Rutherford at the Cavendish Laboratory opening up a new era in nuclear physics, and in 1939 the new Jacksonian Professor of Natural Philosophy, John Cockcroft, was procuring a cyclotron for the university. The search for new knowledge was in earnest, but, as the last pre-war Spring Term began, a *Granta* editorial made it clear that the university was not single-minded. "The May Sunday excursions are crowded with purple lovelies," it reported. "They walk down through Kings and back through Trinity and the sun glows. A cape of pale Russian lynx, an off-shoulder dress of emerald tulle . . . a world of lawns and punts, neckties and shirting-patterns, crème brûlé and paprika salad." No wonder the elementary school product on a grant felt he had problems.

3. John Steegman: *Cambridge as it was and as it is today*, Batsford, 1940.

CHAPTER FIVE

Farmers in Revolt

IT IS difficult to imagine a more unlikely group of people in which to plant seeds of militancy and protest than East Anglian farmers. Yet on 1st February 1939, nearly two thousand of them "invaded" London, marched from Tower Hill to the Thames Embankment, and later staged a protest rally in the Central Hall at Westminster. Many of them had never been to London before and they were resolved to have an enjoyable day out, despite the serious purpose of their visit, and they were quite ready to look and act the part of countrymen "up for the day". Almost all of them wore sprigs of wheat or barley in their hats or buttonholes, some carried whole sheaves of corn, battered trilby hats and leather gaiters were a favourite type of dress, and some even carried their lunches in knotted red handkerchieves. The newsreel cameramen had a field day.

As they marched through the City of London, headed by a band playing "A Farmer's Boy", "A Hunting we will go", "John Peel" and "John Brown's Body", they exhibited great good humour. But when, later, they re-assembled at Westminster their leaders' words were fierce and bitter. Since the National Government had taken office in 1931, they said, nearly 1,300,000 workers had left the land and nearly three-quarters of a million acres of land had been lost to the plough. The meeting called on the government to give immediate help to agriculture.

The London demonstration was the climax of a campaign which was taking shape from the later months of 1938. At a long series of local meetings, farmers' voices were heard running through the gamut of anxiety, frustration, despair and anger. Essex farmers met at the Corn Exchange in Colchester complaining bitterly that arable farmers had led a hand-to-mouth existence for ten years, that their buildings had become dilapidated and their machinery out of date, so that land had had to be left uncultivated and semi-derelict. The essence of their case was that the prices paid for their products failed to cover the actual costs of production. These complaints were echoed when, in January, five hundred protesters packed the Corn Exchange in Cambridge and passed a resolution calling for guaranteed prices "sufficient to secure a reasonable remuneration to all those engaged in this industry".

The cockpit of protest was in Suffolk. When the National Farmers' Union called a meeting in the Public Hall in Ipswich twelve hundred farmers, farm workers, landowners and representatives of allied interests turned up to demonstrate. Outside the hall sandwich-board men paraded all day through the centre of Ipswich displaying such slogans as "If there's war today, you'll starve tomorrow" and "Give the farmer and his men a fair deal". The resolution passed by this meeting struck an ominous note: unless the government took steps forthwith to ensure that payments made to farmers bore a fair relation to production costs, Suffolk farmers pledged themselves to do everything in their power to oppose the return of the National Government candidates at the next election. This resolution, the press reported, was passed with "a storm of cheering and applause". At about the same time the Suffolk branch of the N.F.U. took the initiative in proposing a demonstration march in London.

Fruit pickers checking in their "chips" at the Hoveton Fruit Farm near Wroxham.
Norwich Mercury series

Unfortunately for the government, a by-election occurred early in 1939 in one of the most deeply agricultural constituencies in the country, and one where feeling was running high — East Norfolk. The sitting member, who had succeeded to the peerage as Earl Beauchamp, had held the seat as a Liberal National — the government headed by Mr Neville Chamberlain was, theoretically, a coalition of Conservatives and Liberal Nationals. The new candidate selected to defend the seat for the government was also, therefore, a Liberal National: a 35-year-old rugby-playing London solicitor, Mr Frank Medlicott. In normal circumstances, he would doubtless have been acceptable to the local Conservatives but the fact that he was not, in a strict sense, "one of them" now made it easier for them to mount a political campaign on an agricultural theme. A well-known Norfolk farmer, Mr J. F. Wright, announced that he would stand as a National Conservative and Agriculture candidate. A new organisation, the East Norfolk National Conservative and Agricultural Committee, was quickly created and it accepted the official sponsorship of the candidate. Its chairman was Captain H. J. Cator, of Ranworth Hall, who was the largest landowner in the constituency. Central committee rooms were opened in Norwich and a network of smaller offices in six other centres, and within two or three weeks there were sixty paid election workers.

Haysel. A cutter at work in Hintlesham Park.   *East Anglian Daily Times*

In atrocious weather conditions, a lively campaign developed. A third candidate, Mr Norman R. Tillett, carried the Labour standard and hopes ran high in that quarter that, with the traditional government vote split two ways, Labour might win the seat—despite the 10,461 government majority at the 1935 general election. There were dramatic developments, however, at the eleventh hour. Despite the fact that he was heavily preoccupied with foreign affairs—he made his visit to Rome to talk with Mussolini during the period of the by-election campaign—the Prime Minister decided that he should intervene. A few days before nominations had to be submitted, Mr Wright received a letter pointing out that the Minister of Agriculture, Mr W. S. Morrison, was in the middle of discussions with the National Farmers' Union. "Whatever legislation is found to be necessary will be proceeded with as quickly as possible," the Prime Minister assured Mr Wright.

This letter was reinforced by action by the government Chief Whip, Captain David Margesson, who summoned Captain Cator to London. It was none too convenient, for the captain was host to King George VI, who had driven over from Sandringham to visit him on the morning before by-election nominations closed. Captain Cator completed his social duties and departed for London, with Mr Wright. There were two meetings between Margesson and Cator—Wright does not appear to have been admitted to them. Margesson, said Cator afterwards, "on behalf of the Prime Minister emphasized to me the imperative need for a National united front at this critical period". Cator and Wright hurried back to Norwich and called a meeting of their election organisation for the following morning—only an hour or so before nominations closed. One hundred and ten people attended. They must have been astonished at the sudden turn of events. Later the same day Captain Cator wrote a letter to the press relating his role in the London meetings with Margesson and subsequently in Norwich. "It was then (in London) I learned for the first time that Mr Chamberlain himself, back from his conference with Signor Mussolini, was prepared to make agriculture an essential feature of our national defence. The Prime Minister's letter . . . coupled with my realisation of the international situation, left me no alternative but to advise Mr Wright to withdraw his candidature. At this morning's meeting of 110 people, including Norfolk farmers and electors of East Norfolk, I used all the persuasive powers I had to influence Mr Wright to refrain from going to nomination. I was successful and I am glad because I believe that I have helped to save the appearance of National Unity".

The majority approving withdrawal was a slender one and there were many unhappy people when the decision was announced by N.F.U headquarters in Norwich, at just about the same moment as the other two candidates were handing in their nomination papers. The decision came, said the local newspaper, as a "bombshell". At Mr Wright's central committee rooms a girl worker went into hysterics. Mr Wright put the best possible face on it. "I am entitled to claim a victory for the cause that I set out to promote," he declared. "There is an assurance in the Prime Minister's letter that has never been given to the farming industry . . . I know I would have won the election all right. But I have always been a supporter of Mr Chamberlain and when he personally asked me to do a thing what else could I do?"

When the by-election result was announced on Friday afternoon, 27th January, the Liberal National Frank Medlicott was elected with 18,257 votes, compared to the 23,108 collected by his predecessor in 1935, and Labour polled 10,785, only a few hundred more than previously. The government majority was reduced from 12,647 to 7,472.

On the same day that Mr Wright withdrew from the by-election battle, the annual conference of the National Farmers' Union opened in London. According to one account, it would have been a flat and uninteresting conference but for the militancy of the East Anglian delegates. Most colourful and eloquent of them was the Suffolk County Chairman, Mr A. G. Mobbs, who farmed at Oulton. He was a lively extrovert, in his early fifties, small in stature — probably not weighing more than ten stone, but a great advocate. As a young man he had been the comedian in an amateur concert party which played in East Suffolk village halls. "He could talk a man and boy to death," recalled one of his associates. Now, at the N.F.U. annual conference, he did his best to talk the delegates into action. He proposed a protest rally at the Albert Hall and a delegation to Parliament. Referring to the Prime Minister's assurances in his letter to Mr Wright, he declared: "I hope this annual meeting will not be gulled by such statements. It's the old confidence trick all over again. Farmers are heartily sick of this sort of talk. They are demanding action."

The official N.F.U. leadership was not impressed. Because of its impending talks with the Minister of Agriculture, it considered it inopportune to demonstrate. The disappointed Suffolk delegates went back to Ipswich, called together the county executive, and it was then resolved that Suffolk would itself organise the London demonstration. The arrangements were completed within a few days; special trains were booked from Ipswich, Colchester and Sudbury, arrangements were agreed with Scotland Yard for the march from Tower Hill, and the Central Hall at Westminster was booked for the mass meeting.

Four days before this demonstration the Prime Minister announced Cabinet changes, one of which was the replacement of Mr W. S. Morrison at the Ministry of Agriculture and Fisheries by Major Sir Reginald Hugh Dorman-Smith, who had been the President of the N.F.U. in 1936-7. The Suffolk farmers, who must have felt that they were now winning on points, speedily adapted their plans: what was to have been a demonstration of protest would now become a demonstration of support for Sir Reginald, they said. They invited him to attend the Central Hall meeting, but he was able to decline politely as a debate on agriculture was to take place in the Commons on the same day. The 1st February programme was carried through successfully. There were more than a thousand farmers, wives and supporters on the special train from Ipswich, two hundred travelled by bus from Norwich, hundreds came from other parts of East Anglia, and there were contingents from Cornwall, Devon and Somerset.

The Grand Ring parade of Suffolk horses at the Suffolk Show, held at Saxmundham.
East Anglian Daily Times

Undoubtedly, however, the government had begun to draw the teeth of some of its critics. The fiasco of the East Norfolk by-election took some of the momentum out of the campaign in Norfolk. The Cambridgeshire branch of the N.F.U. at its annual meeting in February decided to telegraph the new Minister of Agriculture that "there are no more ardent admirers of you and your work than this county branch". On 23rd February, less than a month after taking office, Sir Reginald Dorman-Smith made a first gesture to the farmers; subsidies would be available to growers of barley and oats retrospectively so that they covered the 1938 harvest.

By April, with no further announcement, the farmers were restive again. The Norfolk county branch of the N.F.U. called upon London headquarters to make immediate representations to the Minister demanding a statement of government plans for increased home food production.

Ten days later the Suffolk N.F.U. branch received a report of a meeting between the N.F.U. President and the Permanent Secretary of the Ministry of Agriculture. This said that the President "had been informed of the government's plans regarding food production, labour, machinery, implement and fertiliser supplies, and he was thoroughly satisfied that the Ministry of Agriculture would be in a position to put plans into operation in an emergency on the basis of a number of contingencies, but it would not be wise to publish them. Nor would it be wise to put wartime plans into execution until an emergency arose . . . "

If this was intended to mollify the Suffolk farmers, it had the opposite effect. One, who had had experience as a county delegate to N.F.U. headquarters, observed: "It looks to me as if the President of the Union and his colleagues are being gulled. We don't want to know the inner secrets with regard to agricultural production in wartime, but we do want to know whether we are to have a fair share in providing foodstuffs, whether in a state of emergency or not". Another speaker said it appeared the government was banking on reserve fertility, but there was no reserve of fertility in the land — it had all been cashed. There was, however, much land that could be brought into fertility if the government provided encouragement to do so. The meeting decided that, to focus attention on the plight of farming, a special survey would be made of all Suffolk farmland.

The Minister of Agriculture announced two new measures in the course of May, but neither satisfied his critics. The first was payment of £2 per acre for permanent grassland which was ploughed up before 30th September, 1939; the Minister hoped that 250,000 acres would be dealt with. The objective, he said, was to convert poor or worn-out grassland into more productive pasture and to have the land readily available, if need arose, for arable farming. Mr William Waller, the new Suffolk N.F.U. chairman, commented: "It is no use breaking up land to grow corn unless the corn which is grown is made remunerative. The land was put down to grass for the very reason that corn growing was unremunerative. The sum of £2 per acre will only partly cover the cost of cleaning the land . . . " Other critics estimated it could cost as much as £10 an acre to clean some of the land, and that as much as half of it needed draining. In the markets throughout the region in the week that followed the announcement there seems to have been a general air of bewilderment about the government's thinking. Much of the informal debate took the form of questions: Surely the government *wants* us to produce more food? Then why doesn't it guarantee us prices which will cover the costs of production? What's the use of ploughing up land (at a loss) when there is no follow-through plan to use it productively? In any case, it's now too late to plant again this year.

A week after this first announcement came another, promising additional help to producers of oats, barley and mutton. They were to receive a guaranteed income, the payments would be applied to the 1938 harvest, and this was intended to be "the foundation of a comprehensive long-term policy . . ." An Agricultural Development Bill was introduced in the Commons on 6th June, with a promise that it would become law by mid-August. Mr J. F. Wright, secretary of the Norfolk branch of the N.F.U. — the man who in January had received the Prime Minister's personal promise of "whatever legislation is found to be necessary" — was not happy. The government measures, he said, fell far short of what had been expected.

With an Agricultural Development Bill now going through Parliament, the Minister made arrangements to carry through a promised tour of Suffolk farms so that he could see for himself how things stood. The county branch of the N.F.U. was ready to present to him on his arrival the results of the survey which it had just completed. The essential facts were set down thus:[1]

NFU Branch	Number of parishes embraced	Acreage of derelict land	Acreage of rough grazings capable of being brought back into cultivation	Acreage requiring drainage	Sets of farm buildings badly in need of repair
Beccles	53	1,159	4,126	10,694	109
Bury St Edmunds	81	3,088	3,245	16,260	252
Eye	30	421	446	8,323	74
Framlingham	27	714	2,199	14,417	133
Halesworth	35	1,347	2,028	12,007	178
Ipswich	84	2,674	3,217	17,093	174
Saxmundham	29	3,481	3,190	5,270	59
Stanton	18	1,347	795	1,940	37
Stowmarket	28	634	473	9,120	93
Sudbury	27	988	3,081	10,220	123
TOTALS:	412	15,853	22,800	105,344	1,232

FENCES AND DITCHES: It has not been found possible to columnate the reports in this respect, but it is very obvious from these that at least 50 per cent of the fences require attention and that the percentage proportion is higher in the case of ditches. It is also pointed out in the reports that much work is required by Drainage Boards on the main water and subsidiary courses, to effect a marked improvement in the ditches.

1. Reproduced from P. J. O. Trist: "A Survey of the Agriculture of Suffolk", Royal Agricultural Society of England, 1971.

Crisis on the farms: these semi-derelict stables were still being used to house the farm horses.
East Anglian Daily Times

This Suffolk farm house, almost beyond repair, was still occupied by its owner.
East Anglian Daily Times

These findings had been anticipated, in part, by a one-man survey by the agricultural correspondent of the *East Anglian Daily Times*, "Lavengro". On 11th May this newspaper published a large illustrated feature under the title: "Desolation and waste on Suffolk farms—Some stories of heart-breaking struggles". Photographs showed a farmhouse derelict beyond repair, a semi-derelict old barn, stables with most of the roof tiles missing, and land covered with bushes. "Lavengro" reported that in ten years 85,000 acres of good corn land had been lost to the plough. "Traversing the county from one district to another, almost everywhere it was a case of bush-covered pastures and neglected hedges and ditches, with docks and twitch in profusion," he wrote.

86

On Friday evening, 9th June, Sir Reginald Dorman-Smith arrived in Suffolk to confront these facts. By the time he left for London on the Monday morning, he had covered two hundred miles in the county, tramped over land in parish after parish, and met groups of representative farmers and farm workers. The press reported one of his visits thus:

> "At Brick Wall Farm, Hundon, he saw a derelict farm of some 288 acres whose plight has been attributed to lack of capital, the agricultural depression and to the burden of tithe. In 1930 the pretty farmhouse, consisting of dining room, drawing room, domestic offices and seven bedrooms, and the adjacent farm buildings, were intact. Today they are in ruins and have almost totally disappeared, and the same applies to five cottages attached to the farm.
>
> Overgrown bushes and weeds hide much of the remaining ruins and it is almost incredible that in the space of nine years a once prosperous farmstead has fallen into such a state of decay . . .
>
> Sir Reginald was evidently amazed that such a complete disaster could have overtaken a farm." [2]

The Minister produced a carefully balanced comment as he left for London. "There is plenty of work for any Minister of Agriculture for a long time to come," he said. "It is clear to me from what I have seen that the Suffolk farmers are having a rough time. It is equally clear that the policy which the government is determined to pursue is proving of material assistance to them. The question of getting capital back to the land is clearly a very vital one."

It must be said that farmers who were eloquent when complaining were less specific about the remedies *they* would like to have seen. Sir Edward Ruggles-Brise, the M.P. for Maldon, who was chairman of the Agricultural Committee in the House of Commons, suggested that the brewers should be obliged to use a certain guaranteed percentage of home-grown barley. Eighty per cent had been mentioned, but he reserved his view on that. There was, however, one man who knew exactly what he wanted. Mr Owen Steed, of Long Melford, was a member of the Advisory Committee of the Livestock Commission, and during the autumn of 1938 he had founded the Food Producers' Federation, which had enrolled several hundred members in the Sudbury area of Suffolk and North Essex. He explained his approach in a lecture in London in April 1939. Britain's main food needs, such as wheat, barley, oats, potatoes and meat, could not be produced in this country on a satisfactory commercial basis, he asserted; the financial assistance being handed out proved this. Tariffs and subsidies could not solve the problem. The government had imposed a duty on Argentine beef and had paid a subsidy on home-bred British beef, yet there had been a reduction in the quantity of home-produced beef and veal at Smithfield of three per cent

2. Report in the *East Anglian Daily Times*, 12th June 1939.

between 1935 and 1938. The problem should be approached, Mr Steed said, from the point of view of the consumer, rather than the producer. British food production could not be a commercial proposition, but could the State allow it to perish? His answer was No, and his solution was that the State should subsidise the wages of farm workers.

There was one reform which seemed to have the unanimous support of East Anglian farmers. Repeatedly they called for abolition of tithes. Through time immemorial the producers of wealth from the land had been obliged to surrender one tenth of it annually to a local representative of the church, usually the parish priest. Until 1838 most parsons collected in person, carrying away every tenth sheaf to the tithe barn and every tenth lamb and piglet to be slaughtered. A Tithe Commutation Act of 1836 substituted a rent-charge for this payment in kind. East Anglia, at that time, was more highly cultivated than most of Britain and so, along with a few other fertile areas such as Kent, it found itself carrying a disproportionately high share of the new rent-charges. From time to time legislation was passed amending details, but the system remained in force until the nineteen-thirties, and, as East Anglian farming slipped further into depression, the annual payments roused increasing opposition and bitterness. Tithe payments were a particular irritant to the many small farmers who had bought their land soon after the First World War and had then seen its value drop by half. In 1936 the Tithe Act finally divorced tithe and the Church and ended the principle of rent-charge. Instead, landowners became liable to "redemption annuities", payable to the Crown until 1996, when they will cease, and in return the Crown issued government stock to compensate the tithe-owners. Unfortunately, this did not end the controversy. The National Tithepayers' Association, which was particularly strong in East Anglia, complained that the amount handed to the Church in settlement had been excessive, and far more than had been recommended by a Royal Commission. The annual payments were reduced, but the Association then argued that there should be a moratorium on arrears which had accumulated earlier.

Throughout the 'thirties there had been a "tithe war" in the region. Farmers had refused, or been unable, to pay and their farms, or some part of them, had been sold up to raise the sums of money due. By 1939 the fiercest battles were over, but resentment still smouldered. Two of the most able leaders of the National Tithepayers' Association lived in Suffolk, Mr. A. G. Mobbs (who had led the farmers' demonstration in London) and Mrs R. H. Rash, whose husband was, in 1939, vice-chairman of the County N.F.U. branch. Mrs Rash herself was forty-two and in her prime as an exceptionally able propagandist and organiser. She had been educated at Malvern College for Girls and Somerfield College at Oxford and had taught for three years at

Diss Secondary School before getting married. During the 'thirties, using the pen-name Doreen Wallace, she had become a highly successful author and novelist.

In March 1939 a number of distraints for tithe arrears were carried out in Norfolk and Suffolk. Bailiffs arrived at Hall Farm, Wattisfield, and seized eight fat cattle against arrears of £105. On the same day a number of pigs were seized from the farm at Stow Bedon of a well-known Norfolk magistrate. The battle flared when these pigs were put up for sale at Attleborough market on 6th April. The auction was due to commence at eleven o'clock, by which time the sale ring was surrounded by a large crowd of anti-tithe campaigners. The sale was postponed for two hours and the demonstrators formed a procession and marched, with banners high, through the streets of the town.

At the end of April, at the instigation of the Tithe Commissioners, a bankruptcy notice was served on Mrs Rash. She publicly admitted that she owed nearly £200 of tithe arrears, covering a period of over six years, but the bankruptcy notice was in respect of only £11. 3s. 8d. for one half year's tithe. She announced that she would not pay. Why, she enquired, did not the Tithe Commissioners simply seize a piece of her furniture on a County Court order, rather than seek to make her bankrupt? By the time she faced the Registrar at Ipswich in June the claim against her had been increased to £193. Her affairs were placed in the hands of the Official Receiver and he arranged for the sale of her belongings at her home at Wortham Manor, near Diss, on 20th July. He had already taken over her car and placed a value of £130 on it. The amount that remained to be collected was, therefore, only £63 but it is clear that, by this time, it was as important to the anti-tithe campaigners as to the Official Receiver that the sale should be carried through.

A marquee was erected in the garden of Wortham Manor for the sale. Everything in the house was numbered in lots and placed on display. Mrs Rash, in a floral summer dress and a smart hat, was photographed holding framed portraits of her children which were to be sold with the rest, and the press took other photographs of bedding being thrown from an upstairs window. Around the marquee there was an exhibition of anti-tithe caricatures and posters. From miles around farmers and dealers came, with their wives and children, but the majority of the great crowd was made up of tithepayers from all over the country. Most came from the eastern counties, but there were parties from Wiltshire, Hampshire, Dorset, Kent, Worcestershire, Oxfordshire, Sussex, Berkshire, Somerset, Shropshire, Cornwall and Devon. The Tithe Commissioners, the Official Receiver and Mrs Rash and her supporters had, between them, staged one of the biggest anti-tithe demonstrations to date.

Mrs R. H. Rash, a leader of the campaign against tithes, chaired by a group of well-wishers after a sale of her belongings.

Mrs R. H. Rash

Mrs Rash with some of her supporters.

East Anglian Daily Times

A local Diss auctioneer opened the proceedings. "Someone had to sell these things and Mrs Rash expressed a wish for it to be done by someone locally," he said. "To me, it is rather a sad job. Everything in the house has to be sold. I am answerable to the Board of Trade and everything has to be paid for today." That the proceedings were being effectively stage-managed was evident almost immediately. The auctioneer suggested that the best way for the gathering to show sympathy would be to "give a fair price for the goods and put them back in the house for Mrs Rash for such time as she may want them". The sale began. There were two hundred lots — furniture, linen, books, china, glass, garden effects — and altogether they realised £204. 18s. But there was only one purchaser, and he was Mrs Rash's good friend and fellow campaigner, Mr A. G. Mobbs. The charade completed, a procession was formed, Mrs Rash was carried on the shoulders of her supporters, and speeches were delivered from a farm wagon. Mr Mobbs paid tribute to "a very gallant and courageous lady". Mrs Rash responded: "We have been saddled with this burden far too long, we have paid until we have paid the value of our land over and over again". Then they marched to a "tithe memorial" which had been erected to commemorate an earlier battle and Mrs Rash laid a wreath of field peas on it. To round off the day, there was a giant bonfire. Later in the year, Mrs Rash paid twenty shillings in the pound of her debt and was honourably discharged from bankruptcy.

This episode shows that the battle against tithe payments was fought with energy and imagination, and even a sense of fun; but it was nonetheless a serious struggle which involved passionate feelings. The bailiffs' raids were a potent irritant in a countryside which was already embittered by the hardships endured by so many farmers. The National Farmers' Union, prodded by several of its county branches, called a conference in London to consider what should be done and a new Tithe Committee which it set up to collect evidence was actively at work when the outbreak of war put all such issues into cold storage.

In one area the Ministry of Agriculture displayed unusual energy. It decided to create a national reserve of tractors and implements. The Ministry made bulk purchases direct from the manufacturers and the machines were stored in dealers' premises all over the country. In mid-May it was disclosed that orders worth £1,250,000 had been placed. Several agricultural engineering companies in East Anglia derived some benefit from this programme, but it made no difference to the everyday problems of the region's farmers. Most of them could not afford to buy a tractor. The Eastern Counties Farmers' Co-operative Association arranged impressive displays of the latest machinery at the various agricultural shows during the summer, but at its annual general meeting in 1939 it disclosed that, in a turnover of over a million pounds, machinery sales contributed only £25,546. It is clear that apart from lack of money many East Anglian farmers also lacked conviction that mechanisation could greatly affect their performance. In February 1939 the *East Anglian Daily Times* featured a farmer near Colchester who worked 390 acres with no assistance other than his wife and daughter. With his tractor, he had just ploughed a seventeen acre field, less headlands, in one working day. This, it was suggested, was a record; but a few days later the paper's agricultural correspondent suggested that it was a furrow leading to disaster. Mechanisation, he believed, would encompass the ruin of the industry and cause desolation of large areas of land. It was essential to keep stock to supply humus to the soil. "Compare this farm," he continued, "with one in Suffolk sixty acres less in extent on which, besides the farmer and his family, there are no fewer than seventeen other habitations, which supports no fewer than sixty people." He returned to his theme frequently, and there is no doubt that he was both reflecting and giving a lead to the opinions of many farmers in the region. That such views were not restricted to an "old school" of farmers was shown when several Young Farmers' Clubs in Suffolk staged a debate at Blundeston on the motion "that mechanised farming is more beneficial to the farmer today than horse labour". This motion was defeated. One speaker argued forcefully there there was no point in hurrying over the work on the farm; horses could easily accomplish what had to be done in the course of the farming year, and to do it more efficiently. Capital and running costs were lower with horses, which had a working life of fifteen to twenty years, compared with five for a tractor.

We have already noted that in Suffolk alone there were well over 18,000 horses employed in agriculture in 1939. The strong and compact Suffolk Punch, with its glossy chestnut hide and finely arched neck, was extremely popular throughout East Anglia (though not well-known elsewhere in Britain); it was also becoming well-known to breeders in the United States and Canada. The Suffolk Horse Society established a close working arrangement with an American Suffolk Horse Society and agreed in 1939 to donate special medals for the champions of the breed at the New Jersey, New York and Illinois state shows, and other awards for Suffolks shown at the International Show in Chicago and at the Canadian Royal Show.

They were great work horses, but they were also very much an essential part of the familiar eastern counties scene. Julian Tennyson conveyed the essence of their universal appeal:

> "In Suffolk you will find him in every field, every marsh, every farmyard, striding over the plough, cropping contentedly in the shade of a tree, standing in dreaming and Titanic contemplation with his lovely head lolling over a gateway . . . You have only to show yourself in a pasture and the Punches will thunder towards you, surround you, fumbling, crowding, beseeching, whinnying, nuzzling, like outsize schoolboys

Some of the two-year-old Suffolk stallions in the ring at the Suffolk Show, held at Saxmundham.
East Anglian Daily Times

persuading their master to join in a game. And when you have fought your way out of the gate they will stare wistfully after you, their eyes large and bright with childish disappointment."[3]

Despite the accent on arable farming, East Anglia had a large population of other animals in 1939. Red Poll cattle were especially popular with farmers in Norfolk and Suffolk and although there were complaints that the price of bacon pigs was too low some farmers bred and fattened for the factories and almost every farm kept a few for its own consumption. Growing interest was being shown in the white-shouldered Essex breed. But the best-known beast of the region, after the Punch, was the black-faced Suffolk sheep. The flocks, however, were in decline and at the sales in the summer of 1939 this trend was sadly noted. At Haverhill in July, when four thousand lambs and ewes changed hands, the auctioneer recalled that in earlier years they had sold six to seven thousand. Many flocks in that district had been dispersed, he said. Similar comments came from the auctioneer who sold fourteen thousand lambs at the annual sale at Diss; whenever a flock farm changed hands, he said, it went down to cows. The Suffolk Sheep Society's annual sale, at Chantry Park, Ipswich, was reduced from two days to one because of reduction in numbers, but the auctioneer there tried to strike an optimistic note. In his opinion, Suffolk sheep had been through their depression and were now on the upgrade, with a great future before them.

3. Julian Tennyson: *Suffolk Scene,* as before.

The annual wool sales which took place during June compared favourably with those of 1938—indeed, the twenty thousand fleeces sold at Colchester represented a seven-and-a-half per cent increase. There were sixteen thousand fleeces in the Bury St Edmunds sale and fifteen thousand at Ipswich. "The demand at the moment is for strong wools, attributable to the large demand for khaki, and these showed an average advance of about twopence a pound," it was reported.

June was also the month when most of the big agricultural shows took place, but in 1939 the Cambridgeshire and Isle of Ely Agricultural Society were first in the field with their show at Wisbech on Whit-Monday, at the end of May. Record attendances were reported everywhere: twenty-five thousand at the Royal Norfolk Show at Diss, over thirteen thousand at the Suffolk Show at Saxmundham—and there were at least a dozen major shows in the region. These events were the highlights of the countryman's year. Landowners, farmers, auctioneers, dealers, ploughmen, even "back 'us boys", with their wives, children and sweethearts, enjoyed the spectacle and the excitement provided by milling crowds, horses in best harness with brightly polished brasses, farm machinery in brilliant colours, cattle parading the show rings, teas served under the flapping canvas of the giant marquee, sideshows and amusements.

Farmers, of course, kept in touch at the weekly markets, of which East Anglia had a remarkably large number. Apart from Sunday, there were at least three or four markets on every day of the week.

"Norwich Market was on Norwich Hill. There was one sale-ring for dairy stock, one for bullocks, one for pigs, one for rabbits, one for calves, and so on, and a different auctioneer for each. So you'd do whatever was your business, and spar about like hell. You'd meet various people and say 'See you in . . . '—there were pubs all round Norwich Market.

The Corn Hall was the other side of town. There'd be fifty or sixty merchants' stands there. You'd go in, you'd show 'em your barley, say 'What you give for that', and they'd say 'Oh, I'll give you sixty . . . ' Then you'd go to somebody else and they'd say 'I'll give you sixty-five.' You'd take your samples in little bags. Then afterwards you'd buy, some artificials perhaps. You had your own people you tended to prefer for different things."[4]

Norwich Cattle Market, in the shadow of the Castle, handled 200,000 cattle, sheep and pigs a year.

The harvest of 1939 in East Anglia was a reasonable one, but the traditional grumbles of the farmer were widely heard. On the eastern side of the region fine weather in early August brought about a quick ripening of the corn and it became a rush harvest. Farmers insisted that the corn would

4. Mr Gordon Baxter, of Lowestoft, in an interview with the author, 1980.

involve them all in another loss. In Cambridgeshire, on the other hand, there was abnormal heavy rain in early August and spring oats were battered down, wheat suffered from rust and blight and only the barley held up for yield and quality. There was a heavy crop of fruit, but the growers declared that market prices barely covered the cost of picking and distribution. In some areas farmers had the assistance of soldiers temporarily released to help with the harvest. In the Isle of Ely, where harvesting ran late, the Education Committee authorised the employment of twelve-year-old boys and girls for the potato and beet-lifting season, and were sharply rapped in Parliament for breaking the law.

Stocks of Fordson tractors prior to distribution to the farms.   *Ford Motors*

Concurrently with this harvest, the great transformation of East Anglian farming was put in train by a government which, it now became clear, *had* given some thought to increased food production in the event of war. At the outbreak a War Agricultural Executive Committee assumed authority in each county and appointed district sub-committees and, later, various specialist sub-committees. The first task was to get more land under the plough. Targets were set. Norfolk aimed at 25,000 additional acres under cultivation for the

1940 harvest, Essex at 15,000 acres, Cambridgeshire and Suffolk at 10,000 acres each. The new district committees had the responsibility of getting the ploughs to work quickly, and if persuasion was ineffective they had the authority to issue "cultivation orders" to farmers. When grassland had been ploughed, it was inspected by an officer of the W.A.E.C. who issued a certificate if it had been done satisfactorily, and a government grant was then paid. The tractors which had been bulk-purchased by the government earlier in the year were now at the disposal of the Committees and they were made available to sub-contractors where it was necessary to get the work done. In exceptional cases, when farmers were unable or unwilling to comply with a Committee's directions, the Committee could take possession and farm the land itself.

Overall, things went very well and by mid-November the inspecting officers were issuing their certificates and reporting favourably to the W.A.E.Cs. But the derelict farms were a serious problem. Nearly one hundred cases of badly cultivated or derelict land in Norfolk were reported to the County Committee in November. Some owners could not be traced. There was one instance of one hundred acres of one of the best farming parishes gone out of cultivation. In Suffolk things were worse. There were many derelict farms, some grown up with bushes, and there was a great deal of land which had to be drained before it could be ploughed. The W.A.E.C. organised a mole drainage scheme, with steam power, throughout the county, but some estimates were that it would take three years before all the newly-ploughed acres grew good crops.

Farmers were still very unhappy about the prices they were getting. N.F.U. branches sent deputations to put their case to the County War Agricultural Executive Committees, and these views were passed on to the Ministry in London. Immediately the war began, the farmers' costs began to rise, particularly on implements, ploughshares and seeds. Credit became even more difficult to secure; for example, the petrol companies insisted on cash or monthly settlement. The government, it was strongly felt, was still not playing fair. By mid-October farmers had still not received the subsidy for the 1938 barley and oat crops. Some relief came in the following month, however, when the standard price for wheat was increased from ten shillings to eleven shillings a hundredweight, and the price for oats from eight shillings to nine.

Pressure was continuously stepped up. In October it was announced that the Ministry of Food would take control of all collection, slaughter and distribution of fat-stock, effective from a date to be announced later which would coincide with the rationing of meat. In December the Ministry of Agriculture called for a fifteen per cent increase in sugar-beet acreage; in Norfolk, Suffolk, Cambridgeshire, the Isle of Ely and Essex it was to go up from about 175,000 acres in 1939 to well over 200,000 acres in 1940.

City girls on the farm. Women's Land Army girls training at Cambridge University Farm.
Cambridge Evening News

Perhaps there was one bright feature to relieve the burdens of this first war-time winter on the farms. Back in the spring the government had announced that a Women's Land Army was to be recruited for full-time work in agriculture in the event of war. Before the year was out they were arriving in large numbers to lend a hand on the land. Many were country girls, but many others came from shops and offices in the towns. They were in green jumpers and breeches and wide-brimmed hats. They had all been given a brisk training course at centres such as the Chadacre Agricultural Institute in Suffolk, and they were all ready to get muck on their boots.

CHAPTER SIX

Sailors and Sun-Seekers

A DOZEN East Anglian communities sought to make a living from the sea. The North Sea coastline, with its ports and holiday resorts, was almost as important as the vast farmlands in establishing the character of the region. Great Yarmouth and Lowestoft were two of Britain's most important fishing ports, their harbours . . .

> ". . . chock-a-block, so that you could walk across the river from one boat to another from one side to the other. The quayside would be full of herrings in skeps, herrings on carts being carried away, Scots girls taking the insides out of herrings and salting them for export. There were auctioneers all the way down the quay shouting their wares, the horses and lorries carting them to the various kippering houses."[1]

Harwich, Ipswich and King's Lynn were small ports, but important to the hinterland they served, and each with regular links with the Continent. The estuaries of Deben, Orwell, Stour, Colne and Blackwater were lively with barges and small fishing boats, and luminous with the silver of water and the blue-white of cloud-strewn skies. And at intervals along the shore big entertainment complexes had been created, where every effort was made to concentrate the sun on terraces and promenades, in sheltered gardens and glass pavilions, so that city folk could play and local businessmen could turn an honest penny. There were the resorts of Clacton, Felixstowe, Aldeburgh, Southwold, Lowestoft, Gorleston, Yarmouth, Cromer, Sheringham and Hunstanton.

The herring fishery industry at Great Yarmouth and Lowestoft had prospered through many centuries, had peaked in the years just before the First World War, and by 1939 was suffering a serious decline. The value of catches had halved in less than thirty years, the number of vessels in the fleet declined year by year — by ten per cent between 1938 and 1939. In the herring fishery at the end of 1938 there had been about seven hundred, many of them from Scottish ports, and with crews of nine or ten men on each this meant a labour force of nearly seven thousand. Then there were several thousand women gutting, a couple of thousand men working in the curing houses and probably one thousand making barrels, boxes and cases or seamen's clothing.

1. Mr J. H. Prettyman, of Somerleyton, in an interview with the author, 1979.

Scottish fisher-girls gutting herring at Great Yarmouth.   *B.B.C. Hulton Picture Library*

The traditional herring season was from Michaelmas (29th September) to Christmas. The herring is a migratory fish, never remaining in the same area for more than a few days and the fisherman's skill began with finding a shoal.

"My father described it to me — he was a good fisherman. He used to tell me: 'When you go out of the harbour the skipper will say to the mate — "Steam north-east by east so long and then wake me up." They used to wake him up and he'd be at the side five minutes and then — "Now you can steam again, so and so. Then call me again." Perhaps the same thing again, and then he'd say — "Yes, you can shoot here." He told me: 'I knew the herring were there'."

That was how it was. The word got round quickly when a shoal was sighted and the drifters concentrated there, covering perhaps fifty square miles of sea, and proceeded to fish much as a countryman would harvest a field. The vessels took up position so that they would drift parallel to one another, each boat shot a string of nets, up to a hundred of them strung out on cables and perhaps stretching for miles. The nets hung vertically in the water, usually near the surface. The vessels beat across the tide at right angles to the direction being followed by the shoal and the fish were caught in the nets by their gills. A drifter hoped to return to port with sixty to one hundred cran, which would take up to four hours to haul on board. (The cran was a basket measure holding anything from 1,200 to 2,000 herring, according to their size. The general rule was that a cran would fill a barrel for despatch).

99

The vessel then raced for harbour and as the skipper manoeuvred for a berth:

"The mate would be standing with a round basket, a couple of feet in diameter, with the best herring arranged all round it, with their tails in the middle. The mate would jump ashore, pop straight into the auction room, and straightway the auctioneer would be shouting: 'What am I say? There's a sample, do y' want 'em?' " [2]

Herring which were bought for export — a great many went to Germany and the Baltic — were taken from the auctions to the pickling enclosures on the sand dunes where Scottish girls packed them into barrels which were lidded by coopers and then filled with pickle through the bung-hole, ready for despatch.

"When the Scots girls were due at the start of the season, people in the back streets cleared all their front rooms out and the girls lived in there. They did all the gutting and cleaning. They worked in the open, on sort of big barrows. They wore long black oily coats and black oily over-trousers and woolly hats, but most of them went without hats. They had their fingers all bound up and they worked like lightning. They'd gut the herring and they'd lay them neat round the bottom of a barrel, then they'd put a layer of salt, then away they'd go again. They'd have a heap of gut round them. You could never cease looking at them." [3]

Herrings that were not exported went to the kipper houses, for bloaters, or to be cured as "reds".

Apart from the herring, modern steam trawlers brought into Yarmouth and Lowestoft most kinds of fish required for the British market, caught in large bag-shaped nets which were "trawled" over the sea floor. But for them, too, the good days were over. During the 'thirties plaice, which had once been a very important part of the trawl fishery, mysteriously disappeared from the North Sea. The *East Anglian Daily Times* reported in April 1939: "For years the North Sea grounds have been so over-fished by trawlers of various nations that the seabed has almost been swept clean. Since 1935, when Lowestoft had the worst year on record, catches have been going from bad to worse. Only a handful of the port's smacks are now left and at frequent intervals during the year dozens of the steam trawlers have been laid up when they cannot meet running expenses."

In fact, however, the first few weeks of January produced a false boom and raised unjustifiable hopes in the East Coast ports. This was due to the arrival in Lowestoft of a German vessel which announced that it would buy for trans-shipment as much herring as could be caught. For a few weeks a few boats did well, but then the German purchases petered out — there was not sufficient fish coming forward, they said, to interest them.

2. Rev. George A. Read, M.B.E., B.E.M. of Needham Market, in an interview with the author, 1980. In 1939 Mr Read was serving in the police force in Lowestoft and later he was appointed Deputy Chief Constable of East Suffolk.
3. Rev. George A. Read, as before.

Drifters at Fish Quay, Great Yarmouth, landing their herring catch.

B.B.C. Hulton Picture Library

In March the mackerel fishing began and the drifter-trawler fleet, most of the vessels looking smart in fresh paint, sailed for the grounds off the Cornish and Pembrokeshire coasts. As the year progressed, hope remained alive. The owners of one Lowestoft trawler fitted her out specially for an eight hundred miles, fortnight-long voyage to the Faroe Isles and this initiative caused something of a stir in the fish market and had a crowd cheering lustily as she steamed out through the harbour mouth. Summer catches were up on the previous year, particularly plaice and whiting.

The future of the fleet was being settled elsewhere, however. On 23rd August the Admiralty received Cabinet authority to begin to requisition the East Coast trawlers for war purposes. A few days afterwards all vessels had been summoned back to port. The deep-sea trawlers immediately assumed a new role as minesweepers and auxiliary warships, but the Admiralty decided that two hundred and fifty vessels might continue fishing. Port Fishery Officers were appointed, every fisherman had to obtain a personal fishing permit, and all permits had to be endorsed by the naval officer in charge of the district.

The shrunken fishing fleet made a good start in October and the first herrings of the season sold at Lowestoft at the record price of twopence each. A week later the government imposed price control and undertook that any herring left unsold would be taken by them and stored for sale at a later date. Within a week there was chaos, with such a glut of herring on the market that only sixty of the 250 boats thought it worth while putting to sea. The English Herring Catchers' Association sent telegrams to the Ministers responsible for the three Services: "Two thousand five hundred fishermen engaged in the East Anglian herring fishery are now almost at a standstill because of poor demand for herrings and kippers. Our forces would greatly appreciate this splendid food. Cannot arrangements be made to send kippers to them? These could be delivered in London or any town in England for 5s. 9d. per stone, carriage paid. This would help to keep thousands of fishermen and shore workers in employment." The Admiralty made a gesture; a Fleet Order was issued suggesting increased use of herrings in Navy menus. But by then the moon was waning and the peak period of the fishery had passed.

This L.N.E.R. poster showed the vessels employed on the regular routes to and from Harwich. The L.N.E.R's *Vienna* heads the line at the quay and the Zeeland Shipping Company's *Prinses Juliana* is leaving.
Crown Copyright:
National Railway
Museum

THE DAILY LINE UP

HARWICH FOR THE CONTINEN

DAY AND NIGHT SERVICES
THE HOOK - FLUSHING - ANTWERP - ZEEBRUGGE - ESBJERG
FULL PARTICULARS FROM CONTINENTAL TRAFFIC MANAGER, L.N.E.R. LIVERPOOL STREET STATION, LONDON, EC2 OR HULL: 71 REGENT STREET, OR 59 PICCADILLY, LONDON. W1. L.N.E.R STATIONS, OFFICES OR TOURIST AGENCIES.

Of the commercial ports, the most interesting in 1939 was certainly Harwich, for it had regular links with five Continental ports. Railway freight wagons were shipped to and from Zeebrugge on a train ferry; there was a three-times-a-week freight service to Rotterdam; there were daily passenger services to and from Antwerp and the Hook of Holland; and, since 1927 when it had moved from Folkestone, the Zeeland Shipping Company sailed between Parkeston Quay and Flushing. Between the two wars, until the summer of 1939, the London and North Eastern Railway Company ran regular weekend "luxury cruises" to the Continent. Despite these activities, recession had hit Harwich in the 'thirties and it suffered unemployment. According to a local author, "it was said that the L.N.E.R. could have sent its ships to sea with every member of the crew holding a master's certificate".[4] It was encouraging, therefore, when the Zeeland Company built two new vessels for the Harwich service, each able to carry 1,800 passengers and—a sign of changing needs—twenty-four cars between decks. They came into operation during the summer on a service which had but a few weeks more to run.

No-one was more keenly aware throughout 1939 of the ominous developments on the Continent than the people of Harwich. As a port, it provided the most direct route out of Germany and Austria for the continuous stream of refugees, most of them Jewish, who sought to escape the Nazi extermination squads. Children regularly arrived there in large parties. On 5th January for example, 236 German schoolboys and girls disembarked from the *S.S. Vienna*; the *East Anglian Daily Times* reported: "There were a large number of extremely fine lads of sixteen, most of whom were very smartly dressed and had plenty of luggage, with smart suitcases. The majority could speak English some fluently, and asked for their impressions they remarked: 'We feel we have come to a promised land'." A week later a rather different impression was created when an Austrian party arrived, with many young children, some under two, with baggage labels tied around their necks.

Across the estuary from Harwich, Felixstowe's port activity was on a modest scale, but the Felixstowe Dock and Railway Company showed in its advertising a great confidence in its potential. It drew special attention to the fact that it had the only enclosed dock in the area and also to the extensive back-up area which, it suggested, could be used for storage of timber or for the erection of factories. The dock basin had been built in 1886, was six hundred feet long by three hundred feet wide, and provided twenty-three feet depth of water.

At Ipswich, the Ipswich Dock Commission, a public utility, was making substantial improvement to the facilities in the late 'thirties. By 1939 Cliff Quay had been extended to bring the total length of quays up to 1,800 feet with twenty-eight feet depth of water available. Five new grabs had been installed and an old fire dock had been filled in and an old wooden warehouse

---

4. Leonard T. Weaver: *The Harwich Story*, Harwich Printing Co, 1975.

Refugees from Danzig who arrived at Harwich in August, photographed at Liverpool Street Station when they reached London. *B.B.C. Hulton Picture Library*

demolished, to permit further development. The Commission was a prosperous undertaking, but it had its problems. Its chairman reported in April that combined exports and imports had averaged one million tons in each of the three previous years. One problem was a considerable disparity between imports and exports, so that many vessels, after discharging, sailed light. If we examine the events of three typical days, selected at random in that month, we find nine ships arriving on one day from London—two with timber, two with wheat and one with barley, two with coke, one with nitrate and one with linseed; one ship arriving from Goole with coal; and one from Hamburg with maize. The next day there were three more vessels from London, one with wheat, one with barley and one with oil; and one ship from Antwerp with maize. On the third day there was one ship from London light and another from Huelva with iron ore. But in the same three days, of thirteen ships leaving the port only one had a cargo—a sailing to Antwerp with machinery. The decline in coal traffic was a special anxiety; traditionally much coal from north-eastern England for the southern market moved by sea, but it was now being transferred to rail.

King's Lynn was a much smaller port, handling a combined import-export tonnage of less than 300,000 a year. The largest vessels which could use its dock, at high water of spring tides, were those drawing eighteen and a half feet of water. It had its weekly sailing to and from Rotterdam for general cargo, its summer imports of timber from the Baltic, and regular trade in agricultural products and coal.

There were lively quays at Norwich, to which were brought about half of all the general cargoes which came into the harbour at Yarmouth.

The *Abraham Rydberg* and sailing barge at Ipswich Docks.   *A. Frost*

Steam was, of course, almost competely triumphant by 1939, but the occasional large vessel under sail was still to be seen in East Anglian ports. In April two Scandinavian schooners berthed for a time in Great Yarmouth; in June the Swedish four-masted barque *Abraham Rydberg* berthed in the Port of Ipswich for three weeks to discharge grain, after racing from Port Germein, in Australia, to Falmouth in 117 days; and during the summer months the famous windjammer barquentine *Cap Pilar* — one of the finest surviving three-masters — lay in the Colne at Brightlingsea, being fitted with auxiliary engines before going to Haifa. An historic vessel familiar to generations of holiday-makers at Great Yarmouth was taken out of service during 1939, the *United Service*, one of the last surviving clinker-built wooden paddle-boats. She had been built in 1871, until 1914 had run a passenger service from Yarmouth to Cromer and to Walton-on-the-Naze, and after that had carried passengers up the river to Norwich or around the sandbanks.

With the outbreak of war, Port Emergency Committees, under the direction of the Ministry of Transport, took charge of each of these ports and their efforts and facilities were thenceforth directed to entirely new tasks.

If the 1939 problems of the East Coast holiday resorts were quite different to those of the ports, they were no less real. In May the old London and North East Railway Company launched a big promotion campaign, with the slogan: "Meet the sun on the East Coast". Most of the resorts participated in a joint advertising scheme, there were displays in one hundred national and provincial newspapers, and posters, banners, streamers and sticker-stamps were widely distributed. It was a brave, bold initiative at a time when the sun, literally and metaphorically, was shining only fitfully and briefly.

At many of the resorts the numbers of summer visitors had been declining year by year. At a meeting in Lowestoft in January one local hotelier put his finger firmly on the reasons. "It is time we faced up to the simple truth, he declared. "We have got to recognise the competition of holiday camps, Continental tours, cruises and motor tours at home. We have arrived at a period of great change and we have got to consider the new methods of taking holidays. There are twelve holiday camps on the Norfolk and Suffolk coast within no great distance of Lowestoft."

At the Butlins camp at Clacton a lot of money was being spent on new attractions for the 1939 season, including a miniature railway; it was a pace-setter, but a string of other holiday camps were in hot pursuit. They offered a completely self-contained package holiday; their clients might well remain within the camps and spend nothing with local businessmen. At the same time, a growing number of coach operators were organising tours in Great Britain and abroad. The attractions of these new kinds of holiday were that those taking them could hand over most of the responsibility by putting themselves in the hands of "redcoats" or couriers, and at the same time they could budget precisely for the cost. A holiday in a conventional resort involved booking a hotel or boarding-house, often on a bed-and-breakfast basis, struggling with the luggage between railway station and hotel, deciding each day between beach and concert-hall and cinema and pier and keeping an account of how the pennies and the shillings went. Decisions, decisions, all the way!

Two East Coast resorts resolved to offer their own brand of all-in package holidays in 1939. Felixstowe offered a week's holiday for seventy shillings, including accommodation, meals and all entertainments. That was for the more modest boarding-house room; the charge varied according to the standard of accommodation booked. The scheme was limited to the early and late summer periods. Of the total package price, twenty-five shillings was allocated to entertainments; the Council agreed to provide its share of these for 5s. 6d., which was made up of two shillings for admission to the Pier

Pavilion for an orchestral concert, one shilling for admission to a dance, one shilling for swimming facilities, sixpence for use of the bowls green, and one shilling for the use of beach chairs. Lowestoft started with a more modest scheme. The Council issued ten-shilling weekly tickets offering one admission to each of its Sparrow's Nest Theatre, its South Pier band enclosure, its South Pier Pavilion and its boating lake, plus unlimited use of deck chairs, tennis courts and putting and bowling greens.

The hoteliers everywhere seemed anxiously aware of a need to do more. Clacton Publicity Association early in 1939 launched its biggest-ever campaign. It selected the 300,000 population of Leicester as its special target and aimed at a saturation promotion in this Midlands city.

Felixstowe and Gorleston had invested money in new facilities for the 1939 season. At Felixstowe the Council's development ambitions had caused great controversy and had become a principal issue at local government elections three years earlier. The voters rejected proposals for an extensive new complex around the New Pier and so the Council settled for rebuilding and improvement of the existing Pier Pavilion and Spa Pavilion. The first was completed in 1938, and the Spa Pavilion was officially re-opened by the eminent physician Lord Horder in time for Easter 1939. Its cream walls and royal blue ironwork made it an eye-catching landmark and, inside, up to one thousand people at a time might feel cossetted in a nest of deep blue upholstery, rust-red carpeting and much wood panelling. Gorleston's investment for the new season had been made in a new Floral Hall, with dance floor, and swimming pool.

Despite all the efforts to keep abreast of changing tastes, the pattern of holiday activity at all the resorts was a matter of long tradition. The most distinctive feature was usually the pier. An advertisement of July 1939 gives something of the flavour:

CLACTON PIER
Admitted the most progressive and entertaining in EUROPE.

Three theatres — Royal Bengal Circus — Finest
Ballroom over the Sea — World's Wonder Swimming
Pool — All Amusements for Healthy Happiness.

Twopence admits to this galaxy.

Magnificent steamers connect with the Continent, Sundays, Wednesdays and Thursdays.

The piers were suitable for brisk and bracing walks — the Britannia Pier at Great Yarmouth was 810 feet long — or for a little quiet fishing. All of them had a concert hall, or a dance floor, or a sun lounge. They had penny-in-slot amusement machines and stalls selling ice-cream and pink sticks of rock.

A happy crowd enjoyed the Bank Holiday sunshine at Clacton.   *East Anglian Daily Times*

After dark, coloured lights swung gently in the evening breezes. They epitomised fresh air and frivolity. The pier at Lowestoft had the special distinction that those who walked to the end of it were standing on the most easterly spot in the country.

Several times each summer day excitement peaked for ten minutes or so as a paddle steamer, with several sharp blasts on its siren, approached from the sea and deposited a few hundred holiday-makers on the landing stage. The General Steam Navigation Company's Eagle steamers sailed from Tower Pier in the Thames at 8.30 a.m. every morning except Fridays to Clacton. There, one could change on to another steamer for Lowestoft, spending the whole day at sea and coming ashore at 7.30 p.m. The London to Lowestoft return fare was 12s. 6d. Another steamer service left Felixstowe New Pier at 8 a.m., called at Walton Pier at 8.45 a.m. and at Clacton Pier in time to connect with a cross-Channel service to Calais on Wednesdays and to Ostend on Thursdays. On the Ostend trip it was possible to continue to Ypres and the Menin Gate; right up to the outbreak of the Second World War day trippers went to pay homage to those who had died in the First. The cross-Channel voyages cost 10s. 6d. and gave ten hours cruising and four hours ashore. Ipswich pleasure-seekers could go by steamer at 8 a.m. each day down the river to Felixstowe, Walton and Clacton.

Some holiday-makers arrived by steamer to spend their week by the sea, but the majority travelled by train, though with an increasing number in cars. On August Bank Holiday Sunday road traffic reached a peak of 2,800 cars an hour through Colchester on the road to Clacton and other resorts. That same weekend nearly 35,000 people travelled to Clacton by train, over the three days. Most visitors to the coast, in fact, went for the day, taking advantage of the railways' excursion fares. Clacton drew the London crowds, while the northernmost resorts attracted many from the Midlands. The beaches, the sea, the piers and the cafes and public houses provided as much entertainment as the average day-tripper could require.

Those who came for a week expected a full and varied programme. Music was an essential element. The military bands, though they did not touch quite so sensitive a chord as in Victoria's reign, were still popular. During the summer of 1939 the Band of the Royal Dragoons played at Felixstowe and the Band of the Oxfordshire and Bucks Light Infantry at Clacton. Some resorts had a resident orchestra — at Lowestoft, for example, the Commodore Grand Orchestra under the direction of Harry Davidson. Others had a weekly change; at Felixstowe, during July, for example, it was first a week of "the resident orchestra from the Chiswick Empire", then a week of Harry Fryer's "very fine orchestra of broadcasting fame", and then Don Rico and his Gipsy Girls' Band. Some artists came for a single weekend performance, among them was Alfredo Campoli, the violinist, and Mantovani. The accent was on what was called "light classical" music. The August Bank Holiday Sunday evening programme at Felixstowe exemplified popular taste. Jan Ralfini and his Radio Lyons Orchestra played selections from *Rosalie, Firefly* and *Lilac Time*, the overtures to *William Tell* and *Orpheus in the Underworld*, selections from Verdi, Strauss and Schubert, and special arrangements of "Hit tunes of the day", and then they accompanied "an octet of young vocalists in harmony". That was the most popular performance of the year; hundreds were turned away.

Of course, every seaside resort was expected to have its resident concert party. "A blend of song, dancing, sketches, patter, ballet and piano duets" was the offering made by one of them, and that was a fair description of them all. The comedian in striped blazer and straw boater, the tap dancer, the baritone with a repertoire of traditional English songs, the attractive "soubrette" (dictionary definition: maid-servant or similar, with implication of pertness and coquetry) and the line of chorus girls, these were all an essential part of the 'thirties holiday scene.

Repertory companies thrived as well, balancing their weekly productions between romance, thrillers and farce.

At the weekends, stars from the West End of London theatre, particularly comedians, made brief appearances, Clapham and Dwyer, Tommy Trinder, and the Western Brothers singing:

109

"We're an unhappy breed,
And very bored indeed
When reminded of something that Nelson said.
While the Press and the politicians nag, nag, nag,
We'll wink until we drop down dead.
There are bad times just around the corner,
We can all look forward to despair . . . "

They were right about that. There were three weeks left before the war began.

And yet there seemed an unreal quality to all that was happening elsewhere. Especially in the more exclusive and expensive hotels, like the Felix at Felixstowe, the Royal at Lowestoft or the Royal Links at Cromer, the insulation against the outside world was comfortably efficient. Indeed, a remarkable serenity permeated the whole atmosphere of resorts like Cromer:

"Hotel guests dressed for dinner and when there was a dance for guests only we locals used to go round — if the ballroom could be seen from the the road — to watch and to admire or criticise the dresses. Then we would go for a coffee in one of the numerous cafes which used to stay open until about 11 p.m. The hotels held 'flannel dances' once a week, which were open to the general public, and then we used to put on our prettiest frocks and go along.

When there weren't dances, the hotel guests used to make up parties and walk to the Pier or the Picture Palace or the Town Hall (which always had a good repertory season, with good stars). Apart from the evening shows, there was always an orchestra at the Pier shows; they played for one-and-a-half to two hours in the mornings and again during the after-noons. It was lovely to sit on the Paris Cliff, or to be in a canoe under the Pier, listening to the music.

Then there were variety shows, with stars like Leslie Sarony, Ronald Frankeau and Robb Wilton, at the Olympia Theatre, which was a hall with a corrugated roof and where we sat on deck chairs."[5]

Each resort had its own regular visitors and they, quite as much as the local caterers to their amusement, determined the flavour of the place. Great Yarmouth, with its 130 feet high Observation Tower, its race meetings on the North Denes, its daily motor coach trips from the Marine Parade, its boating pool and its great amusement park, the Pleasure Beach, was something very different to Cromer. And resorts like Aldeburgh and Southwold would have been chilled along their spines at the thought of playing host — as Clacton did in May 1939 — to six hundred delegates to the annual conference of the Civil Service Clerical Association. Clacton was very pleased to have them; conference

5. A Sheringham lady who insists on anonymity, in a letter to the author, 1980.

business, it had discovered, was good business. In August, when traditional holiday business was shaky, it was good to see two hundred delegates and visitors in their town for the annual conference of the National Union of Railwaymen.

The Queen Line steamer, M.V. *Royal Sovereign,* which ran on the Yarmouth-Ostend service during the summer.
Norwich Mercury series

The most important single ingredient of a good holiday was sunshine, and that was something that no amount of initiative or careful planning could ensure. The 1939 season was one of extremes of weather. It began well with an Easter weekend of glorious sunshine—between eleven and twelve hours each day at all the East Coast resorts. That drew out record numbers and the roads, the promenades, the beaches and the steamers were all packed. Only eight days later a freak gale swept East Suffolk for ten minutes, felling scores of trees, smashing windows, blowing cyclists off their machines, forcing motorists to stop, bringing down 'phone wires, and damaging hundreds of acres of growing crops.

Whitsun, at the end of May, was bright and sunny on the coast, but a fresh wind off the sea kept it cool. A spell of good weather in the first half of June, with temperatures up into the eighties in some places, was broken by thunderstorms and the weather then remained unsettled for a few weeks. July was an unsettled month, with below-average rainfall yet with showers most days, overcast and lacking in sunshine. Storms on 20th July cut off the electricity over a wide swathe of country from Cambridge to the Suffolk coast. This was no holiday weather. The first Monday in August was a Bank Holiday and on the Saturday of that weekend the *East Anglian Daily Times* commented in a leading article:

111

"The season appears to be trying strenuously to earn the ultimate description of a complete washout . . . It has been a trying time for holiday-makers everywhere and for all who cater for them . . . There hasn't been any summer worth the name . . . "

This was tempting Providence. On the day the comment was published the weather deteriorated and England, as a whole, had its worst Bank Holiday weather for years. East Anglia took its share of the weather's ill-temper. It was estimated that during the Saturday night a record quantity of over forty-eight million gallons of water fell on Colchester and the fire brigade was kept busy with its pumps. Earlier in the day there were whirlwinds at Chelmsford and Debenham, flooding in Stowmarket and around Maldon, and fierce storms at Lowestoft, Saffron Walden and Bury St Edmunds. At Bury manholes were lifted and water spouted like fountains from the drains and flooded some streets. Most of the coastal area, though heavily overcast, escaped this freak weather.

On the Bank Holiday Monday the overcast skies persisted, threatening rain, and there was some afternoon drizzle at Felixstowe. Lowestoft, after its Saturday storm, enjoyed clear skies and sunshine and big crowds from Norwich and elsewhere joined the all-day regatta and fete at Oulton Broad, and watched the fireworks from the South Pier in the evening.

The first really warm and pleasant evening of high summer along the whole coast came on 12th and 13th August. It was too late. By then, the omens were speaking clearly to all. Holiday arrangements were being cancelled. On 29th August the Home Office circulated instructions that theatres, music halls and all other places of entertainment would close immediately in the event of war, and it was clearly only a matter of how many days of peace remained.

The East Coast resorts had a lively recollection of their sufferings in the First World War, not only as a result of shelling but also because the holiday trade upon which they depended simply evaporated. Now the same thing happened again. Delegations from all the resorts met in Norwich on 14th October to discuss their plight and they decided to seek financial aid from the government. Meanwhile, they could only wear a brave face and keep on trying. An advertisement during December by the Grand Hotel at Clacton showed their spirit:

"Christmas Festivities—Special engagement of London orchestra and entertainers. Tea Dances, dinner dances and Cabaret. Inclusive charges for minimum stay of four days: from 21s. per person (facing sea)."

SPARROW'S NEST THEATRE

NORTH LOWESTOFT   PHONE 593

Sunday, August 20th, 8 p.m.

STANELLI

of "Stag Party" and "Crazy Cruise"

JUDY SHIRLEY

" It's Monday Night at 7 "

MAMIE SOUTTER - PETER
BERNARD - HELENE COONEY
and

"I'VE HEARD IT"

The B.B.C. feature in which all
can join

Monday, August 21st, and all the week

" EVERY EVENING AT EIGHT "

GERT & DAISY'S PARTY

(Elsie and Doris Waters themselves)

ALL SEATS BOOKABLE WITHOUT EXTRA CHARGE

Sparrow's Nest Theatre, phone 593; Information Bureau, South Pier, phone 850;
Molls' Chocolate Shop, 175 London Road South, phone 485

JUBILEE PARADE

Daily at 11.15 a.m. and 3 p.m.

LEN MUSIKANT AND HIS MUSIC

SPARROW'S NEST PARK

Daily at 3 p.m.

JACK MUSIKANT & HIS MUSIKANEERS

Special Request Programmes Every
Thursday

SPARROW'S NEST PARK

Every Morning—11 to 12.30

KEEP - FIT CLASSES

Under the direction of
MISS CONSTANCE CLAY
Admission Free

SPECIAL NIGHTS on SOUTH PIER
Wednesday — AMATEUR TALENT
COMPETITION
(Entries to Pier Master)
Friday — GUEST CONDUCTORS'
NIGHT
Saturday — " Daily Herald " £5000
Prizes FAVOURITE TUNE CONTEST
(Excellent Prizes)

SOUTH PIER

THEATRE

Monday, August 21st, and all the week

ONCE NIGHTLY 8.30

ERIC FINDON

in association with

PAT NYE and WALTER WADE
presents—

LORD BABS

By Keble Howard

Even funnier than " Charley's Aunt "

Popular Prices - 2/4, 1/6, 1/-
All Bookable without extra charge

ORCHESTRA

Daily at 3 and 7.45
Sundays 11.15, 3 and 7.30

Harry Davidson

and his famous

COMMODORE BROADCASTING ORCHESTRA

Leader: Chas. Vorzanger

Pier Toll 2d.

DANCING — Thursday & Saturday,
9-11 p.m. 6d.

Entertainment — newspaper advertisement in August.

Norwich Mercury series

CHAPTER SEVEN

Leisure and Pleasure

IN A society in which almost everyone worked for not less than forty-eight hours spread over five and a half days of the week, the time left to develop leisure interests was limited. Yet the variety of the activities in which East Anglians in 1939 found self-fulfilment, satisfaction or simple pleasure was remarkable. Community service of every kind engaged the energies of thousands of people: local government, Community Councils, hospital, nursing and ambulance voluntary work, Women's Institutes, Rotary Clubs. Cultural activities involved thousands more, whose interests lay in music, drama, painting, natural history, ecology. Hobbies with large followings ranged from photography to gardening, from bird fancying to walking. Sport had its enthusiasts, particularly football. And, for complete relaxation, there was the pub and the club, the village hop and the county ball, the day trip to the seaside and the country house weekend.

There was a close correlation between social status and the pattern of leisure activity. The poor aimed for nothing more ambitious than a night at the cinema or a dance at the weekend. "A night out on the town" in Chatteris, for example, was like this:

"Saturday night was the highlight of the week. Everyone put on their best clothes after tea and 'went up the street'. All the people came up from the Fens; you could be sure of seeing everyone you knew. They'd just walk from one end of the street to the other, then back again, and then they'd repeat it, sometimes stopping to talk in groups. The shops were all open until about ten. The fish and chip shop had a cafe where you had a job to find a seat. So perhaps you'd take some fish and chips home and listen to 'In town tonight' on the wireless, or you'd pay a shilling to go to the dance in the Crown Theatre, or you'd join the queue outside the pictures."[1]

That was one end of the spectrum. As an example of activity at the other end one might enter the beautiful Athenaeum building in Bury St Edmunds, settle in the recently redecorated and refurnished club premises to read the latest journals or to play a game of chess or of billiards. Better still, one might go (but only if one was socially qualified) to the Suffolk County Ball in the same building. That which took place in January 1939 was attended by three hundred and forty members of county families; it was organised and

1. Mrs K. R. Taylor, as before.

Members of the Suffolk Detachment of the British Red Cross under Mrs Humphrey.

East Anglian Daily Times

stewarded by a committe of sixty-six gentlemen, of whom one was a duke, one a marquis, four peers, twelve knights and twenty-nine with service rank. The exterior of the Athenaeum glowed in soft floodlights. The guests came under a decorative awning and over soft carpet to the Adam ballroom. From the greenhouses and conservatories of the big houses around head gardeners had brought palms and pot plants, white hyacinths, lilac and scarlet poinsettias, so that the cool elegance of the room was embellished by a lush profusion of foliage and blossom. Supper in the Masonic Hall nearby was a gourmet's delight.

Most leisure activity, however, was more purposeful and self-fulfilling than either of these extreme examples, and much of it bridged the gulf between the classes. Most of the motive power, indeed, was provided by what was generally thought of as "the middle class". It was they, the professional men, the schoolteachers and bank managers and architects, and the artisans, the master builders and engineers and railwaymen, who were usually found holding office or doing the committee work for the countless voluntary organisations.

115

We have referred, in a previous chapter, to the organisations of supporters of the various hospitals and to the nursing associations and the groups which sought, in one way or another, to ameliorate the hardships of the unemployed and the afflicted. There were many dedicated men and women who gave virtually all of their spare hours for a lifetime to this kind of work. There were others who chose to get involved in youth movements, such as the Scouts and the Guides. The Women's Institutes, naturally, were very strong in this rural countryside — there were 11,400 members in Norfolk, for example. A significant development in the years before the war was the establishment of Rural Community Councils. The Essex R.C.C., at its annual meeting at Chelmsford in May 1939, reported that it had links with forty parish councils, eighty village hall committees, thirty horticultural and allotment associations and over four hundred individual craftsmen. A similar organisation was set up in Suffolk in December 1937 and began by assisting schemes to build three new village halls in the county. By the time of the annual meeting at Bury St Edmunds in 1939 the Council was working with fourteen villages in the preparation of plans and deeds for halls and was in touch with twelve others which showed interest. The Councils were particularly helpful in village hall and playing field projects, but their wider aim was to enrich the life of rural communities in every possible way, and they gave active encouragement to village drama, history recording and to rural industries. The accent here was on the future healthy development of the countryside, and this work was supplemented by preservation groups resolved to conserve what was best of the past. The Suffolk Society, for example (which during 1939 transformed itself into a branch of the Council for the Preservation of Rural England), kept a very close eye on the medieval buildings of Lavenham and when the picturesque group of five thatched cottages between the church and the green at Cavendish was condemned and threatened with demolition the Society raised the money to save them. In June it organised an exhibition of one hundred and fifty photographs of old Suffolk windmills at Ipswich Art Gallery in order to stir public interest and secure the preservation of as many of them as possible. Merging with the interests and activities of Community Councils and preservation groups were those of antiquarian societies and naturalists and natural history groups. The English Folk Dance and Song Society was also well-established in East Anglia, with a steadily growing membership.

Every town and village had its own horticultural society or gardeners' association or rose society and in June, July and August there was no weekend when one could not find a local flower show to provide a wonderful day's outing. As early as mid-April the gardeners of Norwich and district filled two local halls with a blaze of colour provided by mountains of daffodils. When the Colchester Rose and Horticultural Society revived its summer show in June — it had almost died, after a hundred years, for lack of funds — more than four hundred competitors displayed their entries in an outsize marquee. By late July the show season was in full swing, with displays in village halls, in rectory gardens or country house parks, and on village greens. Despite their atmosphere of rural innocence and the lovely settings in the quietest corners of East Anglia, few visitors arrived by car to observe. These were genuinely local events; everyone knew everyone else; excitement was generated by the number of entries, by their quality and by the judges' comments.

The various agricultural shows, horse shows, sales and markets, to which reference has been made in earlier chapters, provided countrymen with some of their keenest pleasures, but they were essentially commercial in character. The drawing matches were something different; though work-related and based upon pride in skill of labour, they were certainly treated by their participants as entertainment of a high order. They were usually arranged in aid of the funds of the local British Legion or a charitable organisation.

"In a ploughing match you 'draw' the furrows. You are given the horses at the end of the field and you draw across. There are three gentlemen called 'stickers'. They put one stick at the end of your furrow and then another where you finish. Then at the middle of the field they put the third stick in direct line between the other two and they measure the distance from that to your furrow, and that's called your 'deviation'." [2]

At the annual drawing match promoted by the Trimley and District branch of the British Legion a lady tried her hand. *East Anglian Daily Times*

2. Mr Gordon Baxter, as before.

The best of the ploughmen often produced "deviations" of only one inch or a fraction more! The drawing match season opened in April and continued to mid-summer. The size of the event and the number of competitors was not related to the size of the village where it took place; districts organised a challenge cup contest. In the eastern counties a peak of excitement came with an annual inter-county match between Norfolk and Suffolk. The tractor was beginning to appear on the farms, and it was now catered for in some of the drawing matches, but most people saw them as opportunities to demonstrate the superiority of horse and man. The teams of horses were turned out at their best: carefully groomed, decorated with shining brasses. Often there was a match for ladies—a thirteen-year-old girl, Shirley Pratt, took the prize at Trimley in 1939—and occasionally a landowner or distinguished visitor would try his hand, as did Lord Stradbroke at the match at Wangford in June. After the competition everyone moved on to the village hall or the inn, where prizes were presented and there was a darts match or bowling for a live pig.

The Cambridge Boat Race crew at practice on the Cam in January, watched by a solitary spectator from the snow-clad bank. *B.B.C. Hulton Picture Library*

In 1939 there was a burst of new enthusiasm for these ploughing matches; forty-five took place in Norfolk and Suffolk during the season, which was more than anyone could remember in any previous year. One held at Benacre Hall at Wrentham in Suffolk was the first in that village for forty years and a match at Westhall, near Eye, was the first there for over thirty years. People seemed to sense that the horse and the ancient skills of the ploughman were being challenged by the tractor, and that a demonstration was called for. Farm workers travelled from wide areas to participate in the matches, if not to plough then to cheer on their favourites. The drawing match at Wissett, near Halesworth, in July attracted competitors from fifty-two villages. The Norfolk-Suffolk championship match in 1939 took place at Lodge Farm, Winfarthing, near the county boundary, on 22nd July. Suffolk ploughmen took twelve of the sixteen awards and the silver challenge cup went to Charles Keable, of Linstead, near Halesworth.

There were a number of Hunts in the region, most with foxhounds, but including the Colchester Garrison Beagles, the Norwich Staghounds and the Eastern Counties Otter Hounds. Hunting and shooting were the pastimes of the well-to-do, but a certain number of other country folk were drawn in, as was illustrated by an event in the village hall at Great Bromley, near Colchester. Fifty people were entertained there at the annual Earthstoppers and Keepers Lunch, after which the Master of Foxhounds thanked them for the way they had carried out their duties during the season. Canine societies also flourished, there was an Eastern Counties Poultry Society, and aquarists and pondkeepers had their own organisation.

There were quite as many organisations of an intellectual cast, ranging from Cambridge's Society for the Protection of Science and Learning to Lowestoft's Literary and Scientific Society; and there were many with artistic or craft character, such as the Fine Art Club and the Watercolour Society at Ipswich, the West Suffolk Camera Club or the East Anglian branch of the Radio Society of Great Britain. In the home a good deal of reading was done, of books as well as newspapers. The paper-back revolution had come to the bookshops and a wide selection of good literature was on offer at sixpence a volume. Public library services were being steadily expanded throughout East Anglia. East Suffolk County Council, for example, proudly reported in June "the beginning of the branch library organisation" in the form of new branches just opened in Halesworth, Southwold and Aldeburgh, with others to follow soon after in Felixstowe and Stowmarket. The annual report of the Norfolk County Library showed 1,418,229 issues of books during the year, to over 72,000 readers registered at 505 local centres. Ipswich Libraries Committee made 754,183 issues, and at Bury St Edmunds it was reported that 3,800 members of the public library were borrowing 12,000 titles each month.

Colchester Carnival: the
Women's League of
Health and Beauty.
East Anglian Daily Times

There was a strong musical tradition in the region, manifesting itself in many ways, from religious cantatas performed by church groups, through choral societies with more eclectic tastes, to Gilbert and Sullivan enthusiasts, and sometimes even to village tavern songsters who kept alive traditonal country ballads. Similarly, music was made by distinguished visiting orchestras, by local chamber music groups and soloists and by brass bands.

Almost every one of the smaller towns in East Anglia had a choral or operatic society, each one offering at least one production each year. Acle Amateur Operatic and Choral Society presented "The Mikado" every night for a week; Woodbridge performed Bizet's "Carmen" and packed the Electric Theatre; Saffron Walden presented the opera "Dorothy" at the Town Hall nightly for a week; Cavendish offered Handel's "Saul" in the parish church. Although most of performances pulled in good audiences, the societies did not usually have large memberships and they often lacked the financial support they needed. Clacton Operatic Society, at its annual meeting in June, disclosed that only three of its productions had ever made a profit and that accumulated losses of £500 had been paid off by the active members.

A whole series of competitive music festivals regularly took place in the eastern counties. The Suffolk Musical Competition Festival was spread over three days in May at Bury St Edmunds, with seventeen hundred competitors involved and one day set apart exclusively for children's choirs. Alan Bush was one of the adjudicators and among the prize-winners was Arnold Vivian, of Woodbridge, a nephew of the Suffolk composer Roger Quilter. Norfolk held its Musical Competition Festival at Norwich a few days later, with a record entry of village choirs, male voice choirs, choral societies and Women's Institute choirs, and with newly-introduced sections for verse speaking and for a solo Shakespearean scene. Several smaller towns sought to emulate these major events; Clare had a well-established two-day Musical Festival and Saffron Walden inaugurated what it hoped would become an annual event with choirs from ten local schools and Women's Institutes.

There were other kinds of music, too. During the summer Cambridge had a season of promenade concerts, the Cambridge Band playing in a special enclosure on Christ's Pieces each Sunday, with the audience seated under the trees. On Good Friday, at Chatteris, eight bands competed in the East Anglian Brass Bands Association eighth annual contest; the premier award went to Soham Comrades Band and after the contest the massed bands of Soham, Fakenham and Chatteris gave a concert. There was an East Anglian Dance Band Contest, judged at Ipswich early in the year; Fred Murfield and his Swing Cats, from Leytonstone, emerged triumphant from this tussle, with Essex Rhythm Kings, from Colchester, as runners-up. The springtime of 1939 also marked the discovery of the Eastbridge Singers, a group which, it was said, had been singing traditional Suffolk songs regularly each week in the Eel's Foot inn at Eastbridge, near Leiston. The B.B.C. went to the village with a recording van and in July transmitted a special programme, with Phillip Lumpkin acting as chairman and Walter Button playing the accordion. The group's signature tune was "The larks they sang melodious" and among the other songs broadcast were "The blackbird", "Indian Lass", "Foggy Dew", "The Old Sow", "The Ship that never returned", and "Duckfoot Sue". When the recording was made, some of the regular local singers were too shy to take part, which afterwards they regretted, when the B.B.C. sent the performers cheques for one guinea for each song broadcast.

East Anglia was not well endowed with theatres. Sophie Stewart, the actress, reminded a meeting in Colchester in support of a project there that there was nowhere between London and Norwich where the living word of drama could be produced in a properly-equipped theatre. At Norwich, an important change occurred at the Theatre Royal in 1939. Mr Jack Gladwin, who had been its sole proprietor since 1931, and who had spent forty years in the theatrical business, decided to take life more quietly. He had seen the theatre through troubled times; in 1934 the original, century-old building had been destroyed by fire, but within a year he had re-constructed and re-opened it. Now he agreed to lease the Theatre Royal for a term of 21 years to Prince Littler, an impresario who already owned six other theatres and ran half-a-dozen touring companies and who was on his way to building an empire. Mr Littler agreed to take over the theatre's resident orchestra and he opened his season in April with the musical "Me and My Girl". Another Norwich theatre, the Hippodrome, presented during the summer months a season of West End plays and comedies, performed by the Regent Players, and the city also had its unique Maddermarket Theatre, which had been converted into an Elizabethan-type theatre in 1926 and where the Norwich Players, mainly amateurs but with a professional producer and designer, presented a new play each month. It opened its 1939 programme with "Geneva", a new play by the nonagenarian Bernard Shaw. Cambridge and Peterborough also had professional theatres but elsewhere, throughout the region (except at the seaside resorts during the summer season), the public had to be content with amateur productions. Colchester, however, had ambitions to open its own theatre. A Repertory Company had been presenting plays in the town regularly from 1937, it had formed a Theatre Project Committee and by February 1939 this had raised nearly £4,000. It was claimed that contributions were then coming in at the rate of nearly £1,000 a week. A theatre with a seating capacity of five hundred was envisaged, occupied by the repertory company for half the year and available for other functions for the remainder of the time. Meanwhile, plays were presented in the Albert Hall and in the season from October 1938 to March 1939 forty-eight thousand of the available sixty thousand seats were sold.

Brave and sustained efforts were made to establish a Suffolk Repertory Company. They had continued over several years with indifferent success, but now Miss Rosamund Norton made an energetic new effort at Felixstowe. On 2nd January, 1939 her Suffolk Repertory Players took the stage for the first time, at the Summer Theatre, in a production of a comedy called "School for Husbands". They promised a new play every week, with a special emphasis on comedy. Their real ambition was to move, when established, to Ipswich which had a population of about 100,000 but no theatrical company. They raised their standard there, for the first time, on 31st January with a one-night presentation of "George and Margaret" at the Art Gallery. The regular performances in Felixstowe continued through most of the year.

As with music, so with drama: very few towns in the region failed to produce an enthusiastic amateur group. During the early months of 1939 there seemed to be hardly a hall anywhere where the ringing voice and the dramatic gesture of the salesman-turned-actor and the housewife-turned-actress were not displayed. Comedies and thrillers were the staple fare. An oddity of the season was a confrontation between a Left Theatre Guild and a rival Right Theatre Movement in Ipswich; the latter, with the support of the local Conservative Association, produced a pageant play called "The Making of England" in Murdoch's Piano House in the Butter Market.

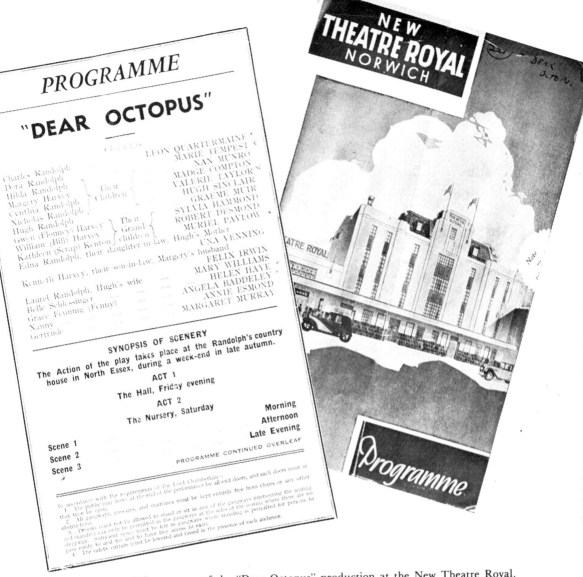

PROGRAMME

"DEAR OCTOPUS"

CHARACTERS

Charles Randolph — LEON QUARTERMAINE
Dora Randolph — MARIE TEMPEST
Hilda Randolph — NAN MUNRO
Margery Harvey — MADGE COMPTON
Cynthia Randolph — VALERIE TAYLOR
Nicholas Randolph — HUGH SINCLAIR
Hugh Randolph — GRAEME MUIR
Gwen (Flouncy) Harvey — SYLVIA HAMMOND
William (Bill) Harvey — ROBERT DESMOND
Kathleen (Scrap) Kenton — MURIEL PAVLOW

Their Children

Their Grand-children

Hugh's Mother — UNA VENNING

Edna Randolph, their daughter-in-law, Margery's husband — FELIX IRWIN

Kenneth Harvey, their son-in-law, Margery's husband — MARY WILLIAMS

Laurel Randolph, Hugh's wife — HELEN HAYE
Belle Schlessinger — ANGELA BADDELEY
Grace Fenning (Fenny) — ANNIE ESMOND
Nanny — MARGARET MURRAY
Gertrude

SYNOPSIS OF SCENERY

The Action of the play takes place at the Randolph's country house in North Essex, during a week-end in late autumn.

ACT 1
The Hall, Friday evening

ACT 2
The Nursery, Saturday

Scene 1 — Morning
Scene 2 — Afternoon
Scene 3 — Late Evening

PROGRAMME CONTINUED OVERLEAF

In accordance with the requirements of the Lord Chamberlain—
1. The public may leave at the end of the performance by all exit doors, and such doors must at that time be open.
2. All gangways, passages, and staircases must be kept entirely free from chairs or any other obstructions.
3. Persons must not be allowed to stand or sit in any of the gangways intersecting the seating and standing can only be permitted in the gangways at the sides of the seating where there are no steppings. Sufficient space must be left in gangways at sides to exits.
4. The safety curtain must be lowered and raised in the presence of each audience.

NEW
THEATRE ROYAL
NORWICH

THEATRE ROYAL

Programme

The cast list and front cover of the "Dear Octopus" production at the New Theatre Royal, Norwich, during November.
Alick Williams and the Theatre Royal

In the late 'thirties the cinema enjoyed its heyday. Between the two world wars Hollywood and its star system flourished and British studios began to build up a special reputation. As the 'thirties opened the sound track added a new dimension of music and effects, and as they ended the big innovation was colour. Walt Disney's "Snow White and the Seven Dwarfs" was shown in East Anglia during the last few weeks before the outbreak of war and it was advertised as "the greatest motion picture miracle since the advent of sound films" — the first full-length colour cartoon. For most people, the cinema was

123

the palace of escapism. It offered vicarious adventure and romance, it set up idols to be worshipped, desired and adored. A list of some of the films being shown in East Anglia during January 1939 will recapture the whole atmosphere for those old enough to remember: "Algiers" with Charles Boyer and Hedy Lamarr; "Sixty Glorious Years" with Anna Neagle, C. Aubrey Smith and Anton Walbrook; "Les Miserables" with Charles Laughton and Frederic March; Deanna Durbin and Jackie Cooper in "That Certain Age"; Clark Gable, Myrna Loy and Walter Pidgeon in "Too Hot to Handle"; Ginger Rogers and Douglas Fairbanks junior in "Having a Wonderful Time". A little later in the year the film fare included Laurence Olivier and Flora Robson in "Fire over England", Rex Harrison and Vivien Leigh in "Storm in a Teacup", and Laurel and Hardy in "Blockheads". And, in the last week of peacetime, films on general release included, apart from "Snow White", Bing Crosby in "Paris Honeymoon", Shirley Temple in "The Little Princess", Basil Rathbone in "Son of Frankenstein", and a line-up of Nelson Eddy, Virginia Bruce, Victor McLaglen, Lionel Barrymore and Edward Arnold in "Let Freedom Ring".

Cinema advertisments in a newspaper during January.
Norwich Mercury series

But it was not only the stars and the scenes through which they moved that offered escape. The cinemas were temples in another sense. The old pioneer halls with their wooden benches had been replaced by Odeons which aspired to set a fashionable new architectural style and a new standard of elegance and comfort within. A manager in full evening dress watched over patrons, concealed lighting enriched the carpeting on wide staircases and in foyers. When the Regent Cinema in Norwich re-opened in September after improvement an enthusiastic newspaper report described a transformation "from old-fashioned red plush and trappings to the peak of modernity . . . warm soothing shades of Pompeian red and buff, enriched by gold and silver . . . . a sumptuous carpet covers all the floors". But an ornamental goldfish pond in the foyer had been retained. A restaurant, also refurbished, offered service all day — "grills served to 9 p.m." Many of the cinemas had their own restaurants; at Ipswich the Picture House's "Cardinal Restaurant" offered "Early morning coffee served in the lounge", "1s. 9d. lunch from 12 to 3 p.m." and "Dainty afternoon teas". Some of the larger places provided an organ recital between the films. These, of course, were the leading cinemas. In the smaller towns one still found the old-fashioned and much simpler establishment, but *they* were gradually disappearing. The Empire at Littleport put up the shutters early in 1939 when the owner, who was drawing only fifty shillings a week from the business, was adjudged bankrupt. He had watched the weekly takings drop from £40 to £16 in two years.

Eric Boon of Chatteris, the British lightweight champion, on the right, in training at Ely in February.   *B.B.C. Hulton Picture Library*

Most people did not aspire to "go away" for a holiday each year, but each Bank Holiday saw a big exodus from the towns. Over 14,000 people travelled from Thorpe station at Norwich on Whit-Monday, and between 20,000 and 25,000 on August Bank Holiday Monday. About two-thirds of them went to Great Yarmouth. The whole railway time-table was scrapped and a continuous shuttle service substituted. The *Norwich Mercury* reported: "The station-master supervised the operations from the signal box. The queue never got out of hand. As soon as one train was filled and off, another was there to take its place . . . The crowd at Thorpe station was considered to be the most soberly dressed ever seen there on a Whit Monday, and the flamboyant beach pyjamas of a few years ago were at a discount. For the most part, Miss Norwich of 1939 wore two-piece suits and looked neat and well dressed. Not many wore hats, while a number favoured the fashion of wearing a coloured handkerchief instead."

Rail travel was, by any standard, cheap and, apart from these special outings, many people regularly used trains for pleasure trips. An evening in London was practicable from any of the principal towns. Excursions from Norwich left at 4.45 p.m., arrived at Liverpool Street station at 7.25 p.m. and returned four-and-a-half hours later, and the fare was 4s. 2d. From Cambridge the fare was only 2s. 8d. and the timings gave five full hours in the capital. Full-day excursions from Cambridge to the coast cost 5s. 6d. to Yarmouth, 4s. 9d. to Felixstowe, and 4s. 2d. to Hunstanton. From Norwich the fares were only 2s. 8d. to Yarmouth and 2s. 1d. to Cromer.

Most popular of all leisure interests, of course, was sport. Almost every village had its football, cricket and bowls teams. Along the coast most places had a sailing club and organised an annual regatta. The Royal Burnham and the Royal Corinthian Clubs at Burnham-on-Crouch, the Royal Harwich, and the Royal Norfolk and Suffolk Club at Lowestoft were the best-known names, but interest in small boats of every kind was growing rapidly and many lesser clubs drew large numbers of enthusiasts to the coast each weekend. Cambridge of course, was identified in the mass mind with the annual Boat Race on the Thames, which in 1939 it won by four lengths. Newmarket was synonymous with horse racing. Tennis had a big following: a crowd of a thousand watched exhibition matches played at Felixstowe in August by professionals who included "Big Bill" Tilden and Donald Budge, and the Felixstowe and Frinton tennis tournaments were very popular. Golf had its enthusiasts, and some Rugby Union football was played, though, in the words of one of the players, they were doing "missionary work".

The government was giving encouragement and practical assistance to those activities which had some direct relevance to the country's defence needs. It had set up a National Fitness Committee in London and in 1939 it was building up regional and local organisations. A newly-formed Norfolk and

Suffolk National Fitness Committee appointed its first secretary and moved into action in March. At Lowestoft a Physical and Recreative Council was set up, to which thirty local organisations immediately affiliated. That was the pattern which it was sought to create in every community. The other new hobby which received official encouragement was flying. Local aero clubs were helped to set up a Civil Air Guard; those who joined it were given instruction for 2s. 6d. an hour. When Ipswich Aero Club entered the scheme in October 1938 it immediately received four hundred applications to join from all over Suffolk and Essex. Over a hundred pilots' licences were issued in the first six months.

Most of those who followed sport, however, were spectators rather than players, and the great spectator sports were cricket and football. Essex was the only first-class county cricket team in the region. Of its performance in 1939, two matches stand out. The opening match of the Chelmsford Cricket Festival, in May, was between Essex and Worcestershire. Essex claimed victory by 295 runs, but everything was over-shadowed by the death of the Worcestershire captain in a road accident at Chelmsford on the evening before play began. It was, therefore, the match which followed immediately afterwards which first roused excitement. On 31st May Essex went in to bat first against a West Indian touring side and their opening pair, Eastman and Avery, rattled up fifty runs in the first twenty-three minutes. But then the great Learie Constantine took the ball. With cunning variations of pace and flight, with deadly spins, he played havoc with the Essex batsmen. In one hour he dismissed six of them for twenty-nine runs. When the whole side was out for 158, West Indies knocked up 219 in their first innings. Much the same thing happened on the second day. Eastman and Avery again started well, holding their own even against Constantine. After lunch, however, he took six wickets for forty-two runs. His match record was thirteen wickets for ninety-one runs and the West Indies won by two wickets.

Felixstoweferry regatta.   *East Anglian Daily Times*

County Cricket week at Colchester with the chairman, C. Stewart Richardson, inset.

East Anglian Daily Times

The 1938-39 football season was a particularly interesting one in East Anglia. Ipswich Town on its way up, and Norwich City was fighting for survival in the Second Division, to which it had been promoted in 1934. Colchester United was out to win the cup in the Southern League. The decisive games on the same day at the end of the season had their fans in a frenzy. Colchester United had had a great season. Between 3rd December and 2nd March they played thirteen games without defeat and put themselves well in the lead for the championship. Then the tide turned. They were beaten first by Swindon, and then by Cardiff, and there then followed a gruelling period when they played twenty-one games in seven weeks and, not surprisingly, they flagged. So it came to the final game. Colchester United began with 65 points, while Guildford City had 64. Colchester needed a draw in order to win the shield. Their opponents were Ipswich Reserves, who gave no quarter. At half-time United were leading 2-1, but thirty minutes into the second half Ipswich scored again and maintained a strong attack. United, however, rallied and took the score to 3-2 before the whistle and this put them one point ahead of Guildford at the head of the league. When a motor coach returned them to Colchester that evening, they found the Mayor and a crowd of several thousands waiting to greet them as heroes.

Norwich City, meanwhile, was going down to disaster in a home match at Carrow Road against Nottingham Forest. The Canaries, as they were known, had been a professional team since 1905, but they were now completing their fifth season in the Second Division under the threat of relegation. They had spent a lot of money on transfer fees, to no avail. As they lined up for this final match, the Canaries knew they had not only to win but to secure a four goals lead over Forest, in order to beat their goal average. They went straight into the attack, and they went on attacking persistently, with the seventeen thousand crowd roaring encouragement. But the goals did not come: one in the forty-ninth minute, and that was all. So at the end of the day, and of the season, Norwich had won the match, they were level on points with Forest, but their goal average was .549, against Forest's .597 — a margin of .048 — and it was upon that that the Canaries lost their Second Division status.

The football heroes of the eastern counties were Ipswich Town. Their team had become professional only in 1936. It had then had two very successful seasons in the Southern League and had been elected to the Third Division (South) in time for the 1938-9 season. It finished that season in seventh place, the highest position which had ever been achieved by any team in its first season in the League. Ipswich was in the grip of football fever. The pitch at Portman Road was claimed to be one of the best in the country, the squad was full of skill and enthusiasm, and the Supporters' Club, with just on ten thousand members by April 1939, was the biggest in the country. They were at a pitch of excitement when the team won the first two matches of the season, but then followed nine games without a victory, and only one point gained, for a goal-less home match. After that bad spell, in September and October, the team found itself twenty-first in the League table, with only five points from eleven games. Then fortune smiled and they gained more points from the next thirty-one games than any other side in the League, and shot up to seventh place. In the F.A. Cup they found themselves in a third-round tie with Aston Villa and when they travelled to Villa Park, with three thousand fans in attendance, they forced a 1-1 draw. After that, anything seemed possible. Portman Road had never before seen a gate like the 28,194 who turned up on 9th January for the replay. Mulraney, who had been injured at Villa Park, was missing from the forward line and for most of the second half they were down to ten men, after Dave Bell left the field with a leg injury. This gave the supporters an explanation when the home team went down 2-1 to Villa, and everyone agreed it was a splendid, thrill-packed game. Easter provided the next major excitement. On Good Friday Ipswich drew with Queens Park Rangers in an away game. The next day they beat Bristol City 4-0 at Portman Road. On Easter Monday, before a crowd of 19,120 in another home game, they won the replay against Q.P.R. 1-0. When, a fortnight later, they beat Clapton Orient 3-0 they made certain of staying in the Third Division. The last game of the season was against Bournemouth Town at Boscombe. Chadwick, the most prolific scorer throughout the season, was missing because of injuries sustained in the match a week earlier and Ipswich did not show their usual power of attack. The best they could do was to hold the match to a goal-less draw, but they had consolidated their League position. In twenty-one League games during the season, the team drew attendances totalling 250,770, an average of 11,941 a game.

Football was played again in the region during 1939, but it was on a make-shift basis. The new season was launched in August, Ipswich played a public trial game at Portman Road, and the crowd went away happy with the new players who had been signed and optimistic about promotion. A week later the team beat Norwich City 2-1 and then, at the official opening of the season on 26th August, it drew at Leyton 2-2. There was one more game, when it beat Bristol Rovers 2-0 at Portman Road, and then the curtain descended. It was lack of transport which caused the first cancellations, at the weekend when all the defences were being mobilised and the school-children evacuated, but on 9th September the Football League competition was officially suspended.

Leisure and pleasure were much more difficult to come by after that.

In spite of the war the Lowestoft Sea Angling Festival took place during October.

Norwich Mercury series

CHAPTER EIGHT

Belief and Behaviour

THE mechanics of a society can be observed and described, and the earlier chapters have sought to do this for the East Anglian community of 1939. The dynamics of a society are much more difficult to identify. How did people *feel*? What did they *think*? What instinctive beliefs sustained them? What convictions motivated their behaviour? Some evidence emerges from the facts we have already reviewed, particularly about the class structure of the society we are examining. Most people had an innate sense of class, and each class had tastes and standards which it felt to be peculiarly its own. Cambridge intellectuals were ready to argue the benefits of *élitism*; in the council chambers and the country houses of the counties to the east such discussion would have been considered futile, if not dangerous — they *knew* the natural order of things. Those who enjoyed privilege readily accepted responsibilities, and not only local administration but a multiplicity of organisations of every kind could count upon donations and voluntary work to advance their purposes. The working class, however, was beginning — even in East Anglia — to question this state of affairs and seeking to re-define its role.

Politically, East Anglia was overwhelmingly Conservative, as the polling figures set out in Appendix II make clear. A National Government headed by Mr Stanley Baldwin had been elected in November 1935 and was supported by 432 Members of Parliament, which gave it a majority over the combined Opposition parties of 247. Though it stuck to the "National" label which had been introduced in crisis circumstances in 1931, this was essentially a Conservative administration; some of the M.Ps who supported it avoided formal identification with the Conservative party, but were nonetheless consistent and dependable allies in the division lobbies. We have already seen how a "Liberal National" carried the Conservative Prime Minister's banner in the East Norfolk by-election. The Eye division of Suffolk was represented by Mr Edgar Granville, who described himself as an Independent — but no Conservative had opposed him in the general election and in 1939 he declared: "I stand or fall by our Prime Minister".

After the general election of 1935 there were only eighteen Opposition M.Ps (fifteen Labour and three Liberal) elected by constituencies in the whole of the southern half of England, if one excluded London. In May 1937 Mr Neville Chamberlain succeeded Mr Baldwin as Prime Minister. And, as

The High Sheriff of Norfolk, Sir William Gentle, with Mr Frank Medlicott (left), the victor, and Mr Norman Tillett at the declaration of the poll in East Norfolk during February.

Norwich Mercury series

usually happens between general elections, the government lost seats in a series of by-elections. One of these was Ipswich, which swung from Conservative to Labour at a by-election in February 1938 and elected Mr Richard R. Stokes. He polled 27,604 votes, to his National Conservative opponent's 24,443. It was a mere dent in the armour-plating of Conservative East Anglia. There was also a solid body of Labour support in Norwich, where well over thirty thousand people had voted for either Labour or Independent Labour Party candidates (against 36,000 supporting a government candidate). There was a Liberal tradition in the region, but the vote appeared to have collapsed and the only

Liberal elected to Parliament from East Anglia in 1935 was Mr James de Rothschild, in the Isle of Ely. In a straight fight with a Conservative candidate, he had a narrow majority of 699 in a total poll of nearly 35,000. East Anglia, then, offered as solid support of the government as could be found anywhere in Britain. Cambridge borough and county constituencies provided comfortable Conservative majorities. The university, which was entitled to two seats in the Commons, elected two Conservatives and there was only a single Opposition candidate standing against them, to make a fight of it. In Essex, every constituency except Romford returned an M.P. supporting the government, including Mr Winston Churchill at Epping and Mr R. A. Butler at Saffron Walden. The Harwich M.P. described himself as a Liberal National. The Conservatives were deeply entrenched in Norfolk, though the M.Ps for the Eastern and Great Yarmouth constituencies used the Liberal National label. In Suffolk a Bury St Edmunds farmer, Major Frank Heilgers, was returned unopposed for that constituency, and apart from the government-supporting Independent at Eye, the county was solidly Conservative.

It is not possible to make any similar analysis covering local government elections. Labour, when it fielded candidates for council elections, insisted that they were party nominees fighting on a party policy, but most other candidates maintained a stance of political independence, even though most of those who were elected were well-known as local Conservative supporters and sometimes activists. Labour members were almost exclusively elected by urban voters; in the rural areas a declared Labour candidate was lucky if he or she collected a three-figure vote.

Without doubt a deep pacifist vein ran through the Labour movement in East Anglia. Fenner Brockway, the I.L.P. candidate who polled 6,737 votes in Norwich in the 1935 general election was a leading figure in the anti-war movement, and in the May Day demonstration in Norwich in 1939 Labour and the I.L.P. shared a united platform, for the first time. Also in May, the executive of the Cambridgeshire Trades Council and Divisional Labour Party passed a resolution declaring "opposition to the conscription legislation of the present National Government because it is not, as they assert, a defence measure against fascism, but a treacherous attack on the industrial and civil liberties of the people". After war had begun the Ipswich M.P., Mr Richard Stokes, though he was certainly not a pacifist, argued for a negotiated peace settlement rather than a "fight to a finish" and the Ipswich Labour Party at a meeting on 8th October attended by the M.P. agreed to send a telegram to the Prime Minister: "Crowded meeting of members of Ipswich Labour Party passed unanimously a resolution urging that an armistice be called at once and the British government immediately put forward wide constructive alternative peace terms for basis of discussion in reply to the German Chancellor's vague generalities . . ."

May Day was the occasion on which the Labour movement celebrated its progress, and the demonstrations in Norwich and Ipswich on Sunday, 5th May were colourful and impressive. The Norwich parade, which assembled in the Cattle Market and then marched through most of the central streets, was headed by banner-bearers and the Drayton and District British Legion Band. In the provision market speeches were delivered from twin platforms.

The agricultural workers' union had a tough task to recruit on the farms, but it was making steady progress. Early in 1939, its president, Mr Edwin Gooch, reported 2,000 recruits in a year in Norfolk alone. The union's general secretary, Mr William Holmes, who was a native of Norwich, was elected chairman of the T.U.C. in September 1939 and a couple of months later he was received by King George VI at Buckingham Palace, where they had an informal 45 minutes fireside chat.

The annual May Day procession in Ipswich, headed by Rickingshall Silver Band.

East Anglian Daily Times

Children were usually present in large numbers at any demonstrations, but it must not be supposed that their impressionable minds were influenced entirely in one direction. When Empire Day was celebrated in all schools on 24th May, it was done in most places with considerable dramatic effect. In most towns Mayors and councillors visited the schools, and there were ceremonies of raising and saluting the Union Jack, poems were recited (Kipling's "Recessional" was very popular), and there were visits to war memorials, services in churches, processions, physical training displays, tableaux devised and presented, maypole dancing, ringing of bells. A report of a visit to one school by the Deputy Lord Mayor of Norwich indicates the strong flavour imparted to these occasions: "After the National Anthem, the hymn 'O Beautiful our country' was sung, followed by Purcell's 'Fairest Isle' and Gustav Holst's 'I vow to thee, my country'. John of Gaunt's famous patriotic speech from Shakespeare was recited."

During 1939 the British Union of Fascists tried from time to time to gather some support in East Anglia, hoping to link their activities to the campaign of the disaffected farmers. They had no success. In January their leader, Sir Oswald Mosley, addressed a meeting in Eye Town Hall, promising his audience that, if he had his way, "nothing would be imported into England that could be produced in this country". Outside the hall there was one of the demonstrations that marked fascist meetings everywhere: boos and catcalls, thudding on doors, fireworks. During July Mosley appeared in Norfolk, telling a crowd divided between the town hall and the market place in Aylsham that "the home market could be secured for British farmers by the exclusion of the £200 millions of foreign foodstuffs imported each year to pay the interest on financiers' loans." Once or twice the B.U.F. roused a rumpus at meetings organised by other parties and during the early hours of a Saturday morning in August, only a few days before war began, they swamped the main streets of Stowmarket with propaganda leaflets and painted the slogan "Mosley for Peace" and swastikas across roads near the centre of the town.

As war came closer, considerable embarassment was caused by links which had been established between some East Anglian communities and towns in Germany. Lowestoft and Ipswich found themselves in the forefront of controversy. Lowestoft had a well-established link with Frankfurt and in three successive years the Turnverein Sachsenhausen hockey team had travelled from that city to play a team of Lowestoft boys in the Easter Hockey Festival. Over the same period an interchange of schoolboy football teams had been developed. In 1939 the Frankfurt hockey team had been invited to visit Lowestoft again, while a Lowestoft football team was to visit Frankfurt. The arrangements were made by the Lowestoft Schools Sports Association, with financial support from the local Education Committee. Much had happened, however, since the previous visits: Munich, the invasion of Czechoslovakia, Hitler's evident inclination to expand further the frontiers of the Reich.

135

At the Norwich May Day procession a tableau by the Independent Labour Party Guild of Youth opposed conscription.

Norwich Mercury series

How far should "politics" be allowed to interfere with international sports exchanges? — it became a subject of acute division of opinion. The President of the Schools Sports Association, who was also the Deputy Mayor of Lowestoft, Major S. W. Humphrey, announced that he would not go to Frankfurt with the boys "as a protest in my humble way against what happened recently". He added: "Personally, I would not send the children at any price". An opposite view was published in the *East Anglian Daily Times* on 21st March in the form of extracts from a letter which the festival organisers said they had received from "a leading businessman in Lowestoft". The exchanges should go ahead, he argued, if only for the sake of retaining Lowestoft's trade with Germany. "Last year the German Control purchased from Lowestoft alone herrings, cured and fresh, of the value of £274,736, of which sum one third represents labour and wages," he wrote.

In the end, the exchange took place. The chairman of Lowestoft Education Committee accompanied fifteen local schoolboys on a football tour in Germany, sailing from Harwich on 6th April, after the committee had approved the trip by eight votes to six. The Turnverein Sachsenhausen hockey team arrived in Lowestoft from Frankfurt (along with the Daring Club de Bruxelles, from Belgium) and, at a dinner on Good Friday, presented the Mayor of Lowestoft with an amber paperweight, declaring: "May it prove to be a continuation of comradeship and unbroken friendship".

During May the Royal Ocean Yacht Club organised a race from Harwich to the Weser, and nine British, nine German and three Dutch boats competed. On the eve of this event the R.O.Y.C. held its annual dinner at the Hotel Alexandra in Dovercourt, with the German and Dutch crews as their guests. Toasts were drunk to the King, the Fuehrer, and the Queen of the Netherlands. Reports of this event drew a letter from an Essex county councillor who was a life vice-president of the Amateur Athletics Association, Mr Herbert F. Pash, in which he protested: "If the Harwich yachtsmen are capable of shame, I hope they may be convinced that in entertaining the representatives of a nation which imprisons, tortures and kills people without trial, they have committed a blunder of the first magnitude".

Others faced similar problems, but escaped with minimal publicity. The Headmaster of Framlingham College cancelled a return visit which his school's hockey eleven was due to make to Dusseldorf. In June a party of twenty farmers from West Norfolk and South Lincolnshire made a ten days tour in Germany studying agricultural conditions.

There were some, of course, who did not believe that a war was imminent, and they included at least two of the M.Ps for the region, as we have noted in an earlier chapter. Others gave more reliable guidance, although few were as forthright as the Chief Constable of Huntingdonshire, who told a National Service recruiting meeting in March: "I think we are almost certainly due for another world war, either this year or next". There was a general concern about events on the Continent, which found expression in many ways. In January 1939 the Bishop of Ely appealed for £50,000 from his diocese for Earl Baldwin's Refugee Fund for Christian Refugees from Central Europe. Committees were set up in many towns, including Cambridge, Norwich, Ipswich, Bury St Edmunds and Felixstowe to raise money for this Fund. Many of the refugees were settled, on arrival in Britain, in reception centres along the East Coast. One of the first was established, before the end of 1938, in a holiday camp at Dovercourt Bay; the Shaftesbury Society's Retreat at Dovercourt also took in many arrivals; and just before that Christmas about two hundred German Jewish boys moved into St Felix School at Southwold.

By early February there were nearly six hundred German and Austrian Jewish refugee boys at the Dovercourt Bay holiday camp and some of them had been there for weeks. It was a rough winter of intense cold, and the accommodation was designed to be used only in the summer months. Conditions became difficult. During the Christmas period problems were relieved by assistance from teachers and student volunteers, but this was a temporary expedient. And more refugees were on the way; they continued to arrive throughout the year until war began: from Berlin, from Austria, from Danzig, and elsewhere. Goodwill was widespread, but the volunteer reception organisations were in danger of being overwhelmed, and there were anxieties about the long-term financial commitments that might have to be shouldered.

137

Some of the major problems were solved by the acquisition early in the year of a former workhouse, the eighteenth-century Barham House, at Claydon, near Ipswich, for use as a transit hostel. It had been unoccupied for four years and required cleaning and furnishing, but volunteers came forward and an appeal for second-hand furniture was successful. By this time the holiday camp proprietors wanted their premises returned, so that they could make preparations for the coming season. By the end of March the first boys were transferred from Dovercourt to Claydon and within a month one hundred and sixty boys were settled in, and more were on the way from the Continent. The place was organised on public school lines and divided into four "houses", and the whole operation was financed by the Earl Baldwin Refugee Fund. Dozens of parcels arrived at Barham House every day, many from British well-wishers, but some from parents abroad containing German sausage, pastries and sweets.

Later in the year, in August, the most distinguished refugee of them all, Dr Edouard Beneš, the ex-President of Czechoslovakia, was given a wild reception when he appeared at a Cambridge summer school. The Arts Theatre was packed and the audience rose to its feet and cheered for minutes when he entered. He refused to discuss current events but, in a philosophical vein, argued that "democracy cannot die".

The victims of war in Spain also aroused the sympathy and support of the East Anglian public. In January three bishops—Ely, Chelmsford and St Edmundsbury and Ipswich—were among the signatories to an appeal for aid to send an Eastern Counties foodship to Valencia. "It has been established that over 100,000 children are actually starving in Eastern Spain," they wrote. "The Eastern Counties foodship has been allocated to Valencia in view of the special urgency of the food problem there, through the influx of refugees from Madrid . . . " They appealed for gifts of cash, tinned milk and meat, soap and dry groceries, and for sacks of potatoes from farmers. The response was generous, the foodship sailed from Wisbech in February and reached Valencia soon afterwards. Local Spanish Aid Committees, linked by an Eastern Counties Co-ordinating Committee, continued to work energetically until war came to Britain, too.

These responses reflected a concern and sympathy felt by the broad mass of the people; they were but one manifestation of human emotion, however, and perhaps we should balance against them the familiar aspects of envy, selfishness, frustration and violence which were as commonplace in this society as in all others. Crime was not significantly more serious that it had usually been in the past, but the extent and the nature of it caused concern. The Chief Constable of Norwich, in his annual report in March, reported an increase in the number of criminal prosecutions, by 104 to 721. "When endeavouring to trace the reason for this increase, we again encounter the problem of

Empire Air Day: a section of the 9,000 spectators at Stradishall. *East Anglian Daily Times*

unemployment, where so many young men are without work and with no interest in life apart from walking the streets and associating together," he wrote. In the single month of June 1939 a group of Harwich juveniles appeared in court after they had climbed into railway carriages parked in a siding at Parkeston and systematically smashed all the electric light bulbs; two Ipswich boys aged fifteen and sixteen came before Woodbridge magistrates after they had demanded "£200 or your life" in a note to a local businessman; there was a smash-and-grab raid on a jeweller's shop within one hundred and fifty yards of Colchester police station; and Saffron Walden town council heard complaints of regular disturbances in the market square after Saturday evening dances in the town hall. The following month an insurance agent had pepper thrown into his face and his wallet stolen in the middle of Dovercourt High Street at mid-morning. And the year produced a wife-killing in Colchester which led to an Old Bailey trial and a sentence of fifteen years penal servitude for manslaughter.

There was some public discussion about "the spiritual state of the nation", but it was muted and diffuse. Schoolmasters tended to express stronger views than Churchmen. The Head of King Edward VI School at Chelmsford, for example, put this point of view at the annual dinner of Old Chelmsfordians:

"There are many reasons for the belief that the sense of responsibility is growing feebler. Our amusements have increased enormously as a result of the progress of science—wireless and the cinema, for example—but they call for very little exertion on our own part. We do not have to put anything into them. Our games are getting the same way—there is an ever-growing tendency to pay experts to amuse us. Even the government is doing more and more for each of us. How long they can go on doing it at such enormous public expense I don't know. Until recently they have demanded nothing in return. These influences seem to lead to the kind of feeling that we demand our rights and do not think of our duties."

A quite different aspect of moral welfare caused concern to some Church workers. The organising secretary of the St Edmundsbury and Ipswich Diocesan Moral Welfare Association explained the problem at a meeting in Beccles rectory garden one June afternoon: aerodromes were being built in many areas round them, she pointed out, and now there were suddenly appearing very attractive young men who quite turned the heads of the village girls. "One of the things we need to consider is what we can do to give these young men proper recreation and decent opportunities for meeting girls, rather than have things left to chance," she said.

The theologians had certain preoccupations at the time. The Upper House of Convocation of the Church of England had recently debated the interpretation of certain clauses of the Creed. The Bishops of Ely, Chelmsford and St Albans had found themselves in a small minority and the Bishop of Ely, writing in the March issue of his *Diocesan Gazette*, reported:

"The upshot of all this is that the House of Bishops of the Convocation of Canterbury prefers not to declare that the historical clauses of the Creed mean what they say, and has no word of reproof for those of the clergy who lead their congregations in these confessions of our faith and then explicitly deny some of the truths, e.g. the virgin birth and the resurrection on the third day, which with their lips they have affirmed.

I do not deny that the situation thus created seems to me to be serious. Christianity is an historical religion. It is based on events in history and if these events did not occur the whole foundation of Christianity is imperilled . . . Just two years ago I said that I could foresee that my own loyalty to the province to which the diocese of Ely belongs might be strained almost to breaking point. It was no idle forecast."

An opposite point of view was presented by the crusading Bishop of Birmingham, Dr E. W. Barnes, when he lectured at St-Mary-le-Tower in Ipswich on Sunday afternoon, 18th June, on the subject "The Faith of a Modernist". He told his audience that they should be ready to accept the results of modern study: scientific, historical, literary or critical. "The increase of knowledge of the nations contemporary with Israel showed that much Bible history was unhistorical folklore," he declared. He thought the new knowledge strengthened Christianity.

A quick, sharp retort came from a freelance evangelist, Mr W. Simpson-Moor, who was running a campaign in Norfolk and Suffolk. In Ipswich Public Hall the following Sunday he preached against the theory of evolution. "Man was made in the image of God and has no near relatives in the Zoo," he summed up.

Growth of population in certain areas and, in particular, the movement of slum-dwellers into new housing estates had placed heavy financial burdens on the Church of England, but it had built some new churches and halls. For example, one at Ipswich All Hallows, with seats for 460, was opened on the new Gainsborough housing estate at Whitsun 1939.

Apart from the provision of new churches, the preservation and care of the historic cathedrals and churches in the region presented a daunting challenge. At Ely during 1939 the Friends of the Cathedral, with almost 1,000 members, raised the money to install electric light. They had already helped with the cleaning and repair of the Lady Chapel, begun the previous year. At Norwich over 300 bosses in the vaulting of the nave of the cathedral were cleaned and restored during 1939 to expose their original colouring. These fifteenth century carvings, which had last been cleaned and restored during the 1870s, were "the Bible of the people who could not read", telling the story of the history of the world, from the Creation to the time of Solomon, and from the Annunciation to the Last Judgement.

In the Diocese of St Edmundsbury, which was fairly typical in this respect, the Chairman of the Board of Finance reported "a really serious financial position". One hundred and fifty of the four hundred parishes had failed to pay their quota to diocesan funds. Shortage of cash produced all kinds of stresses and strains, sometimes with almost bizarre consequences. It was perhaps natural that the parishioners of Drinkstone and Tostock should become militant when their bishop proposed to unite the two benefices, but the evidence presented when a Commission appointed by the bishop held its hearings during March might have suggested to a stranger that they were a continent apart, rather than a matter of one and a half miles. Then, during May, there was the spectacle of the Vicar of Haughley auctioning his home on his front lawn because he had not received his supplementary grant from the diocese. "We shall even sell our beds and sleep on the floor," he proclaimed.

The most astonishing situation arose in the village of Bramfield; it illustrated not only the inability of the Church to escape the harsh consequences of financial stress, but also the subtle balance of power in the smallest rural communities.

Soon after a new parson had arrived in Bramfield he saw, one February night, a light in the vestry and, going to investigate, he came face-to-face with the people's church-warden and the sexton, who was holding an empty cash-box which had just been taken from a safe. What followed then led to a two-day hearing in the Kings Bench Division in London in the spring of 1939. The trouble arose over the supply and sale of the deanery magazine. The vicar, when he took over the parish, had agreed to be personally responsible for the magazines, paying for supplies and retaining any money from sales. One day the treasurer of the rural deanery called to collect payment and the vicar, not having cash on him at the time, took the money which was in the church safe. Some of it was the proceeds of magazine sales, but a sum of 12s. 1½d. represented the church collections on the previous three Sundays. His action was noted — it was not stated clearly by whom, but there was ground for supposing that it was by the vicar's housekeeper. The sexton was told, and he informed the people's church-warden. The safe was checked, the money had gone — and the vicar arrived on the scene at that moment to enquire what was going on. After this encounter the church-warden wrote to the vicar a letter which began: "Dear Sir, With reference to the 12s. 1½d. which you have admitted taking from the church safe and which consisted of church collections, I have no doubt that, being familiar with the law, you realise you are laying yourself open to a charge of misappropriation of church funds . . . " A rowdy meeting of the Church council followed within a few days, held in the vicarage, and — according to the prosecution case as it was later presented in court — the church-warden said to the vicar on that occasion: "If I had done what you have done, I should be under lock and key . . . " The Church council invited the vicar to seek another living. The vicar sued the church-warden for libel.

Having heard the facts set out above presented by the prosecution, Mr Justice Charles, who presided at the hearing, remarked: "They are very touchy people in Bramfield . . . " But when the defence opened its case, things quickly took on a different complexion. Defence counsel was a barrister from Lincoln's Inn who, although only thirty-one, was rapidly making a name for himself, Mr Quintin Hogg. He had been a brilliant scholar at Oxford and in 1938 he had been elected to Parliament as the M.P. for Oxford City. He had a clear analytical mind and a direct and probing style. Some said he would one day follow the example of his father, Viscount Hailsham, and become Lord Chancellor of England. (He did).

The nave of Norwich Cathedral was restored under the direction of Professor Tristram. *Norwich Mercury* series

"Is this the first quarrel you have had in the parish?" enquired Mr Hogg.

"Out of 531 people, I have quarrelled with four, and on each occasion I considered it my job to quarrel with them."

"Isn't such an action as this by a priest a deplorable thing?"

"I regard it as a most wholesome thing. It is the only way in which a clergyman can re-establish his character. I am a useless factor in the parish until then."

The questions continued, until he admitted that some years previously he had brought an action against another clergyman, a canon, for money. Although that action had been settled amicably, his bishop had written him a letter of strong comment.

Next he agreed that at Bramfield he had had a misunderstanding with the headmistress because she would not allow him to take prayers in the village school. He had paid for a statement in the local newspaper apologising for having alleged incompetence on her part.

At this point, the judge's attitude had clearly changed. Commenting upon a letter which the vicar had written to the headmistress, he observed: "It was a very stupid, disagreeable letter and unworthy of the vicar of the parish".

Quintin Hogg pressed on. Yes, the vicar agreed, he had had two disputes with the sexton — disputes, not quarrels. But he insisted he was popular in the parish. Mrs Mason, who was the most important person in the parish — if importance was represented by money — was a most generous donor to the church and he had had no quarrel with her.

Hogg rapped back: "Did you write to her — 'I think you might be more mannerly and less truculent in your method of writing to me, seeing that I am the vicar of Bramfield, the most important person in the parish'?"

"Yes," said the vicar.

On the second day of the hearing, Quintin Hogg began with a presentation of his client, the church-warden, not as a great landowner, as had been represented, he said, but as a working farmer who had lived in Bramfield for twenty-two years and done much voluntary work for the village.

The church-warden, called to give evidence, declared that the vicar had upset everyone in the village. When he arrived he had turned out all the grown-ups from the church choir. Congregations had become very small indeed. There had been a lot of fuss about the village school. The vicar had insisted that he was the head man of the village and he wanted to be top dog in the school, as well as everywhere else. The vicar had started a rival school of his own. "He made a lot of noise about it," said the church-warden. "There were special caps for the boys and it ran on for three weeks or a month, but the whole thing was so irregular that the education people stepped in and shut it up."

The jury had heard enough. While the church-warden was still being cross-examined, they stopped the case and the judge entered judgement for the defendant, with costs. The action, he said, should never have been brought to court.

Such public disclosures were rare, but they lifted a curtain on a way of life which was not particularly unusual in some of its features.

The other churches were also strong in the region. Catholic support was concentrated in particular areas. The last new church opened in East Anglia before war began was a Roman Catholic church in Braintree, dedicated on 31st August. At Sudbury an outstandingly successful priest, Father Gerard Moir, created something of a legend. During the winter of 1937-8 there had been public disquiet in the town because of the aimless way in which young people were roaming the streets. Father Moir opened a social club in the sacristy of his church and then, during the following winter, transferred it to a public hall. Within a few weeks 250 youngsters were regularly turning up and so he transferred again, to the largest hall in the town. Those who came paid threepence for admission which covered dancing to the Blue Serenaders Dance Band, games and refreshments. At the final club night in March 1939 the youngsters spontaneously made a presentation to the priest and sang "For he's a jolly good fellow", and he then promised that the club would re-open one night a week from the first Monday in September. In that week, by government decree, there were no gatherings for public entertainment; the blackout ruled.

The non-conformist churches had their strengths, and their problems. The Suffolk Baptist Union and the Norfolk Baptist Association held a joint assembly in May. Suffolk reported an increase in church membership for the first time in six years and an increase in Sunday School pupils for the second successive year. Total membership was given as 2,391 — up on the previous year and ninety members more than there had been in 1919. On the other hand, the Norfolk Association reported its membership down by 188 to 3,048 and the number of Sunday School pupils down by 129 to 3,203. Its report asserted: "Unless they gave themselves to aggressive evangelism and sought to gain new recruits from the rising generation, the future for Norfolk Baptists was very dark." The Norfolk president thought it "a first-class disaster that we have lost tens of thousands of boys and girls from our Sunday schools in recent years". The Suffolk Congregational Union, at its annual assembly, also reported a declining membership, but was more reticent about statistics. Methodists reported 1,735 members in the area between Chelmsford and Harwich, compared with 1,688 a year earlier. The Strict Baptists of Norfolk and Suffolk mustered over a thousand members of forty-three churches at their annual meeting in June, in a big marquee pitched in a meadow at Horham.

The mayoral procession when the Mayor of Ipswich, Mr E. L. Hunt, accompanied by members of the Town Council and Corporation officials, attended divine service at St Andrews, Rushmere. *East Anglian Daily Times*

The war began, and the churches faced a greater challenge. At the outset the Bishop of Ely gave clear counsel: "Sing no hymns of hate . . . Vast numbers of Germans must hate the war as we hate it, and are kindly, good-living folk. Pity them and give them a place in your prayers." There was a National Day of Prayer in all churches at the beginning of October. At Lowestoft the Rector, Canon L. Whytehead, echoed the Bishop of Ely: "So far we have little malice against the German people. I hope we shall maintain that attitude, because the greatest defeat would not be a defeat of arms, but that we should become a hating and therefore hateful people." There was a different emphasis in some other sermons. The Bishop of St Edmundsbury and Ipswich told his cathedral congregation: "God is summoning us to do His Will. He has called us to stand for His righteousness". A former Bishop of Durham, Dr Hensley Henson, preaching in Ipswich assured his listeners that it was a Holy War, God's War, and thus they were called to be God's fellow workers.

Later, as the first war-time winter set in, the Bishop of Chelmsford wrote: "I do plead that war sermons shall be few and far between. People do not go to Church in these days to hear hymns of hate and denunciation of Hitler. This not only does no good, but does real harm." The warning was timely. At that time the sinking of ships began to make the headlines and the government published a White Paper detailing the nature of cruelty in the Buchenwald concentration camp. Talk of "the age-old, unchanging Hun" was beginning to be heard.

CHAPTER NINE

Preparing for War

A^T A number of meetings in the early weeks of 1939 the British Cabinet authorised a series of measures which ensured that, henceforth, the nation's energies and will would be concentrated on preparation for war. Recruitment to all three Services was to be expanded as rapidly as possible; the Army was to be built up to thirty-two divisions — six regular and twenty-six Territorial Army. Aircraft production was to be pushed to the limit; factories were to make as many planes as they could in the shortest possible time, regardless of cost. Increasingly during the 'thirties the government had concentrated its thoughts on national defence, as a response to the build-up of armed forces in Germany and the Soviet Union. Even before the Munich crisis of 1938 visual evidence of re-armament was to be seen widely in East Anglia. New airfields were being built: Honington, near Bury St Edmunds, and Debden near Saffron Walden, were commissioned in 1937, and Wyton, Huntingdonshire, and Stradishall, Suffolk, soon after. There was much discussion of "air raid precautions" and an A.R.P. Officer was appointed in each of the big centres to organise the protection of the civil population.

Permanent A.R.P. shelters under construction on Midsummer Common in Cambridge during March. *Cambridge Evening News*

Other measures taken were cloaked in great secrecy, such as experiments which began at Orfordness in the mid-'thirties and were later concentrated at Bawdsey Manor, on the Deben estuary, leading to a system of radio-location of planes approaching the coast. A chain of "radio direction finding" (R.D.F.) stations had been created by the summer of 1939. Despite the secrecy, those who lived near the installations realised they had special significance; they devised their own, often fanciful, explanations of what was going on.

"The activities at Bawdsey Manor encouraged some very remarkable rumours in the district. One theory was that some sort of 'death ray' was being developed there. When a seaplane, approaching from the sea, crashed close at hand, it was said that an invisible screen had been created through which aircraft could not penetrate. Another story which circulated widely in Woodbridge was that visitors to Bawdsey beach one summer Sunday afternoon found they were unable to start their car engines when they were ready to leave. They were all cranking away with starting handles at the front of their cars when an officer emerged from Bawdsey Manor, took in the situation at a glance, disappeared inside again and, immediately afterwards, all the cars started without trouble! Nobody really knew what was going on, but there was no shortage of theories." [1]

A Wellington bomber over its pre-war aerodrome at Marham, Norfolk, during the last days of peace.   *Mrs M. Martin*

The new airfields and the increasing activity there gave the clearest indication of the scale of rearmament. In 1935, when the decision was taken to expand the Royal Air Force significantly, the established air bases in East Anglia were at Felixstowe, where the Marine Aircraft Experimental Establishment had been based since 1913; at Martlesham Heath, first established as a fighter station in 1916 but later the principal experimental and test airfield; and at Duxford, which was opened in 1918 as a training station and later became a fighter base. By early 1939 the planes which saved this country in the Battle of Britain were being introduced and tested at these stations. The first Hurricane fighters came off the regular production line in October 1937, but ran into some trouble. Martlesham undertook further intensive testing, including test dives at 380 m.p.h., between September 1938 and January 1939, and deliveries were then resumed. The first Spitfire fighter was delivered to Duxford in September 1938 and by early 1939 the two squadrons there had been fully re-equipped with this plane. These planes represented a revolutionary advance. Before them the R.A.F. fighters had been biplanes—the Gauntlet, with two machine-guns and a top speed of 230 m.p.h. and, later, the Gladiator, with four guns. The Hurricanes and Spitfires had eight machine-guns and maximum speeds of 316 and 355 m.p.h. respectively. Comparable developments took place in the bomber fleets. When Stradishall was opened in February 1938 it was equipped with Handley Page Heyford biplanes. Honington's four squadrons had Heyfords, Harrows, Harts and Wellesleys. During the early months of 1939 the biplanes were banished, so that by the outbreak of war Bomber Command's No 2 Group, based in East Anglia, had six squadrons of Mark IV Blenheims and No 3 Group, also in East Anglia, had six squadrons of Wellington 1 and 1a aircraft. The Blenheims could carry 1,000 lbs of bombs for 1,460 miles, the Wellingtons up to 4,500 lbs of bombs for 1,200 miles.

As the Air Force was expanded and the new planes were introduced, there were inevitably crashes and forced landings. Reports appeared regularly, week by week, in the East Anglian newspapers. In January a bomber from Stradishall crash-landed in Yorkshire. In February a Hurricane dived into the ground at Debden at 400 m.p.h. and another crashed nearby at Radwinter, a Blenheim crashed on take-off at Wyton, a flying boat sank at Felixstowe, and a Harvard trainer from Martlesham crashed near Woodbridge. Some of the accidents were attended by special drama. In June a bomber force-landed one evening on the North Beach at Great Yarmouth and those on the beach had to run and duck. A few weeks earlier another bomber had ended up across a busy road near Lowestoft. During large-scale air defence exercises in August in one night three Blenheim bombers made forced landings in harvest fields near Dunmow and a Wellington bomber was brought down safely in a plantation of young trees at Roundham Heath, near Thetford, by the pilot, after four other crewmen had parachuted. No-one was hurt in these incidents.

1. Rev H. d'A. Cullen, B.A., in an interview with the author, 1980.   149

An Avro Anson narrowly missed the Rogerson Hall Holiday Camp and crash-landed across the Corton-Hopton road during May.   *East Anglian Daily Times*

On "Empire Day" in May many R.A.F. stations were opened to the public. Empire Day displays had been given every year since 1934 and had always had a frankly propagandist purpose. In 1939 they became an important part of the R.A.F. recruitment campaign which was then in full swing. The crowds which converged on the airfields broke all records: twenty thousand at Martlesham Heath, fifteen thousand at Marham, twelve thousand at Duxford, eight to nine thousand at Stradishall and Debden, five thousand at Bircham Newton. Whole villages emptied as people walked or cycled or travelled in special buses to watch programmes of aerobatics designed to give maximum excitement. The new Hurricanes, Spitfires, Wellingtons and Blenheims dominated the displays, but the planes they had supplanted—a Gauntlet at Mildenhall, a Gladiator at Stradishall, a Harrow and an Oxford at Wyton—appeared, too. There was formation flying, mock combat, parachute dropping. At Felixstowe the crowd watched Sunderland experimental flying-boats—the first of which had arrived there for testing a year earlier—fly past in formation, and they were allowed to inspect a four-engined Singapore flying-boat at close quarters.

Another recruitment aid during this period was a film called "It's in the Air", starring George Formby, which was shown at cinemas in most of the towns in the region. Officers and men attended in uniform for the first night's showing each time and aircraft engines and R.A.F. equipment were displayed in the cinema foyers. At Cambridge the Commandant of the R.A.F.

The Cambridgeshires leaving Ely for camp in summer 1939.
                                          Colonel J. G. A. Beckett   ▶

Volunteer Reserve went on to the stage to appeal for 1,100 men. At Bury St Edmunds an R.A.F. plane flew overhead, in direct radio communication with an operator in the cinema foyer, and a "guess the height" competition was featured. Public interest was also stimulated by linking particular squadrons to particular towns; No 9 Bomber Squadron at Stradishall, for example, was "adopted" by Ipswich.

The Army's recruitment efforts were no less determined. There was a lot to be done in a short time. The Regular Army had been organised since 1881 on the basis that each county should raise its own regiment, with two battalions of infantry; after the formation of the Territorial Army in 1908, these were supplemented by additional battalions of part-time volunteers.

In 1939 the 1st battalion of the Royal Norfolks and the 2nd battalion of the Suffolks were both serving in India. The 2nd battalion of the Royal Norfolks returned to England in January 1939 after two years' service in Gibraltar and settled in at Aldershot, and the 1st battalion of the Suffolks returned in July after two years' service in Malta and was stationed at Devonport, as part of the Eighth Infantry Brigade of the Third Division, commanded by one Major-General Bernard Montgomery.

Cambridgeshire did not have its own regiment in the same way, but raised a battalion of Territorials who were given the title of the Cambridgeshire Regiment, but received their training as the 3rd battalion of the Suffolks. The Suffolks also had their own battalion of Territorials, the 4th. The Royal Norfolks had a 4th battalion of Territorials drawn from Norwich, Yarmouth, Attleborough and Harleston, and a 5th battalion drawn from Dereham, Aylsham, North Walsham and Holt.

Such was the picture when, on 29th March, the Prime Minister announced that the Territorial Army was to be doubled in size and put on a war footing. A month later, after initial hesitation, the government accepted the Army chiefs' recommendation that men aged twenty to twenty-one should be conscripted.

In East Anglia the recruiting campaign achieved remarkable results. Suffolk set an all-England record by signing on 2,060 volunteers in two months, and a new 5th battalion was formed. In Norfolk, the 4th, 5th and 7th battalions were quickly brought up to strength and a 6th battalion was created, raising its strength in Norwich. In Cambridgeshire the sole battalion was joined by a second, raised in the Isle of Ely. Intense pressure was brought to bear on men of military age in order to achieve these results. Two Territorial officers drove around Saffron Walden, Dunmow and Stansted in a lorry on 26th April urging young men, through a megaphone, to volunteer before they were conscripted. The same evening at Saffron Walden drill hall they signed up 54 recruits. At a rally on Angel Hill at Bury St Edmunds on 6th May the British Legion band opened up with stirring marches, the Army gave a demonstration of equipment and arms, and Major-General Lord Loch, from the balcony of the Athenaeum, called on men to come forward and be enrolled and medically examined on the spot. "Two doctors were kept busy until a late hour," according to a newspaper report. The technique of "instant commitment" now took hold everywhere. On 11th May a platform was raised beneath the Gainsborough memorial on Sudbury Market Hill, soldiers with field guns formed up in the square, the Mayor and the local M.P. appealed for one hundred men — and twenty-five volunteered within ninety minutes. On 15th May Hadleigh staged a market square rally and again recruits were medically examined and attested on the spot. On 19th May the Ipswich Territorials marched through the town, shopkeepers (in response to a request from the Mayor) decorated the route with flags and streamers, and men between seventeen and thirty-eight were urged to fall in behind the column and march to the drill hall to be signed up. Twenty-five did so. A few days later the Ipswich T.A. Association sent a telegram to the War Office: "All Ipswich units, first and second-line, recruited to full establishment". It was the first provincial town to achieve this result. In Cambridge there were displays on Parkers Piece and in the Cattle Market, with band and drums, and tours of towns and villages nearby by a small tank and several platoon trucks, and by 1st July the total strength of the Territorials had grown from 667 to 2,028 in three months. Any suggestion of foot-dragging roused ire. When a Committee of Norwich City Council imposed conditions for a recruiting demonstration in the city market, the vice-chairman of the Territorial Association commented angrily: "We shall have Hitler here before we get the Market Place".

A recruiting advertisement published in August.   *Norwich Mercury* series

A Fleet Air Arm recruitment advertisement.
East Anglian Daily Times

As the summer came, the intensity of the recruiting campaign grew. All the big agricultural shows had Service displays and centres to sign up volunteers. The charity fetes and carnivals were used, too. Colchester's three-day carnival kept national service to the fore throughout the programme; the customary procession through the town was this year headed by six motor-cyclists of the 27th Field Regiment R.A. and included the bands of the 5th Royal Inniskilling Dragoon Guards and the 2nd Lancs Fusiliers. Recruitment also took place at factories and other large establishments. The

Chairman of the Bury St Edmund brewers, Greene King, told his company's annual meeting that eighty employees had joined the Territorial Army, their wives and pensioners having volunteered to stand in for them during training. Maximum publicity was given to the various summer camps and manoeuvres. One of the most colourful ideas was a mock invasion of Clacton-on-Sea, when troops wearing foreign uniforms appeared in the town and "captured" the police station. An alarm was sent to the 5th Royal Inniskilling Dragoon Guards at Colchester and they turned out from their garrison, raced over in lorries and "intercepted the invaders" near Thorpe. The manoeuvres continued there. A more impressive ceremonial occasion was at Cambridge on 16th July, when thirty thousand members of the British Legion from ten counties, including two thousand women, paraded at an Eastern Counties rally on Jesus Green, with twenty thousand more as spectators. The town had never before seen a parade of such a size. The Defence Minister, Admiral of the Fleet Lord Chatfield, made a speech and the vast crowd sang "Land of Hope and Glory".

Before the Territorial recruitment campaign had reached its targets, a new call was made. In July it was announced that ex-Servicemen between forty-five and fifty-five were urgently required to volunteer for a Home Defence Corps which would undertake armed guard duties; but the organisation of these Local Defence Volunteers (subsequently renamed the Home Guard) was not properly under way as the year ended.

In February the Defence Chiefs had recommended the setting up of a Ministry of Supply to co-ordinate orders to industry for every kind of equipment, but the Cabinet did not accept this recommendation until the end of April, the new ministry was barely functioning when war began and the flow of tanks and guns — and Service clothing — began slowly. The sort of thing that resulted is indicated by a report of a Suffolk Territorial Association meeting in July: "The Secretary reported that clothing for new recruits was arriving at a fairly satisfactory rate, except for great-coats. The 5th Suffolks when they went to camp shortly would be provided with great-coats borrowed from the 55th Anti-Tank Regiment". Some engineering factories in East Anglia, such as the firm of Richard Garrett of Leiston, worked a great deal of overtime on armaments, but Mr Richard Stokes, the M.P. for Ipswich, complained in April that his constituency "had no armament contracts worthy of the name for engineering work".

Civil defence had become a matter of serious public concern in 1937, when Parliament had passed an Air Raids Precautions Act. Many plans existed on paper, but not a great deal of action had resulted. The Munich crisis of September 1938 brought matters to a head. The government's basic thinking was that poison gas was the greatest danger, then incendiary and high explosive bombs. In 1938 it gave absolute priority to the distribution of thirty-five million gas-masks to the public, the creation of a network of sirens

The 412th (Suffolk Yeomanry) Field Battery with an anti-tank gun on Westleton Common.   *Norwich Mercury* series

to give public warning of danger, and the digging of shelter trenches in parks and open spaces. In November 1938 Sir John Anderson was asked to take charge of civil defence, expenditure was increased dramatically, evacuation plans were worked out, and the recruitment and training of volunteer forces was at last tackled seriously. It was decided to compile a National Register. And in each county new National Service Committees were set us, charged with the responsibility of reshaping and improving the rather scrappy organisation which had struggled into existence.

These committees met for the first time in January 1939 and had before them guidance from Whitehall on how they should proceed. At Cambridge the existing A.R.P. Committee reported: "The training of volunteers has been going forward and now that we have got the instructions from the government we are at once to organise the whole of the necessary measures. It means we have got to divide this town up into small sections . . . " It was divided into twenty-four sections, two in each ward, and in each section permanent accommodation was found for mobile pumps and first-aid posts were designated, each with its equipment, materials and schedule of volunteers. This was the pattern followed generally in all the towns. In March Norwich City Council took over one of the most modern factories in the city, in Sussex Street, as its A.R.P. headquarters, training school and central store and it went ahead to organise a network of 80 air raid wardens' posts.

While a new start was being made, there were tasks begun in 1938 still to be completed in many places. Colchester and Haverhill were two of the towns which had not yet distributed gas-masks, and this became a top priority everywhere. The authorities were extremely worried about the possibility of gas attack if war came. Every possible preparation was made. Every civilian received a black rubber mask with a metal "snout", packed in a small cardboard box which could be carried on a sling over the shoulder. Respirators were supplied to mothers of young babies in which the infants could be completely encased, with a screen through which observation could be maintained. Servicemen were issued with respirators, eye shields and gas capes, and Civil Defence workers with gas-proof suits in which, when fully kitted out, they looked like miniature barrage balloons. Farmers were urged to keep a supply of damp cloths and sacks to hand, which could be drawn across cowsheds, kennels and chicken coops in the event of gas attack. A special paint which changed colour in the presence of poison gas was splashed across the tops of pillar boxes, on the sides of Service vehicles and on special "detector boards". When war began, most people conscientiously carried their gas-masks for at least the first few weeks.

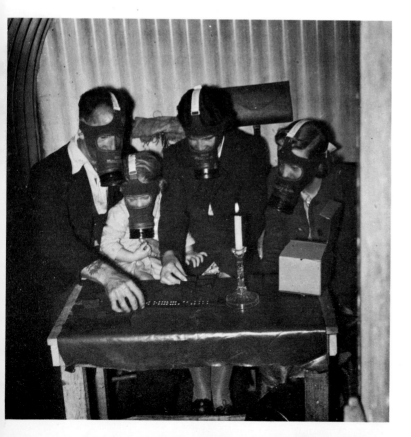

A family wearing gas-masks in their air-raid shelter.

B.B.C. Hulton Picture Library

Many of the shelters which had been dug during 1938 were nothing more than simple trenches; if they were to be made permanent they had to be lined and roofed with concrete. The government now indicated that public shelters should be provided able to accommodate some ten per cent of the population, and that represented a formidable task. In some places, air raid sirens had still to be installed and tested, and during the first few months of the year people were introduced to the long oscillating wail that signalled danger and the sustained monotone that became known as "the all-clear". There was an acute shortage of equipment for Civil Defence. There was only one "gas van" available for Norfolk, parts of Suffolk and the Isle of Ely and it was "totally unable to cope with the immediate training requirements". The War Office was urged to supply a second van, quickly. An initial supply of stretchers had arrived from the Home Office on the scale of 25 for every 100,000 of population.

Some areas were relatively well ahead with their preparations, even before the new National Service Committees were set up. The Norfolk A.R.P. Committee reported in January that it had enrolled over 5,000 wardens and had appointed four full-time A.R.P. Officers, on a temporary basis, at £350 a year salary. They were all ex-Army officers. Voluntary first-aid commandants had also been appointed, and 2,902 volunteers enrolled in the casualty services. Training was well advanced.

East Suffolk already had far more A.R.P. wardens than the establishment proposed by the Home Office: 11,222 had volunteered, whereas the establishment was 3,999 with a reserve of 1,072. Ipswich, on the other hand, had only 481 trained wardens, of 1,122 required, and to try to arouse interest a procession was formed of auxiliary firemen with two pumping appliances, ambulance men with full equipment and decontamination squads in their lorries and this paraded the town. Appeals were now being made for volunteers for a variety of different services — a national service guide was distributed to every house in the country setting out the alternatives — and in the months that followed there were often problems in directing the flow so that appropriate numbers found their way into the A.R.P., the fire service, the police, nursing, first aid, the Women's Land Army, and others. Mildenhall was one of the places where complaints were heard that volunteers were no sooner recruited for one purpose than they were solicited to do something else.

Once they had enrolled, the volunteers were impatient to "do something". Claydon air raid wardens held a "test mobilisation" on 27th January; they tied white handkerchiefs around their arms — they had no other means of identification. On that same day Bury St Edmunds organised a major exercise, with the town and its surroundings blacked out from midnight until 1.45 a.m., the R.A.F. flying overhead and reporting by radio on the effectiveness of the black-out, and over three hundred wardens and special constables in action.

The sirens sounded at midnight and six separate "incidents" were simulated. The R.A.F. plane dropped a parachute flare and this was interpreted as a high explosive bomb on a local school. Elsewhere, a fire escape was used to rescue a man supposed to have been trapped eighty feet up on top of the local brewery. The following day Sandringham staged a mock air raid and the King, the Queen and the two princesses watched from a distance as two hundred members of their staff and estate workers donned gas masks to deal with smoke bombs.

Amid all these activities, the Registrar General wrote to local authorities asking that an organisation be created in each borough so that, if necessary, a national register could be compiled at short notice. Some officials came under considerable strain. The Clerk of the Cosford R.D.C. remarked wrily at mid-January that he had just been designated Registration Officer. He was already A.R.P. Organiser, Evacuation Officer and Food Control Officer and it seemed to him that he was becoming a regular Poo-bah. Cambridge Town Council was told on 2nd February that its officers were badly over-burdened and that routine matters would have to be sacrificed to give an absolute priority to civil defence. A little later in the year the Clerk of the Depwade R.D.C. flourished a bundle of correspondence several inches thick and told his councillors: "I've received all these circulars relating to the question of Civil Defence during the last month. I've had time only to glance through them."

The provision of air raid shelters for the civil population was a subject which caused a certain amount of debate, and this led to delays. To protect people while they were at home, the government offered what became known as the Anderson shelter (named after Sir John Anderson). This was a corrugated sheet-steel construction in the form of an inverted "U", which was intended to be sunk several feet into the earth and then covered with sandbags. It was large enough to hold four bunk beds, and some people managed to squeeze in six. It was offered free to all homes with a suitable garden and where the income did not exceed £250 a year, and it arrived in 21 pieces, including a bag of nuts and bolts, and was to be set up by the householder himself. The first 300 Anderson shelters reached Norwich a fortnight before war began, and Ipswich did not receive any until early in September.

The public shelters, sufficient for ten per cent of the population, were intended for those who were caught in the streets during a raid. In most cases there was a disposition to plan these shelters on a more ambitious scale than the government considered practicable. The Norwich committee at first proposed to cut tunnels into the chalk ridges on which the city stands and also considered the possibility of tunnels into Castle Mound. The cost was estimated at nearly £2¼ millions and the committee was asked to think again. When war began, work was still going on to provide shelters on the Cattle Market for 3,500 people. The trench shelters which had been dug earlier were

Spitfires at Duxford. The first Spitfire was delivered to Duxford in September 1938 and by early 1939 the two squadrons there had been fully re-equipped with this plane. *Imperial War Museum*

being supplemented by sixty shelters above the surface because, as the Town Clerk explained on 8th September, "they are quicker to build than trenches". They had 14-inch brickwork, were claimed to be blast and splinter-proof, and each could hold 50 people. Ipswich drew up plans for an underground car park and shelter in Tower Ramparts for 800 people, a tunnel shelter for 800 in Alexandra Park, and another shelter for 600 in the Wherstead Road area. Withholding sanction, the Home Office hinted that trenches for 200 people on parks and open land should be sufficient. At Saffron Walden there was a "ginger group" which wanted to supplement the official scheme by taking a thousand volunteers with spades to dig shelters into the sides of the hills around the town. At Bungay a popular outcry just stopped the local enthusiasts digging tunnels into Castle Hills, which was scheduled as an ancient monument.

For several months there was uncertainty whether schools would try to remain open during wartime, and decisions about shelters at schools were therefore postponed. It was 31st July before the Norwich Education Committee, for example, authorised the expenditure of £37,000 to provide covered trench shelters for its 10,800 school-children over eight years of age (it was still believed that children under eight would be kept at home). Few state schools had adequate shelters — many had none — when war began. By contrast, the headmaster of Ipswich School announced at its speech day in July: "The school proved themselves so proficient with the spade that trenches were dug in two days sufficient to provide its whole 350 members with cover."

Some rural areas were worried that not enough was being done for their protection. The Home Office offered guidance during March. The main risk, it said, was of bombs dropped at random. This did not justify organised and equipped parties in every village. Each rural parish should depend upon (1) a police constable with protective clothing; (2) two or three volunteer "special constables" with protective clothing; (3) air raid wardens—three for each 500 of population—with some protective clothing and a first-aid box; (4) a first aid post; (5) voluntary help from the men of the village; and (6) "the trained sense of the village".

Complaints continued to be heard that not enough was being done. At Stowmarket in March the Medical Officer of Health resigned because he considered the Ministry of Health's ideas for air raid protection of Stowmarket to be "inadequate, unimaginative and some of them almost frivolous". He had indented for things he needed for training and after three months he had received nothing. The local carpenter had made him a set of splints, but he had failed to get his hands on any of the fifty stretchers which he understood were being held in store at Wickham Market. An ambulance unit at Diss related that it had dealt with a real accident, in which a cyclist fractured a leg, with three pieces of string, a piece of wood, two handkerchiefs, a linen tablecloth and a wooden shutter used as a stretcher.

Sandbags to protect the police station at Felixstowe.   *East Anglian Daily Times*

Some people had more specific complaints. The Labour Party in East Suffolk objected to the fact that no-one was accepted as an air raid warden in that county unless he was first sworn in as a special constable. Questions were asked in parliament, but the rule stayed. Yarmouth was upset by a recruiting film called "The Warning", for which the Home Office was responsible. In many towns in East Anglia its showing was accompanied by a tableaux and parades and civic ceremonies. When it was screened in Yarmouth there was consternation. It depicted an air raid, the film showed what was plainly the coastline near Yarmouth, and the commentator announced that the enemy bombers were dropping bombs on Yarmouth. This was all very well *in* Great Yarmouth, where it was intended to stimulate recruiting; but the film was also being shown in cities in the Midlands from which the seaside resort hoped to be drawing thousands of holiday-makers over the following three months. The film, it was contended, negated the effects of £4,000 Council expenditure on promotion of the resort.

During April the government appointed Sir Will Spens, Master of Corpus Christi College, as Regional Commissioner for Civil Defence. It called upon everyone involved to see that all national service organisation was complete by 1st July. That was demanding too much, it seemed. Ipswich said plainly that it could not comply — they still needed to recruit 420 more wardens, 125 more rescue workers, 103 more auxiliary firemen, 145 more special constables and 99 more for the medical services to reach establishments. At Cambridge the wardens met on 6th July, under their Chief Warden, Lord Rothschild, and passed a resolution viewing "the condition of A.R.P. services in this borough with the gravest concern." In Norwich they were still calling in June for 800 more air raid wardens, 150 first-aid workers and ambulance drivers, one hundred for rescue and decontamination squads, and 550 auxiliary firemen. There were some, however, who preened themselves on their success. The chairman of Felixstowe A.R.P. Committee thought they could *almost* say that they were the first town in the country to be *practically* ready (the italics are the author's). They had even got the details worked out, what each person was to do, with the hours of duty, for the first seven days of war, he said.

The passage of events, the growing certainty that war was about to begin, redeemed the situation everywhere. Complaints and frustrations disappeared as the various services became involved in regular training sessions and frequent rehearsals of an emergency. Several thousand civil defence workers took part in a series of mock air raids during the night of 15th-16th April. Wailing sirens warned towns and villages as R.A.F. planes flew overhead. Thunder flash fireworks represented bombs, flares represented major fires, smoke clouds represented gas bombs. There were eleven simulated "incidents" in Lowestoft, where six hundred wardens and three hundred special constables were on duty in the streets. Three hundred more turned out at Beccles to deal

Bury St Edmunds Observer Corps at practice with their gas-masks during May.

East Anglian Daily Times

with eight "incidents" there. Bungay staged an "incident" in the area of each warden's post and in every village. Halesworth had eight "incidents". When Aldeburgh held its big exercise in May, it spiced the affair by imagining Barclays Bank to have been bombed and "the securities were in danger of looting". "The public had been requested to keep indoors," the press reported, "but the temptation was too great and at most points where the incidents were staged there were large crowds of interested onlookers". When Leiston A.R.P. Committee planned its mock raid it urged its residents not to be unduly alarmed by the explosion of fireworks and announced: "Parts of the town where any people suffering from nerves live will be avoided and the committee would like to know of any reasons why there should not be any incident staged outside any particular house".

Cambridgeshire and Norwich staged large-scale Civil Defence exercises in July. At the control centre in the Guildhall in Cambridge, the Regional Commissioner, the Chief Constable and the heads of the various services received and despatched messages on eighteen telephones and plotted events on a large-scale map of the county. Outside in the darkened streets special constables rushed round placing red hurricane lamps and smoke candles to indicate "incidents". White hurricane lamps represented high explosive bombs. Volunteers lay down on pavements with labels tied to them showing the injuries they had sustained. One lady, it was recounted afterwards, was not found and waited for several hours before making her way to a 'phone to ask for guidance. In early August there was a second, similar exercise, but this time there was special emphasis on testing the links with outlying villages.

Cambridge was the centre of activity in East Anglia for the proposed war-time hospital service. All local authorities were represented at a conference in the town in April which heard the plan drawn up by the Ministry of Health. Two hundred and fifty of the 315 beds in Addenbrooke's Hospital would be cleared immediately on the outbreak of war. The Public Assistance Committee was asked to reorganise its Cambridge County Infirmary to provide 248 beds for some of the first casualties from London; a new operating theatre was to be installed there. Addenbrooke's was asked, later, to staff and supervise an ancillary hospital of one hundred beds which it was proposed to establish in the Examination Hall of the University.

No feat of organisation involving the whole population of Britain has ever equalled the desperate rush during 1939 to get ready for war. Mistakes were made, plans went adrift, delays occurred, but in less than twelve months every national resource of skill and energy was effectively mobilised and re-directed to defensive purposes. It was a very remarkable achievement.

The 27th Field Regiment R.A. about to leave Colchester for exercises in Kent during August.
East Anglian Daily Times

CHAPTER TEN

Hail, Strangers!

THE problems of evacuating civilians from London and other big cities in the event of war had been studied during 1938 by a committee under Sir John Anderson and an outline plan was ready. Early in January the Minister of Health, Mr Walter Elliot, broadcast an appeal to householders to help with a survey of available accommodation in the countryside, which the government wished to complete by the end of February. Because of its proximity to London, which had by far the greatest concentration of population in the country, the message particularly concerned the people of East Anglia. Many of them felt, however, that their region was not a suitable one for evacuees.

Before the survey of accommodation was even begun, Whitehall had made some provisional estimates and these were circulated. The most provocative feature was the apparently arbitrary choice of some areas as being suitable for the reception of evacuees, while others were designated neutral and excluded. The *East Anglian Daily Times* on 12th January commented:

"Whereas the towns and urban districts of both Essex and Norfolk are scheduled either for evacuation or as neutral areas, those of East and West Suffolk are classified as suitable for the reception of refugees. In view of past experience and known possibilities the arbitrary division of East Anglia along these lines is neither explicable nor defensible. There is neither rhyme nor reason in the belief apparently held by the Home Office that, of the entire coastal area from the Thames to the Wash, Suffolk is the least exposed to attack from the air. Everything, in fact, points in the other direction. During the Great War both Ipswich and Felixstowe suffered frequently from the attentions of enemy air raiders, while Norwich enjoyed comparative immunity. Yet Norwich, and not Ipswich, is now listed as a 'neutral' area. Again, while the borough of Harwich is considered to be a danger zone, the adjoining Felixstowe urban district and the densely populated county borough of Ipswich — only two minutes away as the bomber flies — are regarded as so safe as to be suitable for the reception of refugees. In no less a degree the same paradox applies to the position of Lowestoft and Yarmouth. Only ten miles (by air) separates them; yet one is officially 'safe' and the other dangerous."

A special edge was given to the controversy because only a few months before Mr Richard Stokes, the Labour M.P. for Ipswich and a prominent local industrialist, had offered to manufacture shells for the government in his Ipswich factory on a no profit-no loss basis and his offer had been rejected principally because Ipswich was too vulnerable to attack for siting a munitions factory. Ipswich sent its Town Clerk to Whitehall to try to change their thinking there, and meanwhile delayed the accommodation survey for which the government had asked. The eventual upshot was that it was agreed that Ipswich had some degree of vulnerability, but that evacuation plans were not determined by relative safety of particular areas, but were designed to spread population as much as possible. Preparations to receive evacuees must therefore proceed.

Other areas produced sound reasons why *they* should not be expected to receive evacuees. Mr P. C. Loftus, the M.P. for Lowestoft, remarked at the annual dinner of his constituency Conservative Association: "It does seem curious that Yarmouth, which was never attacked in the last war, and has never been a naval base, should not have to receive any of the children, while Lowestoft, which was bombarded from both sea and air during the war and is a naval base, is scheduled to receive eight thousand."

Newmarket A.R.P. Committee did not want evacuees "in view of the numerous aerodromes and ammunition dumps in the vicinity". Haverhill Urban District Council suggested to the ministry that it should not have any because it was surrounded by four aerodromes. Whitehall replied to all such representations in the same terms as it had done to Ipswich: safety under conditions of modern warfare was relative only and dispersal in areas which might to some extent be vulnerable was better than congestion in large cities. Individual voices continued to protest.

Despite these initial apprehensions, however, councils proceeded to appoint an official to organise the surveys of accommodation. Usually it was their Education Officer, who now took the additional title of Evacuation Officer or Billeting Officer. Callers visited every house to collect the information and to explain that payment would be made by the government at the rate of 10s. 6d. a week where one child was taken and 8s. 6d. for each child where more than one was taken.

The surveys were completed expeditiously. Bury St Edmunds reported its local survey of accommodation complete by early April and Cambridgeshire County Council soon afterwards. A conference of representatives of all local authorities in the eastern counties was called at Cambridge on 28th April and the Parliamentary Secretary to the Ministry of Health, Mr Robert Bernays, M.P., announced to them that their response to the government's appeals for provision of accommodation was better than that of any other region in the country.

Children from London boarding one of the buses which distributed them around the Norfolk countryside.

Norwich Mercury series

The government produced window cards which could be displayed by all homes which had agreed to accept evacuees. In one or two areas these were not distributed. In the Cosford council area in Suffolk, Sir William Brunyate explained that ill feeling might be aroused if some houses displayed cards and others did not. Some people were too old to accept evacuees, he said, while in other cases offers of accommodation had been made but not accepted.

In exchanges between the councils and Whitehall quotas were agreed for each area. The borough of Cambridge expected to receive 16,000 evacuees: 8,000 unaccompanied schoolchildren and 8,000 "others". The general idea was that they would be placed in about eight thousand different homes, and that left a good deal of available accommodation in reserve. The Chesterton rural district expected to receive 10,000; the South Cambridgeshire villages a further six thousand; the Newmarket rural district 3,600. East Suffolk planned to receive 23,000. There were detailed plans showing where and when the children would arrive and how they would be fed and dispersed to their new homes. At Ipswich railway station 15,755 were to be received over a period of three days, at Saxmundham six thousand would detrain and then be distributed to Saxmundham, Aldeburgh and Leiston and to dozens of small villages. In West Suffolk 12,000 were expected by train at Bury St Edmunds and 3,000 at Brandon.

With the broad outlines of an evacuation scheme now completed, there was a great deal of detailed preparatory work to be done. The experience of Cambridge illustrates the kind of activity. The Education Officer appointed thirteen ward billeting officers, all of whom were head teachers in the borough and the Women's Voluntary Service named a Senior Voluntary Worker for each ward, who would assist with after-care when the children had moved in. A group of "Friendly Visitors" was appointed for each ward—from twelve to thirty-six in a ward—and they were expected to make regular visits to billets and to report on progress and problems.

One difficulty was immediately evident. Many of those who promised to take in evacuees did not have enough beds and bedding and their offers were conditional on these being supplied. Cambridge Council applied to the Ministry of Health for them, but little had arrived when evacuation began, and it became necessary to take beds from infants' schools and to buy blankets locally wherever they could be found. Everyone who had agreed to accept children was invited during the summer to lectures given by experts on health, nutrition and the possible reactions of children suddenly moved into a strange environment.

The next problem to be faced was that there were only eight thousand school places available and sixteen thousand children to educate. A double shift system had to be devised, and that meant the children would have long hours away from the classrooms. During these periods, it was decided, there would be "recreation under discipline" in local halls, with volunteers taking charge. A further eighty volunteers were next recruited to supervise recreational activities in the evenings and at weekends.

All of these plans were detailed in a memorandum dated 23rd August which was circulated, just in time, to everyone involved in any way in the scheme. It is doubtful whether there were many other authorities which completed such a sophisticated programme and schedule, but efforts proceeded on similar lines everywhere. On 24th August school-teachers were recalled from their holidays to report for duty. On Saturday, 26th August, schools throughout the length and breadth of the densely-packed East End of London opened their doors and thousands of children turned up, their gas-masks strung around their necks in cardboard boxes, to be told what was going to be done with them. On the Monday there was a partial rehearsal of evacuation, inasmuch as the children were asked to come to school with a change of clothing in a case and with labels giving names and addresses. Meanwhile, in the reception areas reception teams put the final touches to their plans.

Evacuation began on Friday, 1st September. According to the press reports which appeared at the time, it went off like clockwork. A school-teacher who travelled on one of the first trains to Ipswich reported on arrival: "The children have behaved like angels. All the way down they have been singing,

167

waving and keeping us all cheerful." At Bury St. Edmunds the evacuees were received in "a holiday mood". But a reporter who watched the first parties of the 20,000 who came to Thorpe station at Norwich over a period of four days was perhaps more sensitive to mood: "The children did sing popular choruses occasionally, but on the whole they were quiet and quietness from children in bulk is surely rather a sign of unhappiness. There were hardly any tears but one sensed tiredness and a sort of suppressed sadness . . . It was pathetic later on when families of several children had to be split up among several houses."

At each railway station an official reception officer established the name of the school, what sort of school it was, and how many boys, girls and adults had arrived. Parties were then usually directed to buses which took them to dispersal centres in nearby schools. Scouts and Guides, as well as school-teachers and W.V.S. workers, helped with these movements. At strategic points, the children were paraded through specially-constructed temporary W.Cs, handed emergency rations for forty-eight hours in a carrier bag (one can of beef, milk, two four-ounce blocks of chocolate and one pound of biscuits each), and given a quick medical inspection. Heads and tongues were inspected. Those with sore throats were made to gargle. At Cambridge one child was found to have scarlet fever and was taken to hospital.

Some of the "Barnado boy" evacuees at Euston Hall, complete with gas-masks.
East Anglian Daily Times

Some parties travelled on steamers which brought them from the Thames. Many thousands of evacuees disembarked at Claremont Pier in Lowestoft, at the Fish Wharf in Great Yarmouth, and at Felixstowe. They spent most of a day on the water, for most of them it was their first sea voyage, and some had never *seen* the sea before. But there seems to have been no sea-sickness and when the steamers berthed their rails were lined by cheering, waving children.

On the first day the whole operation went quite smoothly. The first party of about one thousand arriving at Norwich were settled into villages during the afternoon. Colchester moved two train-loads to their new homes by early afternoon. On the second day, Saturday, things began to go seriously wrong. Reception officers found that the parties arriving were quite different from those they were expecting. What had happened was that many of the East Londoners for whom evacuation had been planned simply opted out. Very few unaccompanied school-children arrived on the Saturday. Later it was established that fewer than half the expected number of school-children and only about a third of expectant mothers with young children had turned up. Some made their own alternative evacuation plans, but most simply stayed at home.

As trains discharged only pregnant women, mothers and young babies, with some older children in tow, reception arrangements had to be quickly adapted and sometimes they faltered.

"The organisation at the station had been more difficult, confused as it was by the arrival of a great number of eager volunteers who carried luggage hither and thither and led parties off with no clear directions. Owing to the kindly zeal of porters at exchange stations, the mothers' often ill-labelled luggage was piled into vans with the result that in a number of cases it took several weeks to recover it for the owners . . ."[1]

That was at Cambridge, where an additional, unforeseen, problem was that many of the mothers were not English and quite a few of them did not speak English—or, at least, did not appear to understand it in the special circumstances at that time. One observer noted among the arrivals one or more of Austrian, French, German, Greek, Hungarian, Irish, Italian, Polish, Rumanian, Russian, Siamese and Turkish nationality, plus a Yiddish-speaking Jew. A refugee German scientist who spoke Greek was found living in Cambridge and he took charge of a group of nearly sixty Greek evacuees and supervised their settlement in a local youth hostel. The billeting officers found it much more difficult to get mothers with young babies accepted into homes, even where offers had been made earlier in the year, and eventually five hundred mothers and children were found accommodation in five different colleges and halls.

1. *The Cambridge Evacuation Survey*, edited by Susan Isaacs, Methuen, 1941.

Much the same thing was happening throughout the region:

"I lived in Chatteris and I was sixteen when war broke out. On a Saturday night the evacuees came from the East End of London. At nine o'clock at night my aunt was brought a woman with a nine-months-old baby and two young boys around seven and five years old. The billeting officer said he could not get them in anywhere. So he brought a large mattress to place on the bedroom floor to make extra sleeping space. They had been going since early morning, with their few rations and their gasmasks. It must have been awful for them to have to go into strange people's houses as they had to do. The next morning we all grouped round the wireless set and heard Chamberlain say 'We are at war with Germany' and this woman from Bethnal Green said 'Oh, my Gawd . . .' Chatteris was full of these strange people. My grandparents had been taken a woman and six-months-old baby. A neighbour of theirs had two Czechoslovakian boys, wearing odd-looking grey suits more like plus-fours. Mum had a Polish lady. The schoolmasters were walking along the High Street in homburg hats and with umbrellas—they were Jewish gentlemen." [2]

That same day, at Cambridge, the Evacuation Officer in the Guildhall was inundated with complaints. For many it had been a dreadful night.

"It was a pitiful sight in the school. We were packed with women at the fag end of their endurance, anxious, afraid of the unknown. But a cup of tea worked wonders. There was no hysteria, they were sensible. Their morale, even with babies crying in their arms, and toddlers at their feet, was excellent. On the other hand, other mothers were on that same night trying to return to London, demanding return fares under the impression that this was their due." [3]

On the Sunday another unexpected difficulty arose:

"Everyone was doing some rebilleting: local head teachers, London head teachers, voluntary workers, school helpers, and mothers and children themselves, whilst householders would exchange children amicably without notifying any in authority. Tracing people was a time-consuming job and full of minor irritations to all concerned . . . There was a very real possibility at first of losing track of a child." [4]

For some weeks afterwards, in fact, evacuees were being moved from their initial billets into other accommodation, and this often caused irritation or anger. At Cambridge many had been put into university lodgings, in the belief that there would be many fewer undergraduates at the university in the new term; in the event, far more than usual came up and between five and six hundred mothers and children had to be hurriedly moved on. There were

2. Mrs K. R. Taylor, as before.
3. *The Cambridge Evacuation Survey*, as before.
4. *The Cambridge Evacuation Survey*, as before.

some cases where whole schools had to be relocated. Parmiter's school from Bethnal Green, for example, was at first sent to Aylsham, in Norfolk, where there was no secondary school with which they could establish a working arrangment, so they had later to be transferred to North Walsham. In many such cases foster-parents who had accepted children and coped with initial problems were incensed when the children were taken away from them. Their viewpoint was presented by a South Cambridgeshire councillor when there was a proposal to move evacuees from the village of Ickleton to nearby Sawston:

"Thirty children arrived in Ickleton and the nurse who was put in charge of them was horror-stricken. They were dirty, filthy, badly clothed and badly cared for. It was a very difficult question to know what to do with such verminous children. They were put into cottages which were clean, bright and healthy and the cottage people have changed them. They are now clean and tidy, their manners have improved. Peace reigns for the moment. But if they are going to be taken to Sawston, there won't be any more evacuees taken in our village."

The peaceful invasion. Child evacuees, with teachers, arriving in Cambridge on the eve of the outbreak of war. *Cambridge Evening News*

171

That statement summarises something of the ordeal of those at the receiving end before things settled down. It needs to be balanced against the experience of some of the evacuees for whom things did not go smoothly:

"We started from school in Dagenham on Friday morning, while it was still dark. We steamed down the Thames and we landed at Yarmouth and they took us to a school there. They were not well prepared—there were no blankets or bedding. People came and peered at us through the railings and then they lent us blankets. We had no hot food; they brought in trays of rolls and bread, sausages and apples. It wasn't very clean lying on the school floor and there was only cold water for washing, and straight away impetigo started to spread.

On Saturday they still didn't know what they were going to do with us. Local school-teachers came in to help, but there was only cold food again.

On Sunday nothing; we were just a nuisance. During the night the sirens went. The children sat bolt upright and began getting their gas-masks out.

On Monday morning we lined the children up, stood there for a time, nothing happened, disbanded them again. Eventually some buses arrived and we started a northward trail through the coastal villages of Norfolk. In each village we stopped and some of the children and staff were accepted. I remember that in one school where we lined up in rows in the sunshine there was an over-powering smell of new asphalt on the playground. We were the last party and we got to West Runton and asked if they had any accommodation for us. They said they hadn't—they'd already taken people from Grays. The owner of a little olde-worlde café came out and asked if we had had a hot drink that day. We hadn't, and she invited us to have cups of tea. We sat in the garden while efforts were made to try to accommodate us. I sat there singing camp fire songs with the children, their numbers gradually decreasing, until it was quite dark.

Next morning we re-assembled at the café and tried to sort out where all the children had gone—to make lists. I was twenty-one and to me it was all a great adventure. In the end, we were very happy there; I could have stayed in West Runton for ever."[5]

In October officials were still trying, in a state of some desperation, to compile card indexes of the evacuees in their areas. The Chief Billeting Officer of the Hartismere Rural District Council confessed to a meeting in Eye that matters were chaotic, adding: "For some unknown reason, three buses I sent off from Lowestoft with evacuees have not yet arrived, and that was three weeks ago."

5. Mrs Thelma Wolfe, of Woodford, in an interview with the author, 1980.

Once everyone had settled down, the main complaints concerned cleanliness and health. Bed-wetting as a problem became part of the folk-lore of the time, but investigators at Cambridge did not rate it highly important. Mackintosh sheets were not available to foster-parents during the first few weeks and by the time they came through the problem seems to have been cured with most children. At Ipswich the Acting Medical Officer of Health reported to his Education Committee that he had been "astonished to find a large amount of vermin among evacuated children". Ipswich, he remarked, had got rid of vermin, impetigo and ringworm among its own children fifteen years before. At Bury St Edmunds the County Education Officer reported; "A great deal of distress has been caused by the fact that London children in many cases came down suffering from dirty heads, impetigo and, in a few isolated cases, infectious diseases." The position was aggravated when dirty children infected clean children. Nurses were sent to East Anglia by the London County Council to help the local medical resources.

Another major problem was that a high proportion of the children were facing the winter in rural surroundings without suitable clothing, particularly footwear. Communication with the parents was not easy, nor calculated to produce much result, and the question was: who was to assume responsibility for the expense of re-kitting? Even after the W.V.S., in most centres, had organised depots at which to receive gifts of clothing and then to distribute it, it was a continuing problem. The cost of shoe repairs and of additional garments for nightwear or as "Sunday best" was often beyond the capacity of parents and foster-parents.

The clash of two cultures produced interesting consequences. The London women greatly missed their familiar street markets where they could buy food each day, and this accentuated problems which would have been bound to arise in any case with two women sharing a kitchen.

There was a patronising tone to many of the anecdotes which circulated at the time, though they were usually well-intentioned. The *East Anglian Daily Times* related, for example:

"London's evacuees, especially the children, are having the time of their lives 'somewhere in the country'. They are having not only fresh air but some of them are enjoying fresh vegetables and real butter for the first time. At the same time, the folks who are billeting the children are enjoying original Cockney humour at first hand . . . At eight o'clock one night a youngster was asked if he did not think it was time he went to bed. 'Wot, in daylight'?' he retorted. 'Well, what time do you usually go to bed?' enquired his host. 'I allus wait till the old man comes home from the boozer'."

173

The authorities issued this poster when large numbers of the mothers and children began to drift back to their homes.

Imperial War Museum

TAKE THEM BACK!
TAKE THEM BACK!
TAKE THEM BACK!..

DON'T *do it,* *mother—*

LEAVE THE CHILDREN WHERE THEY ARE

ISSUED BY THE MINISTRY OF HEALTH

Another story concerned a young mother who threatened to return to London because she had to wash her two babies in "dirty water", referring to the rain-water which was collected in a tub outside her new home. She was assured that this was a great luxury, sought after by beauty queens and film stars, and she then settled down happily!

It was true that very many of the evacuees quickly returned to their own homes in London, particularly the women. A newspaper report on 18th September said: "Inquiries in the Melford district on Saturday indicated that on average at least 25 per cent of the evacuees received a fortnight ago had returned to their homes. In some parishes, the percentage was put as high as fifty. Some left within twenty-four hours of their reception. Cars arrived and without any explanation to the householders concerned they departed . . . "

It proved even more difficult to monitor the movement of evacuees back to London than it had been to establish a reliable register of their whereabouts when they first arrived. Many of the statistics quoted did not match up, but there was no doubt that there was a tidal movement southward.

Bury St Edmunds Education Committee was told on 13th October that of 942 children, mothers, teachers and helpers received in September, only 526 remained (55.8 per cent). Blyth R.D.C. was told on 6th November that a half of the 1,500 received in its rural district had departed. Ipswich Town Council received a report on 9th November that of 4,810 unaccompanied children received 3,270 (68 per cent) remained, and of 3,315 mothers and children 2,576 remained (77.7 per cent). The East Suffolk Education Committee heard on 28th November that only 8,633 of 13,500 elementary schoolchildren received in September were still in the county (63.95 per cent).

By the end of 1939, over eighty per cent of mothers evacuated with young children were generally believed to be back in London, and about forty per cent of the unaccompanied schoolchildren.

The Cambridge Evacuation Survey workers who investigated the motives of those who returned concluded that they were many and complex, but identified as dominant: 1, the feeling of family unity and an intense resistance to its being broken; 2, complaints about foster homes and foster parents; and 3, the financial burden which the billeting allowance was insufficient to ease. There is no doubt that husbands missed their families, and that wives were concerned about the welfare of husbands left alone in London. During the first few weekends there were bus trips bringing husbands and fathers to visit their families in East Anglia. There were stories of some fathers cycling from the East End — and one case of two small children hitch-hiking back to London on their own initiative. Some of these visits were not helpful. Foster-parents were heard complaining that several adults would arrive without food, accept hospitality and offer no payment. Alternatively, the visitors would make an impetuous decision to take their wives and children back with them, at a moment's notice. There had been none of the expected air raids on London, and from 27th October parents were required to start paying towards the cost of maintaining the evacuees. It seemed much easier to take a chance in London.

Just before Christmas parents visited their evacuee children in several Norfolk reception areas.

Norwich Mercury series

175

A suitable postcript to the great evacuation of 1939 is provided by the Cambridge Evacuation Survey, whose conclusion is applicable to experience throughout East Anglia:

"The public response to this emergency had been generous and devoted. The planning and preparation for the work had, on the whole, been carefully done . . . A considerable body of practical women had been found who could devote part of their time regularly to aiding and supervising the billeting arrangements. And the bulk of the households who had been willing to receive children had proved themselves sensible and friendly, indeed in many cases astonishingly helpful, to the strangers . . . Yet the most casual inquiry, after the first month of evacuation, showed that everybody concerned with billeting—officials, voluntary workers, parents and teachers—was heavily overworked and over-burdened with the acute personal problems of parents and foster parents and children. And there were exceptions, some of them outstanding exceptions, to the general satisfactoriness of the billeting . . . "

Evacuated children gather at Ipswich station to await parents arriving on an "evacuation special" cheap day excursion from London in December 1939.   *B.B.C. Hulton Picture Library*

CHAPTER ELEVEN

From Peace to War

WAR did not come suddenly to East Anglia. The groups gathered around wireless sets in virtually every home on Sunday, 3rd September, heard the Prime Minister pronounce that "this country is at war with Germany" but already, throughout that fevered summer, war-like activity had become very familiar to them. No dramatic action followed Mr Neville Chamberlain's broadcast. People talked together quietly and the realisation came to them that their lives had already been transformed. Month by month, gradually but at an accelerating pace, they had grown used to the patterns of war: the increased air activity, the recruiting rallies and call-ups, the drilling and rehearsals of enemy attack, the mysterious construction work—all were now seen to have significance as part of a grand design.

Earlier in the year many people had been unwilling to understand the significance of events; what Winston Churchill later called "a wave of perverse optimism" swept across the scene. When six French destroyers visited Harwich for a week in May, it was organised as a fête. BON ACCUEIL A NOTRE VILLE read a banner stretched across Church Sreet, there were French flags flying everywhere, and the Mayor was piped aboard and the town provided generous hospitality to the visitors. Not long afterwards, however, three British destroyers arrived and it was announced that a minesweeper flotilla was to be stationed at Harwich for three months, and no-one could interpret these developments as an expression of goodwill.

The atmosphere of war settled on the land during July and August. For the first four hours of Sunday, 9th July, 16,000 square miles of eastern and southern England, covering fifteen counties, were blacked out for a combined R.A.F.-Civil Defence test. Sirens wailed, air raid wardens manned their posts, ambulances moved in streets where the lighting had been dimmed, searchlights played across the sky, and anti-aircraft guns could be seen in position at many points near the coast. A month later another large-scale exercise approximated . much more closely to "the real thing". It continued for three days and nights. An attacking force of five hundred Eastland bombers took part in about seven hundred raids on Westland territory between the Wash and the Thames estuary. Five hundred fighters, plus three hundred planes of various kinds, formed the defence. On the ground street lights were turned off, trains ran into darkened stations with all blinds drawn, traffic lights showed only tiny crosses of light and homes were completely blacked out. Coloured flares were dropped and hurricane lamps placed at various points to signify "incidents" of every kind: red indicated a fire, yellow meant gas (for which smoke bombs were also sometimes used), and green signalled obstruction by debris after a high explosive bomb.

French sailors from visiting destroyers photographed on the Pier at Harwich.

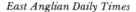

East Anglian Daily Times

In July the first conscripts reported to barracks and began their training.

Apart from these developments, which were well publicised, stories sometimes went into circulation which the authorities showed some reluctance to discuss, as when, early in August, Lowestoft skippers returned to port with descriptions of the way the German *Graf Zeppelin* had been cruising near the East Coast. A short story appeared in the *East Anglian Daily Times:*

"Skipper W. Bridge, of the steam trawler *Witham,* said he had seen it so low over Smith's Knoll, the famous herring ground 22 miles from Lowestoft, that he plainly saw the swastika on its hull. Skipper Nelson Hood, of the smack *Lustre,* also saw it. Skipper Beamish, of the Lowestoft drifter *Peacemaker,* reported that during the night *Graf Zeppelin* had swept the decks of his and other craft with her searchlights."

The *Graf Zeppelin* photographed near Mundesley during the summer.   *David Hill*

A few people also saw it from the coast. There had been an earlier, similar flight in May.

Defence authorities in London knew about them, but they would make no comment. As *Graf Zeppelin* flew parallel with the coast, R.D.F. (radio direction-finding) stations monitored its movements throughout and understood its purpose, which was to listen with special equipment to any British R.D.F. transmissions. They were unsuccessful, Winston Churchill later declared. The R.D.F. screen, which was completed just before the war began, was a top secret. Pioneer development which began at Orfordness in the middle 'thirties was later transferred to Bawdsey Manor, where laboratories were set up in the stables and outbuildings. Plans were completed during 1937 for a chain of R.D.F. stations along the east and south coast, which were to be ready by the end of 1939. In fact, they were completed ahead of this schedule. Those in East Anglia were in isolated positions at Darsham, between Southwold and Aldeburgh; at Stoke Holy Cross, south of Norwich; at West Beckham, south of Sheringham. Winston Churchill, who was a member of the Committee of Imperial Defence on Air Defence Research (despite his exclusion from the government at that time), visited them on 20th June, flying around all day "in a rather disreputable airplane" (as he later reported to the Air Minister), and finding his visits to Bawdsey and Martlesham "profoundly interesting and also encouraging". [1]   By this time, the R.D.F. stations could detect aircraft approaching over the sea at distances up to about sixty miles. The air defence commander was thereafter authorised to intercept any aircraft making unauthorised flights over British territory.

1. Sir Winston Churchill: *The Second World War, Vol. 1, The Gathering Storm,* Cassell, 1948.

If the Lowestoft skippers' stories started tongues wagging, tales brought back to Harwich by those coming from the Continent also stimulated gossip. As early as April these "personal experience" accounts were being related. Travellers described unusual activity in the Hook of Holland port area: warships berthed at the quays, their searchlights turned on any incoming ships, soldiers with fixed bayonets or manning sand-bagged machine-gun emplacements, the River Maas closed to all shipping for twelve hours so that (it was believed) mines could be laid.

On Thursday, 24th August, Parliament, which had adjourned for its summer recess twenty days before, was hurriedly recalled to be told by the Prime Minister: "The country finds itself today in imminent peril of war". An Emergency Powers (Defence) Bill was passed that same day, giving the government unlimited powers to set the war machine in motion. Holiday-makers hurried home. They came flooding through Harwich on Saturday and Sunday from a procession of steamers from the Hook, Flushing and Antwerp. There were many Central European refugees among them, bringing stories of congestion on the European railways. In the reverse direction, many Europeans hastened home from Britain.

The Services were moving even more swiftly and decisively. On the evening of 23rd August the holiday amusements were in full swing in Lowestoft and in the Sparrow's Nest Theatre Elsie and Doris Waters ("Gert and Daisy") had the audience roaring with laughter. Twenty-four hours later the Navy had commandeered everything, the theatre had been renamed H.M.S. *Pembroke*, the White Ensign flew over its roof, the seats were being removed and the building was in business as the war-time headquarters of the Royal Naval Patrol Service. Two days later Southend Pier was taken over by the Navy as headquarters for the Thames and Medway Control and became the assembly point for East Coast convoys, and some time later some other piers along the East Anglian coast had planks removed so that they could not be used for landings. Trawlers were called back to port, requisitioned by the Admiralty and equipped with Asdics and formed into a minesweeper fleet. At Harwich the Admiralty took over the old Great Eastern hotel on the quayside, which had been empty for years. Air reconnaissance of the North Sea began on a regular basis. Reservists were called up. Coastal defences and anti-aircraft units were brought to full readiness. The A.A. Gun Operations Room for the Harwich area was in the Landguard Fort, on the Felixstowe side of the estuary, a strongpoint since the days when a Spanish invasion had been feared.

The 18th East Anglian T.A. Division was deployed along the East Coast to defend it against invasion, and the 5th battalion of the Suffolks was assigned to guard duties at various isolated vital points in the region, as part of the 54th East Anglian Division. Back at the regimental depots, meanwhile, a stream of conscripts was being trained. Often they appeared on their first parades wearing suits and trilby hats, while awaiting the issue of uniforms. They were paid two shillings a day, but married men had to remit half of this to their wives.

Whitehall sent instructions to every kind of authority in the regions to put themselves on a war footing. A.R.P. Committees and Controllers assumed their full powers from 31st August. The evacuation of school-children and mothers was in full swing. Hospitals were cleared for emergency use. Within a couple of days the Norfolk and Norwich Hospital cleared 284 beds for emergency use (later this "reserve" was reduced to 150 beds). During the evening of the 31st fifty of the patients in the West Suffolk Hospital at Bury St Edmunds were sent home and their places were taken by serious cases transferred from Addenbrooke's Hospital at Cambridge, which then took in similar cases moved out of hospitals in London. The government feared that there might be heavy casualties in air raids on the capital. The Cambridge Infirmary was also used for patients from London:

"On the first of September the Emergency Medical Service, headed by John Ryle, Regius Professor of Physick at the University, appointed me surgeon-in-charge at the Cambridge Infirmary, Mill Road, which was then raised to the status of County Hospital . . . At once the Hospital was flooded with cases evacuated by motor ambulance convoys from infirmaries in North London. Most of them were old and enfeebled; some arrived moribund; a few died on the way, and others had gangrene of the extremities requiring amputation." [2]

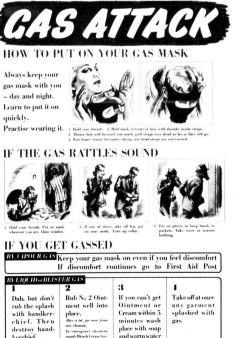

Protection against poison gas. During 1939 urgent action was taken to distribute gas-masks to the civilian population and posters regarding their use were displayed.

Imperial War Museum

181

All over the region hospitals and other institutions were similarly cleared and refilled from London. Sitting cases were all sent to their homes; the seriously ill often had to be moved.

There was frantic last-minute effort to tie up loose ends and to complete tasks which were in hand. Many public shelters remained to be constructed — Lowestoft Education Committee did not formally accept a tender for construction of trench shelters at its schools until 25th August. It was late in November before Norwich had completed enough school shelters to permit any significant number of its over-eight pupils to return to their classrooms. Newmarket called an emergency meeting on 30th August to appoint a Food Control Committee and to confirm the appointments of a Chief Billeting Officer and a Fuel Overseer. Police stations, hospitals and other public buildings were hastily surrounded by sandbags; volunteers were called for in advertisements and by street broadcasts and thousands came forward to fill sandbags in all the larger towns. The Suffolk Territorial Army Association advertised in the local press: "Personnel required immediately for Ipswich Light Anti-Aircraft battery" — just as though they were looking for a clerk or a cook-general. A combined Army, Navy and R.A.F. recruiting centre was opened in the Assembly Rooms at the Agricultural Hall in Norwich on 5th September, and immediately a queue formed up. Workmen moved into King's College chapel in Cambridge and delicately, piece by piece, removed the priceless medieval stained glass from the Great East Window. Street lighting was extinguished and cars forbidden to use headlights.

Headlamp masks were an essential black-out precaution for every car.
East Anglian Daily Times

Every household was advised to erect an air raid shelter in the garden. *Norwich Mercury* series

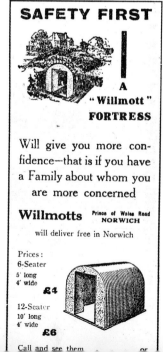

Some individuals made their own last-minute preparations, as a report in the *East Anglian Daily Times* on 31st August indicated:

"The Food Officer for the Eastern Area calls our attention to the fact that there is at present a certain amount of buying of abnormal supplies of essential foodstuffs by a section of the public . . . It is pointed out that the nation's food resources today are probably greater than at any time, and this fact, together with the arrangements made to meet emergencies, render the selfish action of a comparatively small number of people as unnecessary as it is undesirable."

That this was not directed specifically against East Anglians was made clear within hours, when an Order was made under Defence Regulations making it illegal to acquire or purchase more food than was required for one week.

At 11 a.m. on 3rd September the war began—officially. Less than an hour later a Blenheim bomber of No 139 Squadron, piloted by Flying Officer A. McPherson, took off from Wyton, in Huntingdonshire, and flew to Wilhelmshaven. Earlier reconnaissance had shown that units of the German fleet were in harbour there; the question now was: had they moved? Flying Officer McPherson returned with the information that the pocket battleship *Admiral von Scheer* and the heavy cruiser *Prinz Eugen* were at Kiel. A raid was planned forthwith. Blenheims of No 139 Squadron at Wyton and of Nos 107 and 110 Squadrons at Wattisham took part. The planes from Wyton failed to find their way to the target. The Wattisham squadrons, led by Flight Lieutenant K. C. Doran, made their attacks in shallow dives from 500 feet. Several 500 lb bombs hit the *Scheer*, but they were set with an eleven seconds delay fuse and they simply bounced off her armoured decks. The Germans, though they had been surprised, quickly brought their ship and shore-based anti-aircraft guns into action and shot down five of the fifteen British planes. One crashed into the cruiser *Emden* and killed and injured some of its crew, and that was the only real damage inflicted on the German vessels. It was a discouraging start. A decision was made that, in future, attacks would only be launched against ships at sea. Thereafter, for several weeks, the main R.A.F. activity was the dropping of propaganda leaflets over Germany.

There were fifteen active military airfields in East Anglia at this time and four others under construction. Work was speeded up. All landing strips in the past had been grass; now new concrete runways began to be laid. There were five satellite landing grounds, one of them just beside the race-course at Newmarket. Bomber crews were put through intensive training courses at Stradishall and elsewhere, Spitfires and Hurricanes flew regularly from Martlesham, Watton and Duxford, Coastal Command Ansons maintained convoy protection flights from Bircham Newton over coastal waters.

During the early days of September the air raid sirens wailed occasionally in different parts of East Anglia, but no-one sighted an enemy plane. Radar stations, fighter bases and ground units gained experience in co-ordinating their efforts—and sometimes learned the lessons the hard way. On 4th September the Ministry of Information announced: "The warnings given early this morning were due to the passage of unidentified aircraft over the Eastern Counties and Midlands. Fighter aircraft went up and immediately a satisfactory identification of the aircraft was established, the All Clear signal was given". Two days later German planes attempted a reconnaissance off the East Coast, but turned tail before reaching the coast when British fighters went after them. The British machines failed to make contact with the raiders, but when returning were themselves mistaken for the enemy and met with fire from coastal batteries.

A family entering an Anderson shelter, gas-mask boxes in hand, following an air raid warning siren.
                                                                    B.B.C. Hulton Picture Library

Those who were still civilians were preoccupied with completion of their air raid shelters, with black-out curtains for their homes and with protection from flying glass by fitting shutters or criss-crossing their windows with lengths of adhesive paper tape. This was a major task in every private home, but for large public buildings it was enormously difficult. At the Norfolk and Norwich Hospital there were 1,600 windows to black out. Cinemas and all other places of amusement closed down completely for ten days. When the government decided that those in neutral and reception areas could re-open, most cinemas in the region fixed their closing time at 9.30 p.m. but in the eastern area, considered to be more vulnerable, all places of entertainment closed at 7 p.m. As far as sport was concerned, the government ruled that friendly local games could be played, subject to police approval, provided they did not gather big crowds. Ipswich F.C. directors met on the 13th September and decided to suspend the club's activities indefinitely. It was the first League club to make such a decision and some of its supporters, particularly those who had bought season tickets (and were not offered their money back), were indignant. The Club explained that any other decision would involve it in substantial losses. On 16th September Norwich City and Southend United played a friendly game at Southend and after that football began to be played again, fairly regularly, in most of the region.

Bus and train services were severely curtailed, particularly in rural areas. The last trolley buses left Ipswich Cornhill at 7.30 p.m., but there was soon agitation to keep them running until 10 p.m. People got used to the blackout. Kerbs, walls and the corners of buildings were painted white and soon it was only on completely moonless nights that people hesitated to go out. The Mayor of Ipswich made a public appeal; the Council, he said, was concerned at the danger occasioned by the number of people using the streets after dark. "At the suggestion of the traders, I ask all tradesmen to close their shops not later than seven o'clock each evening," he said. Rail services were cut by half; cross-country routes, like that between Ipswich and Cambridge, were reduced to skeleton time-tables. Newspapers reduced their size to conserve newsprint. The Post Office announced that there would be only two daily deliveries in future and that head post offices would only be open between 8.30 a.m. and 6.30 p.m. (instead of from 8 a.m. to 7.30 p.m.) Advertisements like this one began to appear in the papers:

"Corders regret that owing to nearly the whole furnishing department staff having been called to National Service, it is impossible to give the usual prompt attention to orders and enquiries . . . Blackout curtains, 54 inches wide, Navy Blue only, 4s. 6d. a yard."

The British Expeditionary Force began to land in France, and it included the 1st battalion of the Suffolk Regiment and the 2nd battalion of the Royal

Norfolks. Their families back home learnt little of their activities during the closing weeks of 1939, but there was nothing dramatic about them. They were mainly engaged in a round of patrolling, digging, wiring—and waiting for a sight of the enemy. It was a bitter, freezing, dismal period.

In Britain enemy aliens were rounded up, put through a screening process, and many of them held for a time in Butlin's Holiday Camp at Clacton, before being dispersed to the Isle of Man or overseas. That, too, was a bitter, freezing, dismal experience. Some people began to listen to Lord Haw Haw broadcasting war propaganda from Hamburg and purporting to tell the British what their own government concealed. Petrol rationing was re-introduced, from 16th September, and a single grade, called "Pool" was retailed at 1s.6d. a gallon. A month later this was increased to 1s. 8d. and by the end of the year it was 1s. 10d. Advertisements began to stress the petrol economy of small vehicles. The East Suffolk County Council made this announcement:

"Owing to the Rationing of Motor Spirit, it is believed that many Residents in East Suffolk are intending to use Horse-Drawn Carriages and the County Council beg to remind such persons that Licences must be taken out for these vehicles. The Licence duty payable each year is: carriage with less than four wheels 15s.; carriage with four wheels drawn by one horse £1. 1s.; carriage with four wheels drawn by two horses £2. 2s.; Hackney carriages 15s."

There were prosecutions for petrol hoarding. A number of eminent landowners and farmers found themselves in court because they had not realised that they required a permit to maintain their customary stores of petrol. Offenders against the black-out regulations also appeared regularly in court, from the very first week of war. In October the Wisbech borough magistrates sent a nineteen-years-old girl to prison for a month for flashing a torch; there was an outcry about this, but the girl had been defiant when approached, and the sentence stood. The maximum penalties for breaking the black-out were two years imprisonment and fines of £500. Among those fined at Norwich for showing a light was the Bishop—the poor man was not directly to blame, but it was the "householder" who had to accept responsibility.

It was difficult for people to decide how seriously to take the air raid warnings, because after the sirens no enemy planes ever appeared.

"The first few months of the war were quiet here. The local policeman, he'd go about with a whistle and if there was anything near . . . We all got annoyed with him, because you were going down the road with a wagon-load, he'd tell you you had to stop under some trees so the enemy aero-plane didn't see you. When we got more used to planes coming over, nobody took any notice, just carried on." [3]

3. Mr J. H. Prettyman, as before

In the towns some people went into garden shelters and put on their gas-masks and failed to hear the all-clear sirens, and stayed there until someone went to look for them. In the countryside there was considerable difference of opinion as to whether one was safer under cover or out-of-doors. In some areas during the first weeks children were led out of school into fields when the sirens sounded.

The government decided that students below the age of twenty might defer their military service and the result was the arrival in Cambridge that term of the largest number of freshmen since 1919. In addition, about two thousand undergraduates from London colleges were granted the use of Cambridge University facilities. Students from St Bartholomew's and London Hospitals used the laboratories of the Medical School; the London School of Economics moved into Peterhouse, with some of its social science students working at Addenbrooke's Hospital; Bedford College went to Newnham; Queen Mary College to Kings.

Other forms of education in East Anglia suffered for many weeks after war began. Cambridge had re-opened all its senior and junior schools by 18th September, but elsewhere the fact that shelters had not been completed meant that children could not be accepted. Colchester managed to get all children over eight back to school by the end of October, and Norwich by the end of November. Ipswich Education Committee was told on 20th November that only 56 per cent of the children in the town were receiving satisfactory education. The evacuees, it was added, were "receiving some sort of education." Schools were either seriously over-crowded or they were working a two-shift system.

Keeping children interested and occupied when they were not in school was a major problem for teachers everywhere. Keeping evacuated mothers and expectant mothers amused was also a problem. The third, associated, problem was to facilitate visiting by parents or husbands from London in such a way that the visits did not unsettle the evacuees. Saffron Walden was a pioneer in solving these problems, and its example was later followed by many other towns. On Saturday, 21st October, the Mayor of Saffron Walden invited over a thousand parents of evacuee children billetted in the town, most of them from Tottenham, to pay a visit. The Londoners came in nine large motor-coaches and a procession of private cars, about five hundred of them in all. In the Town Hall and the Corn Exchange they were introduced to the foster-parents. The Saffron Walden Borough Band played selections and the Tottenham Girls High School Prize Choir sang songs. Tea was served and a good time was had by all—despite the fact that there were speeches, too. The local M.P., Mr R. A. Butler, praised the organisers. Miss Florence Horsbrugh, M.P., who was Parliamentary Secretary to the Ministry of Health, declared it was the best day she had had since evacuation began. Saffron Walden councillors fraternised with the two Tottenham M.P.s, and the Mayor, the

Deputy Mayor and the Director of Education of Tottenham. After this successful beginning, the Mayor of Saffron Walden formed a Town Entertainment Committee to arrange entertainment for the evacuees during the winter.

Within a few weeks, too, several play centres, a nursery school, a schoolboys' football league and a folk dancing group had been started. The W.V.S. was busy collecting clothing for children who were in need of it. Regular monthly meetings were set up in the Town Hall for parents coming down from London to visit.

Before the year was out, most towns and villages had done something of this sort. Cambridge opened three social centres in schools on a Sunday in December and the Mayor and Mayoress met 175 parents from London. In many village halls evacuated mothers met local mothers at regular tea parties. Exchange visits by M.Ps, mayors and officials became a regular routine. In Cambridge undergraduates helped groups which had already been established and "adopted" particular schools. Small groups of evacuated children were invited to colleges for music and play-reading, to make model planes from wood, to discuss stamp collecting, to dance, and to play chess and other games.

Two young soldiers study the King's Proclamation calling up all services at the outbreak of war.
B.B.C. Hulton Picture Library

When war began, many local authorities resolved that their normal administrative procedures would need to be changed, that there would not be time for the usual democratic discussions, and that small emergency committees should be given wide powers. East Suffolk County Council elected a committee of three men — the Earl of Cranbrook, Lord Cranworth and Mr J. W. H. Bird — and delegated to it complete powers to act on its behalf in matters of civil defence, and powers to act in other matters "in the event of the interruption of communications, on the understanding that the committee would only exercise these powers if, in their opinion, it was not reasonably practicable for the County Council to meet." Beccles Town Council used a more cautious formula, appointing a committee of seven "with power to act in all matters except the raising of a loan, the making of a rate, the engagement or dismissal of a permanent official, or any other matter which, in the opinion of a majority of the members of the committee, is of major importance and requires consideration by the whole council". Harwich Council met on 9th September and decided to disband, appointing a three-man committee to deal with everything. A little later, however, dissident councillors created stormy scenes and the council decided to hold quarterly meetings. Beccles Council met quarterly, and at the first such meeting there were protests that "dictators" were having too much of their own way. Eye councillors flatly refused to hand over any authority to an Emergency Committee. After two or three months, during which no air raids or other serious disturbance of normal activity had occurred, councils everywhere went back to their usual monthly meetings and regular meetings of committees; but the chairman of the key committees and their officers continued to carry much greater responsibilities for decision-making than is normally the case.

It is interesting to note that during these same months when the normal democratic processes were suspended and the free flow of information restricted, a good deal of potentially demoralising rumour began to spread. The most serious manifestation was a widespread belief that many of the Civil Defence workers were receiving payment and were "on to a good thing". The chairman of the Depwade R.D.C. said in October: "I have been plagued with telephone calls concerning the salaries, honoraria, etc. paid for work in this emergency. In this district there is not one person doing voluntary A.R.P. work on a paid basis, other than divisional organisers". Similar formal denials had to be issued in a number of places.

The demands from Whitehall did not slacken. During September and October enumerators were recruited and set to work collecting information for a National Register, and identity cards were prepared for every civilian. In October and November ration books were prepared and delivered to every home. This was an immense task; in Norwich between 80 and 100 schoolteachers and volunteers worked for ten days in committee rooms at the City Hall to get it completed.

189

Everyone was required to register with retailers by 23rd November and a first announcement was that bacon and butter would be rationed from mid-December. There was a postponement, however; rationing began on 8th January, 1940, with each person getting twelve ounces of sugar, four ounces of bacon and four ounces of butter, and it was extended to cover meat a week later, with a ration of six ounces per head per day.

Allotment associations were formed in most places, the War Agricultural Executive Committees maintained the closest scrutiny of progress on the farms, but there were some features of food production and distribution which roused criticism. The outstanding example was a disastrous government scheme for the handling of fish landed at East Coast ports. Because heavy and sustained air attack had been expected, it was decided in advance to disperse inland all marketing and distribution arrangements. East Coast catches were to be taken to Norwich for sale. In mid-September the M.P. for Lowestoft, Mr P.C. Loftus, gave the Commons an account of what was happening. He spoke of "complete chaos" and of "an absurd and unworkable scheme". Hitherto, he said, fish landed at 6 a.m. at Lowestoft or Yarmouth had been bought in markets there by the merchants, and the fishermen knew the same day exactly what they were getting for their catch. Now the fish was being carried twenty-five miles to Norwich and in some cases being kept for several days before it was sold. The fish merchants had to follow it to Norwich, wasting petrol, and had to form a long queue and take what fish was offered them. Before, they had bought fresh fish, within an hour of its being caught; now hundreds of tons of good fish were being wasted. "Last week," said Mr Loftus, "there were thirty-two tons of fish landed at Lowestoft, and seventy-eight officials to deal with it." The Minister of Food, Mr W. S. Morrison, found he could not resist these arguments. Within a week the government's marketing scheme was wound up and fish auctions were resumed at the ports on Saturday, 23rd September.

When the next herring voyage was imminent, in October, no official scheme for its control had been completed. Licences for drifters were issued provisionally, so that crews could be signed on, but only a small fleet was able to put to sea. The Colne Oyster Fishery, when the season opened in September, was also a shadow of its usual scale, but tradition was maintained to the extent that there was a ceremony on board a fishing smack, when the Loyal Toast was drunk in gin and small cubes of gingerbread were eaten.

This was one of the early examples of the stiff upper lip, "let's carry on as usual" attitude which was widely taken up. At Norwich the problem was to get St Andrews Hall effectively blacked out. Once that had been done, a programme of events was quickly arranged: four Saturday evening municipal concerts before Christmas and three performances by the Philharmonic Society, as well as Thursday afternoon concerts in the Stuart Hall. The

The Colman House Soldiers' Club in Norwich catered for Civil Defence workers, as well as soldiers.   *Norwich Mercury* series

Norwich Chamber Orchestra also carried on. The Norwich Players — some of them now in uniform — resolved to present four new productions during a season which opened in November 1939 and Mr Nugent Monck encouragingly pointed out to the public that the first performances would take place "during the week of a full moon". The Colchester Repertory Company produced a new play each week, and, when they presented "French without Tears", over three thousand people attended performances in one week. At Ipswich the Chamber Music Society carried on, and held its first war-time event on 18th November — a Beethoven, Brahms and Hugo Wolf recital by the Menges String Quartet. The Ipswich Male Voice Choir followed suit, then the Bury St Edmunds Operatic Society decided to rehearse every Thursday evening at the Angel Hotel for a production of "Trial by Jury", and then the Ipswich Public Hall had its first full-scale concert early in December, when the performers included the pianist Mark Hambourg.

191

Organisation after organisation announced its continued activity, even including golf clubs and other sports associations. From mid-November the football pools were back in business — though there was only a single, unified pool and it was not allowed to post any material to clients, but only to print coupons in the newspapers. At Newmarket, however, there was a major disturbance of routine. Many of the best-known personalities went off to the Services, as did many of the stable-boys, and five hundred acres of land at the various stud farms were ploughed up for food production. But racing was considered to be crucially important to breeding and selling, and the bloodstock industry was a very valuable one. During the early weeks of the war trainers waited anxiously to hear from government and owners what they should do. The government had requisitioned the Old Course and some of the training grounds. Many trainers were performing Civil Defence duties by night and exercising the horses as usual during the mornings. Eventually it was decided that there should be two race meetings on the Summer Course, with six races each day. The Cambridgeshire was run on 18th October, divided into two sections to cope with eighty-one entries. In fact, only fifty-four horses started — twenty-seven in each race. The class one event was won by Gyroscope, ridden by a sixteen-years-old jockey, R. Lacey, owned by Mrs H. Leader and trained by her husband at Newmarket. There was no advance betting on the race and the tote was not operating, so it was a novel experience, unlike anything previously seen in the one hundred years history of the race. It was probably the sheer novelty which drew many people to Newmarket who otherwise would not have gone. There were big crowds on each of the two days of the first meeting and one newspaper, commenting on the number of cars, observed: "Apparently racegoers had saved their petrol coupons for this special occasion". The second Newmarket meeting, again for two days, was at the beginning of November, when the Cesarewitch was won by Cantatrice II, ridden by D. Smith and owned by Sir Alfred Butt. A few days after this, the Jockey Club announced that the flat race calendar would be back to normal in 1940.

But some things would never be quite the same. When it was announced that bloodstock sales would be resumed at Newmarket before the end of the year, the Aga Khan decided to sell most of his stud there. From 1921 the Aga Khan had built up one of the greatest studs in the history of racing, and it had been in Newmarket since 1931. On 5th December, at Tattersalls, he sold nineteen yearlings and fourteen horses in training. They realised a total of just over forty-two thousand guineas, which the experts said was half the amount they would have fetched in normal conditions. It was the most important sale of bloodstock in England for many years, and it attracted world-wide interest, but prices throughout the three days were seriously depressed — on the first day some bids of less than ten guineas were accepted.

So events ticked quietly on "the home front", as they called it. There was a great increase in reading: all library borrowings went up sharply. W. H. Smith and Sons advertised their library service: "You will need books this winter more than ever . . . For as little as 1s. 3d. a month you can borrow a different book each day—twice a day if you like." Boots offered a similar library service. Electricity undertakings advertised "demonstrations of economy cooking". The despatch of parcels to Servicemen became a popular activity, and clubs and social centres were opened for them almost everywhere. The first in Norwich was the Colman House Soldiers' Club, and in Bury St. Edmunds they used one of the most elegant buildings in England, the Athenaeum. The Ministry of Information issued morale-boosting stories in a regular stream.

A few R.A.F. and Luftwaffe pilots "ditched" into the North Sea. Before the year was out several German airmen's bodies had been washed ashore, and buried in East Anglia. The first such funeral—of three Luftwaffe officers—was at Happisburgh on 2nd November. They were accorded military honours: an R.A.F. party fired a last salute, while the bearer party presented arms. Two of the coffins were draped with the German flag, but no third flag could be found. There was, however, a wreath on each coffin, two sent by R.A.F. officers and men and the third by a local woman resident who had dragged one of the bodies from the sea. Her wreath carried the inscription: "On behalf of all those who must have loved these men in their homes beyond the sea".

Three German airmen whose bodies were washed ashore on the Norfolk coast were buried with military honours at Happisburgh in November. *Norwich Mercury* series

Along the East Coast, the war was a grim reality from the earliest days of September. A lot of shipping regularly used these coastal waters; on almost any day there were over three hundred small vessels of between 500 and 2,000 tons, and few of them had been fitted with weapons. The first victim, however, was a much larger vessel, the 8,641 tons Brocklebank merchantman *Magdapur*. On 10th September hundreds of holiday-makers watched her sink off the coast of Suffolk. They heard a loud explosion, which rocked the buildings around them, saw a column of water shoot into the air, and then watched her go down by the bow. The Aldeburgh lifeboat *Abdy Beauclerk* arrived to find the vessel's back broken, and returned, covered in oil and blood, with seventy survivors, eight on stretchers, and one crewman who had been killed. It was the first war service by any lifeboat in the British Isles, but after that all lifeboats along this coast were frequently called out.

Accounts now began to be published regularly of encounters between East Coast vessels and German U-boats and they showed that, during these early weeks, remarkable efforts were made to try to civilise the practices of war. Skipper after skipper told of being called on board the German submarines to meet their captains, who showed concern that the English sailors should get back safely to shore. The first such story was told by the skipper of the *Alvis* when she returned to port on 20th September. A U-boat commander had ordered him and his crew to leave their ship and transfer to their lifeboat, but had then doubted if they would make it safely to port. So, instead of sinking the *Alvis*, the German crew came on board and smashed the radio and cut away the fishing gear. They left the provisions intact, and the catch of fish, and sent over a bottle of gin. Only a matter of hours later, the trawler *Nancy Hague* came home with a similar story.

In October twenty-three members of the crew of the Norwegian oil tanker *Deodata* were landed at Yarmouth after their vessel had struck a mine and sank. From this time the attack on shipping along the East Coast had a new dimension. German planes flew close in and dropped mines by parachute. In a single weekend four vessels were destroyed. In many cases ships were so close to the coast when they sank that there was insufficient depth of water to cover their masts and funnels. From the promenades of Essex, Suffolk and Norfolk residents watched these grim dramas, when loud explosions were followed by giant spouts of water, and the stricken ships could be seen listing and settling while small rescue craft dashed from the shore.

On 18th November the 8,309 tons Dutch liner *Simon Bolivar* hit a mine off the Suffolk coast. She had sailed from Amsterdam the previous evening, bound for the West Indies, with 383 passengers and crew. On the Saturday morning, in a slight haze, she ran into disaster. There were explosions, which destroyed the bridge and killed the captain, shattered most of the lifeboats and fractured pipes, so that thick black fuel oil gushed over everyone as they were thrown into the sea. The ship quickly heeled over and sank. Trawlers arrived from all directions to pick up survivors. A full-scale emergency alert was raised at Harwich and doctors and nurses and scores of ambulances gathered on the quays. Covered bodies were carried ashore and taken to mortuaries. When the count was complete, eighty-two persons were dead or missing. The survivors were in a sorry plight, many seriously injured, almost all of them black with oil, young children crying for their parents. The majority of them were put on a train and taken to London, where they were accommodated in the Great Eastern Hotel at Liverpool Street. Those who needed hospital treatment were rushed to hospitals at Harwich, Dovercourt, Colchester and Ipswich. They included two unidentified babies between six and eight months old. At Colchester surgeons worked in the operating theatre throughout the day and into the early hours of Sunday.

Only three days later the 12,000 tons Japanese liner *Terukuni Maru* was sunk off Harwich in very similar circumstances, again with promenade spectators viewing with horror the last moments as her prow dipped into the sea, the stern rose high, and the vessel foundered. This time, however, everyone on board was rescued and few were hurt. On the same day, there was another disaster which grabbed the headlines. At 9.23 p.m. a German seaplane approached Harwich, dropped a magnetic mine, machine-gunned a building on shore, and then made off. Three destroyers, H.M.S. *Gipsy*,

H.M.S. *Gipsy* lies broken off the Felixstowe shore of Harwich harbour after striking a magnetic mine on the night of 21st November.

H.M.S. *Boadicea* and *Burza*, one of the Polish destroyers which had escaped to Harwich when the Germans invaded Poland, went out to investigate. Just inside Landguard Point H.M.S. *Gipsy* passed over a mine, there were violent explosions and the destroyer sank almost instantly. Hundreds of people hurried to vantage points as a large number of vessels concentrated searchlights on the scene and rescue operations went on. In the glare of light a dense cloud of smoke could be seen above a huge volume of waves. Small boats were tossing about, shouted commands could be heard above the noise of the sea; it was an outstanding display of courage in the face of disaster. Eventually, about one hundred survivors were brought ashore, but over forty of the Navy men ended up in the cemetery at Shotley.

The funeral cortege of Lieutenant Commander Crossley, commander of the destroyer H.M.S. *Gipsy*.   *East Anglian Daily Times*

Many smaller vessels were victims. In six days of this intensified German campaign, over 65,000 tons of shipping were destroyed. The East Coast lifeboats received constant calls. Harwich acquired a protective balloon barrage. Anyone who lived near the coast now had a dreadful understanding of the realities of war.

And, by this time, so did quite a lot of families living elsewhere in the region, even though they themselves had seen and experienced little war-like activity. We have earlier taken glimpses at the 1939 diary kept by Sir Robert White, the chairman of the East Suffolk County Council, and some entries which he made towards the end of the year provide moving testimony to the fact that grief and suffering might now enter at every door, the palatial as well as the humble. From time to time, Sir Robert noted in his diary the course of events in the Far East, where Japan and China were still at war and where British warships were seeking to protect British interests in the China Sea. In July he wrote: "Saw in the papers the *Duchess* had collected a number of women and children from Fuchow and taken them to a ship outside". Sir Robert was particularly interested in that, because H.M.S. *Duchess* was a destroyer commanded by his son, Lieutenant Commander Robert White.

On 14th December Sir Robert sat at his desk and made another entry. This was it:

"At 8.30 a.m. received a telegram from the Admiralty that our very dear Robin had been lost in H.M.S. *Duchess* . . . So ends the life of a perfect son who never gave us one hour of anxiety or sorrow throughout his life. How well I remember his first cry when he was born and since then he has given us a blessed companionship and all his love. God Almighty bless him, as he has blessed us. Thank God for him."

Five days before Christmas there was a memorial service in Boulge Church with a White Ensign on the altar, the Bishop of St Edmundsbury reciting "The Crossing of the Bar", and a bugler blowing "The Last Post" and "Reveille".

Sir Robert and his wife went back to their home, walked quietly in the park when the weather permitted, reflected no doubt, on the tribulations of the year that was ending, and sought to gather their strength for a difficult year ahead.

Their lives would never be quite the same again. That was equally true for one and three quarter million others who were the East Anglians of 1939, though most of them, for whom the ordeal still lay ahead, had not yet fully recognised the fact.

APPENDIX I

POPULATION FIGURES 1939

Civilians only. Source: National Register of 1939
(Statistics of Population on 29th September 1939, H.M. Stationery Office).

Cambridgeshire	Males	Females	Total
Cambridgeshire Administrative County	74,428	86,088	160,516
Cambridge M.B.	35,178	43,533	78,711
Chesterton R.D.	16,527	18,994	35,521
Newmarket R.D.	10,553	10,390	20,943
South Cambridgeshire R.D.	12,170	13,171	25,341

Ely, Isle of			
Isle of Ely Administrative County	45,038	46,465	91,503
Chatteris U.D.	2,953	2,801	5,754
Ely U.D.	4,672	5,300	9,972
March U.D.	6,843	7,299	14,142
Whittlesey U.D.	4,324	4,157	8,481
Wisbech M.B.	8,261	9,338	17,599
Ely R.D.	7,263	7,322	14,585
North Witchford R.D.	2,672	2,505	5,177
Thorney R.D.	1,495	1,321	2,816
Wisbech R.D.	6,555	6,422	12,977

Essex (Northern part only)			
Braintree and Bocking U.D.	7,918	8,936	16,854
Brightlingsea U.D.	2,253	2,867	5,120
Burnham-on-Crouch U.D.	1,983	1,914	3,897
Chelmsford M.B.	16,119	17,553	33,672
Clacton U.D.	10,201	14,365	24,566
Colchester M.B.	21,989	27,488	49,477
Frinton and Walton U.D.	4,069	5,859	9,928
Halstead U.D.	2,995	3,811	6,806
Harwich M.B.	5,768	6,222	11,990
Maldon M.B.	4,764	5,296	10,060
Saffron Walden M.B.	3,255	4,193	7,448
West Mersea U.D.	1,317	1,738	3,055
Witham U.D.	4,096	4,088	8,184
Wivenhoe U.D.	1,197	1,341	2,538
Braintree R.D.	8,653	9,825	18,478
Chelmsford R.D.	17,068	19,417	36,485
Dunmow R.D.	9,651	10,811	20,462
Halstead R.D.	8,696	9,413	18,109
Lexden and Winstree R.D.	10,776	12,104	22,880
Maldon R.D.	6,856	7,803	14,659
Saffron Walden R.D.	8,441	9,650	18,091
Tendring R.D.	12,170	13,246	25,416

POPULATION FIGURES 1939

Huntingdonshire	*Males*	*Females*	*Total*
Huntingdonshire Administrative County	31,217	34,045	65,262
Godmanchester M.B.	1,136	1,317	2,453
Huntingdon M.B.	2,420	3,138	5,558
Old Fletton U.D.	3,985	4,203	8,188
Ramsey U.D.	2,807	3,074	5,881
St Ives M.B.	1,539	1,872	3,411
St Neots U.D.	2,203	2,481	4,684
Huntingdon R.D.	3,751	4,146	7,897
Norman Cross R.D.	4,030	4,089	8,119
St Ives R.D.	5,427	5,799	11,226
St Neots R.D.	3,919	3,926	7,845
Norfolk			
Norfolk Administrative County	249,341	280,019	529,360
Great Yarmouth C.B.	23,286	28,420	51,706
Norwich C.B.	53,574	64,992	118,566
Cromer U.D.	1,747	2,417	4,164
Diss U.D.	1,728	2,195	3,923
Downham Market U.D.	1,438	1,570	3,008
East Dereham U.D.	3,150	3,560	6,710
King's Lynn M.B.	12,056	13,683	25,739
New Hunstanton U.D.	1,463	2,122	3,585
North Walsham U.D.	2,462	2,715	5,177
Sheringham U.D.	1,767	2,512	4,279
Swaffham U.D.	1,241	1,431	2,672
Thetford M.B.	2,109	2,717	4,826
Wells U.D.	1,138	1,318	2,456
Wymondham U.D.	2,774	3,183	5,957
Blofield and Flegg R.D.	14,655	17,032	31,687
Depwade R.D.	9,139	9,560	18,699
Docking R.D.	8,274	9,207	17,481
Downham R.D.	10,944	10,874	21,818
Erpingham R.D.	10,289	11,153	21,442
Forehoe and Henstead R.D.	10,181	11,426	21,607
Freebridge Lynn R.D.	5,101	5,301	10,402
Loddon R.D.	6,179	6,438	12,617
Marshland R.D.	8,987	8,645	17,632
Mitford and Launditch R.D.	8,589	8,182	16,771
St Faith's and Aylsham R.D.	16,660	18,077	34,737
Smallburgh R.D.	8,710	8,907	17,617
Swaffham R.D.	4,290	4,480	8,770
Walsingham R.D.	8,426	8,630	17,056
Wayland R.D.	8,984	9,272	18,256

POPULATION FIGURES 1939

Peterborough, Soke of	*Males*	*Females*	*Total*
Soke of Peterborough Administrative County	27,776	30,527	58,303
Peterborough M.B.	23,268	25,980	49,248
Barnack R.D.	1,077	1,162	2,239
Peterborough R.D.	3,431	3,385	6,816
Suffolk, East			
East Suffolk Administrative County	152,186	175,219	327,405
Ipswich C.B.	45,317	54,317	99,634
Aldeburgh M.B.	1,199	1,926	3,125
Beccles M.B.	3,499	3,987	7,486
Bungay U.D.	1,462	1,789	3,251
Eye M.B.	835	964	1,799
Felixstowe U.D.	5,615	8,013	13,628
Halesworth U.D.	1,100	1,303	2,403
Leiston cum Sizewell U.D.	2,293	2,366	4,659
Lowestoft M.B.	19,253	23,200	42,453
Saxmundham U.D.	670	802	1,472
Southwold M.B.	1,117	1,701	2,818
Stowmarket U.D.	3,420	4,010	7,430
Woodbridge U.D.	2,429	3,233	5,662
Blyth R.D.	10,229	10,986	21,215
Deben R.D.	13,984	15,355	29,339
Gipping R.D.	10,251	10,151	20,402
Hartismere R.D.	9,527	9,652	19,179
Lothingland R.D.	9,132	9,899	19,031
Samford R.D.	7,353	7,939	15,292
Wainford R.D.	3,501	3,626	7,127
Suffolk, West			
West Suffolk Administrative County	53,720	59,232	112,952
Bury St Edmunds M.B.	7,764	9,751	17,515
Hadleigh U.D.	1,450	1,672	3,122
Haverhill U.D.	1,631	2,100	3,731
Newmarket U.D.	4,571	5,117	9,688
Sudbury M.B.	3,002	3,680	6,682
Clare R.D.	4,219	4,415	8,634
Cosford R.D.	5,031	5,547	10,578
Melford R.D.	5,870	6,847	12,717
Mildenhall R.D.	6,773	7,021	13,794
Thedwastre R.D.	4,573	4,861	9,434
Thingoe	8,836	8,221	17,057

APPENDIX II

MEMBERS OF PARLIAMENT

SITTING IN THE COMMONS REPRESENTING EAST ANGLIAN CONSTITUENCIES AT 1st FEBRUARY 1939 (names in bold type).

(with votes cast for all candidates in the polls at which they were elected. These figures all refer to the General Election of 14th November 1935, unless otherwise stated).

Cambridgeshire

CAMBRIDGE BOROUGH:
**Lt. Com. Richard L. Tufnell, R.N.
(Nat.Con.)** 18,927
Dr W. A. Wood (Lab.) 13,436

CAMBRIDGE UNIVERSITY (2 seats):
Sir John Withers (Con.) 7,602
Sir Kenneth Pickthorn (Con.) 6,917
H. L. Elvin (Lab.) 3,453

CAMBRIDGESHIRE:
Capt. Richard G. Briscoe (Con.) 19,087
Maj. J. R. Bellerby (Lab.) 11,437
J. W. Payne (Lib.) 5,223

ISLE OF ELY:
James de Rothschild (Lib.) 17,671
W. F. C. Garthwaite (Con.) 16,972

HUNTINGDONSHIRE:
Dr Sidney J. Peters (Lib.Nat.) 17,287
L. J. George (Lab.) 7,861

Norfolk

NORWICH (2 seats):
**Sir Geoffrey Shakespeare, Bt.
(Lib.Nat.)** 36,039
Henry G. Strauss (Con.) 34,182
W. G. Hall (Lab.) 24,670
C. J. Kelly (Lab.) 22,055
Fenner Brockway (I.L.P.) 6,737

EAST NORFOLK: (by-election 26th January 1939)
Frank Medlicott (Lib.Nat.) 18,257
N. R. Tillett (Lab.) 10,785

NORTH NORFOLK:
Sir Thomas Cook (Con.) 17,863
Lady Noel-Buxton (Lab.) 14,465

SOUTH NORFOLK:
James A. Christie (Con.) 18,420
G. Clark (Lab.) 13,409

SOUTH-WEST NORFOLK
Somerset de Chair (Con.) 16,060
S. Dye (Lab.) 11,943

KING'S LYNN:
Hon. S. A. Maxwell (Con.) 17,492
F. Emerson (Lab.) 12,062
F. Darvall (Lib.) 5,418

GREAT YARMOUTH:
Sir A. Harbord (Lib.Nat.) 16,998
Dr J. Lewis (Lab.) 11,658

Soke of Peterborough

PETERBOROUGH:
Lord Burghley (Con.) 22,677
E. A. J. Davies (Lab.) 17,373

Suffolk

BURY ST EDMUNDS:
Maj. Frank F. A. Heilgers (Con.) Unopposed

EYE:
Edgar Granville (Independent) 21,606
H. L. Self (Lab.) 7,613

IPSWICH: (By-election 16th February 1938)
Richard R. Stokes (Lab.) 27,604
H. U. Willink (Nat.Con.) 24,443

LOWESTOFT:
Pierse C. Loftus (Con.) 21,064
Maj. F. J. Wise (Lab.) 13,348

SUDBURY:
Col. Henry W. Burton (Con.) 11,700
A. J. Sainsbury (Lib.) 8,344
Lt. Com. H. Denton (Lab.) 3,670

WOODBRIDGE:
Walter Ross-Taylor (Con.) 22,715
A. V. Smith (Lab.) 8,808

Essex

CHELMSFORD:
Col. J. R. J. Macnamara (Con.) 28,314
F. Hughes (Lab.) 11,690

COLCHESTER:
Oswald Lewis (Con.) 19,915
H. Beaumont (Lab.) 14,039

HARWICH:
Joseph S. Holmes (Lib.Nat.) 21,716
A. E. Appelbe (Lab.) 9,170

MALDON:
**Col. Sir E. A. Ruggles-Brise, Bt.
(Con.)** 17,072
W. F. Toynbee (Lab.) 9,264
Miss H. Buckmaster (Lib.) 5,680

SAFFRON WALDEN:
Rt. Hon. R. A. Butler (Con.) 19,669
Mrs C. D. Rackham (Lab.) 9,633

A Selected Bibliography

East Anglia, Peter Steggall, Robert Hale (*The Regions of Britain*), 1979.

East Anglia, Doreen Wallace, Batsford (*The Face of Britain*), 1939.

Norfolk and Suffolk, Cambridge and Essex, Ed., W. Shears, Hutchinson's Pocket Guide, 1939.

Suffolk Scene, Julian Tennyson, Blackie & Son, 1939. Reprinted 1973 by E. P. Publishing Ltd.

A History of the Fens, J. Wentworth Day, Harrap, 1954.

The Oaken Heart, Margery Allingham, Hutchinson, 1941.

Cambridge, F. A. Reeve, Batsford, 1964.

Cambridge, F. A. Reeve, Batsford, 1976 (a different book).

Cambridge as it was and as it is today, John Steegman, Batsford, 1940.

Cambridge between the wars, T. E. B. Howarth, Collins, 1978.

The Story of Colchester, Geoffrey Martin, Benham Newspapers Ltd, 1959.

The Felixstowe Story, Allan Jobson, Robert Hale, 1968.

The Rise of Great Yarmouth, A. W. and J. L. Eccleston, 1959.

The Harwich Story, Leonard T. Weaver, Harwich Printing Co, 1975.

Royal Newmarket, R. C. Lyle, Putnam & Co, 1945.

Norwich and its Region, British Association for the Advancement of Science, 1961.

City of Norwich Plan, 1945, prepared for the Council by C. H. James, A.R.A., F.R.I.B.A., and S. Rowland Pierce, F.R.I.B.A., consultants, and H. C. Rowley, A.M.Inst. C.E., M.I.M. Cy. E., City Engineer.

Norwich — the growth of a City, Barbara Green and Rachel Young, Norwich Museums Committee, 1964.

Industry in the Country Towns of Norfolk and Suffolk, T. Eastwood, B.Com, Oxford University Press, 1951.

A Survey of the Agriculture of Suffolk, P. J. O. Trist, Royal Agricultural Society of England (County Agricultural Surveys, No 7), 1971.

The Contentious Tithe, Eric J. Evans, Routledge & Kegan Paul, 1976.

The Draining of the Fens, H. C. Darby,

A Regional History of the Railways of Great Britain, Vol. V — The Eastern Counties, D. I. Gordon, David & Charles, 1968.

Saved from the Sea, Robert Malster, Terence Dalton Ltd, 1974.

The Herring and its Fishery, W. C. Hodgson, Routledge & Kegan Paul, 1957.

Ipswich — An illustrated history of Ipswich Town Football Club, K. Rice, Wensum Books, 1973.

On the Ball City — An illustrated history of Norwich City Football Club, Ted Bell, Wensum Books, 1972.

The Heath and the Turf — a History of Newmarket, Richard Onslow, Arthur Baker, 1971.

East Anglia at War, 1939-45, Derek E. Johnson, Jarrold, 1978.

The Cambridge Evacuation Survey, Editor, Susan Isaacs, Methuen, 1941.

The Regional Military Histories: East Anglia, Martin Bates, Osprey, 1974.

Action Stations — Wartime Military Airfields of East Anglia, 1939-45, Michael J. F. Bowyer, Patrick Stephens Ltd, 1979.

Aeronauts and Aviators, Christopher Elliott, Terence Dalton Ltd, 1971.

Trawlers go to War, Paul Lund and Harry Ludlam, New English Library, 1972.

Cambridgeshire at War, Jeffrey Barham, Birds Farm Publications, 1977.

Norwich at War, Joan Banger, Wensum Books, 1974.

Cambridge Doctor, Rex Salisbury Woods, Robert Hale, 1962.

Kelly's Directories were published for most of the larger towns in East Anglia in 1939.

Ward Lock Illustrated Guide Books.

Index